IMAGES
of America

BEREA

For Eloise Tressel
1925–2001
–a joyous spirit
–an inspired life

IMAGES
of America

BEREA

Patricia M. Mote

ARCADIA
PUBLISHING

ISBN 978-0-7385-3330-8

Published by Arcadia Publishing
Charleston, South Carolina

Printed in the United States of America

Library of Congress Catalog Card Number: 2004108465

For all general information contact Arcadia Publishing at:
Telephone 843-853-2070
Fax 843-853-0044
E-mail sales@arcadiapublishing.com
For customer service and orders:
Toll-Free 1-888-313-2665

Visit us on the Internet at www.arcadiapublishing.com

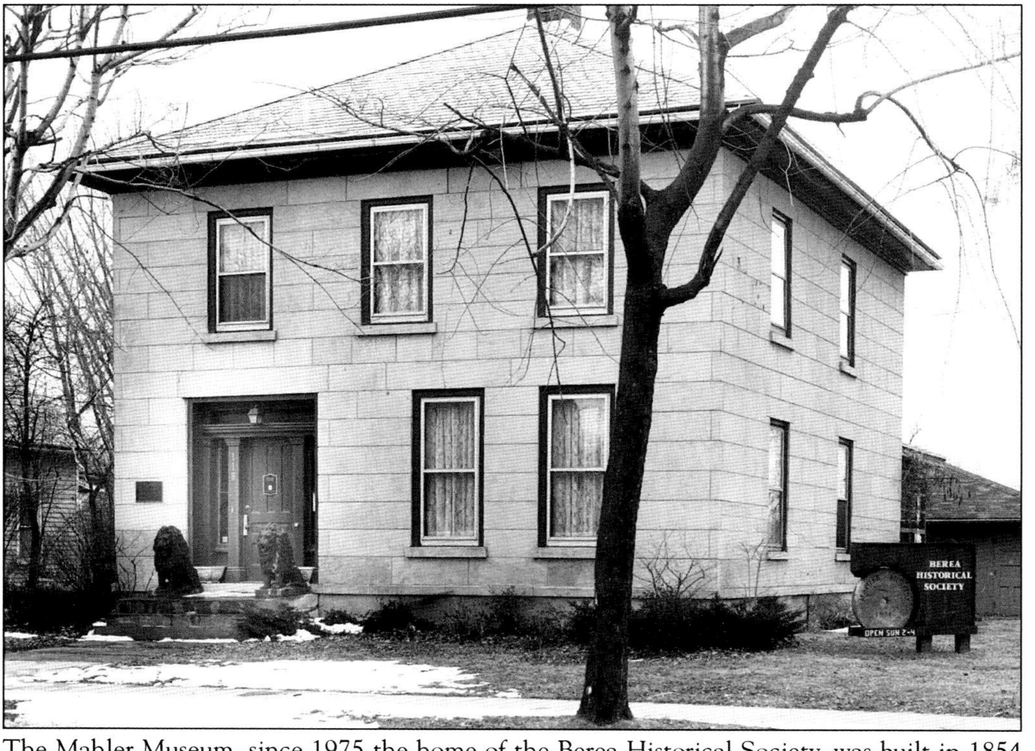

The Mahler Museum, since 1975 the home of the Berea Historical Society, was built in 1854 and was one of only two homes built of native Berea sandstone. Lydia Buehl, a resident in the home all of her life, hoped it could become a museum. The community raised $50,000 to match a gift from Berea residents, Otto and Mabel Mahler, and Mary Buehl Adler, one of the heirs, donated her portion of the purchase price to the Historical Society.

Contents

ACKNOWLEDGMENTS

To the Berea Historical Society—especially Nancy Gillahan and Dave Burnett, administrative assistants; Pat Slater, president; Stanley Maxwell, vice-president; Louise Allen, curator; and Mary Jane Papp and Florence Gardner, volunteers—I am grateful not only for the location and use of many images but also for their enthusiasm and encouragement throughout this project.

To Louise Kiefer, historian at Baldwin-Wallace College, for supplying images and facts about German Wallace College. To the Cuyahoga County Library, Berea Branch, for microfilm access to the *Berea Advertiser* and especially to Mary Ellen Nichols, adult services librarian, for recommending me as an author to Arcadia Publishing. To Susan Lee, photographer, who converted a number of slides into images for use in this book. To Jim Jaworski, who also furnished images and served as a consultant for Chapter Two, "The Quarries." To Father Gerald Keller, St. Adalbert's Catholic Church of Berea, who loaned reference materials and offered insight into the history of the church. To Barbara Sherwood, past president of the Berea Historical Society and columnist for the Berea *NewsSun*, for her encouragement, publicity, and for introducing me to the Polish Village. To Betty Bainbridge Vitez, William Allman, and Betsy Menzel, all longtime Berea area residents, who contributed information and enthusiasm for this project.

I am indebted to a number of published sources: *Of Grit and Greatness* by Walter F. Holzworth (Walter F. Holzworth, 1970, 1986); *And Then There Were None* by Mickey Segal (King's Court Communications, 1996); *The Biography of John Baldwin* by Judge A.R. Webber (The Caxton Press, 1925); *A Collection of Historical Facts Concerning Berea, Ohio*, compiled by Willard H. Shaw for the city's centennial in 1936; and *The Encyclopedia of Cleveland History* edited by David D. Van Tassel and John J. Grabowski (Indiana University Press, 1987). I also made use of the files of *The Cleveland Press*, *The Plain Dealer*, *The Enterprise*, published by the Berea Historical Society, and the *B-W Night Times*.

All images were furnished by the Berea Historical Society unless otherwise credited. Most of the images in Chapter Four, "The German Methodist Orphan's Home," are from the Henry Barr collection housed at the Berea Historical Society.

Introduction

This book could have been called *Tabor* instead of *Berea* since the town was named by the flip of a half-dollar with the two names written on it. As the coin was tossed, John Baldwin called "heads," and so the town became Berea. Both are biblical names, which is not surprising since John Baldwin, a devout New England Methodist, had come here to farm in 1828 and with two Methodist ministers, Reverend H.O. Sheldon and Reverend James Gilruth, founded The Lyceum Society, a cooperative venture to educate missionaries. The school eventually failed in 1844, and John Baldwin, the heaviest investor, faced possible bankruptcy. When he discovered sandstone on his 200 acres, which he found could be used for making grindstones, Baldwin believed that God had led him to a way out of his difficulties. Sandstone became in demand as a building material.

Quarrying in Berea and in surrounding areas was a major industry from roughly 1850 to 1950. By then, sandstone as a building material was being replaced by limestone, and the Berea quarries were largely exhausted. Large numbers of immigrants had come to work in the Berea quarries. First came the Irish, Scotch, and the English; in the latter years of the 19th century many German and Polish arrived.

Baldwin Institute and University (1846) and German Wallace College (1863) created an academic atmosphere for the community into which the immigrants had difficulty fitting. The South Side, where the professors and business people of the town lived, was often referred to by those residents as "God's side of town," while the immigrants lived in their own ethnic neighborhoods on the North Side. A strike in the quarries in 1896 further inflamed ill feeling in the town.

Many of the fashionable South Side homes and the original buildings of Baldwin University were situated upon valuable sandstone deposits. Eventually, the Cleveland Stone Company consolidated all of the quarry operations in and around Berea in 1886, and many homes and all of the Baldwin University buildings were moved to other locations. The two educational institutions merged to become Baldwin-Wallace College in 1913.

When quarrying ended in the mid-1940s, Berea's great quarrying industry passed into history. The concerted efforts of the Cleveland Metroparks System and the City of Berea have transformed the South Side of Berea to a place devoted to recreation and enjoyment. The largest quarry became Coe Lake, a site for fishing, canoeing, art fairs, and band concerts in summer and for ice fishing and skating in winter.

Three times, the downtown business district, the Triangle, was nearly destroyed by fire. Each time its determined residents rebuilt and began again. Today, Berea has a uniqueness that sets it apart from other Cleveland suburbs. Coffee shops, boutiques, and art galleries now thrive in spaces once occupied by livery stables, icehouses, and hardware stores. The second and third generations of the immigrant population have become assimilated into the community, and a dichotomy no longer exists. The two colleges have merged into one institution, and college and community leaders work in cooperation with each other. Many of the grand homes of the 19th century still stand, proudly wearing their bronze "Century Home" plaques.

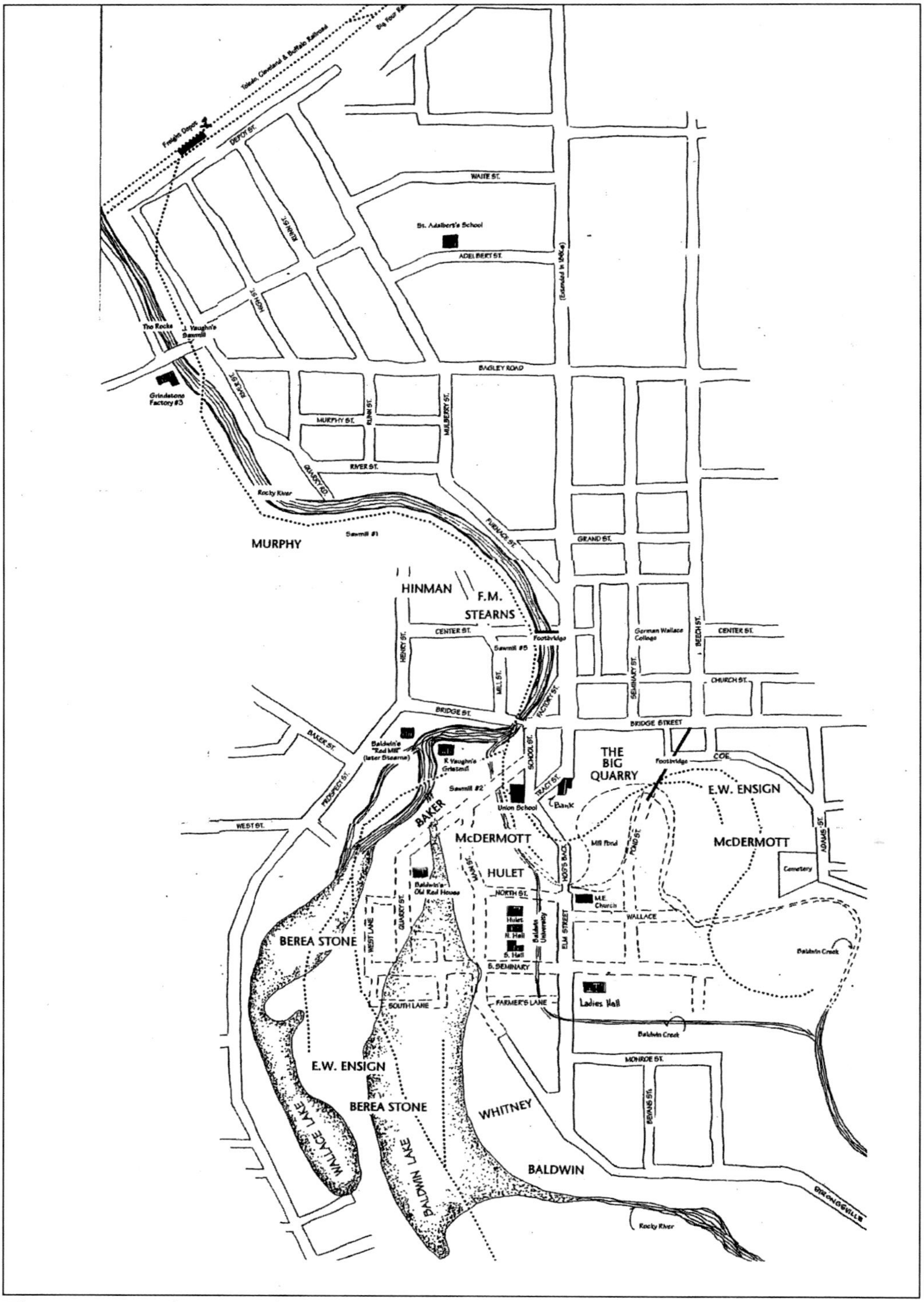

This is a map of Berea, Ohio. (From Mickey Sego's *The Quarry Years* for the Berea Area Historical Society, 1996.)

One

Daily Life in Earlier Times

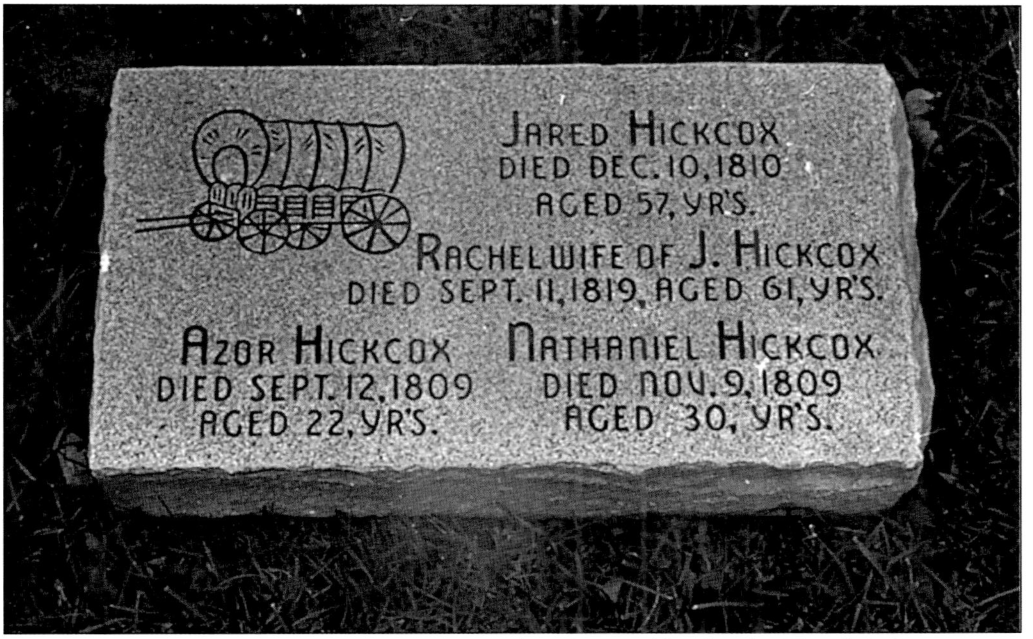

The earliest settlers in the Berea area were Jared Hickox and his family. They left Connecticut in 1809 to take up a 50-acre homestead in the Western Reserve at what is now Bagley Road and Hepburn Place. Native Americans still inhabited the area as well as bears and wolves. Today, an iron fence surrounds their family cemetery in the midst of a shopping mall parking lot. Developers of the shopping center have provided a new marker for their graves. (Courtesy of Jim Jaworski.)

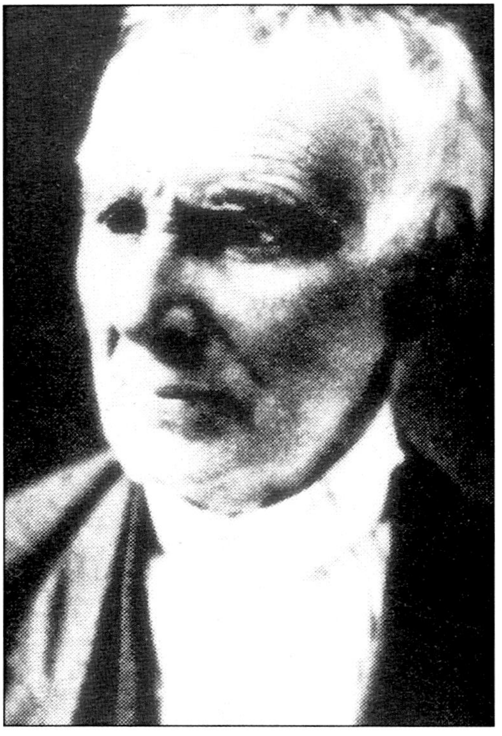

John Baldwin, a Connecticut Yankee and a devout Methodist, settled in Berea in 1828, immediately after his marriage to Miss Mary Chappell. One day in 1842, he discovered a rock on his farm that would put a sharp edge on his pocketknife. That very night he made the first Berea grit grindstone at his home. Baldwin became a man of great influence in the religious, civic, educational, and business life of Berea and beyond.

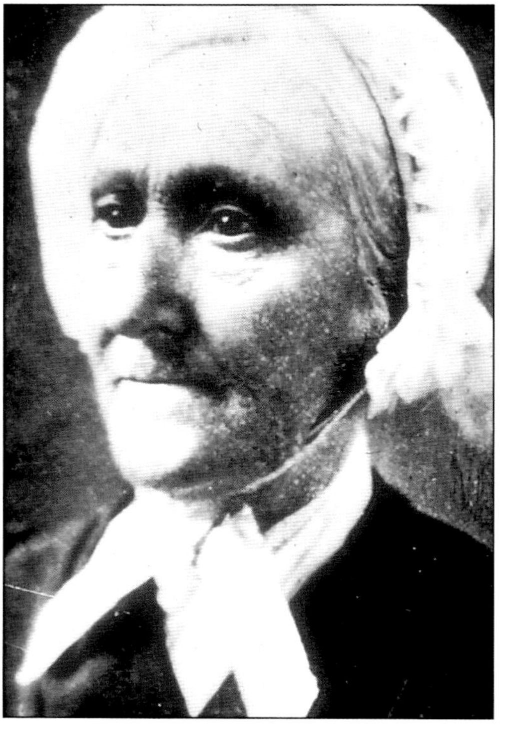

Mrs. Mary Chappell Baldwin came west with her new husband to 200 acres of land they had never seen. A person with little formal education, she had worked as a domestic and a mill worker. Mary Baldwin supported her husband in his strict views on morals and temperance and his efforts to establish first the short-lived Lyceum and later Baldwin Institute, which became Baldwin University in 1855. Later, she moved with him to establish schools in Kansas and Louisiana. The Baldwins had seven children.

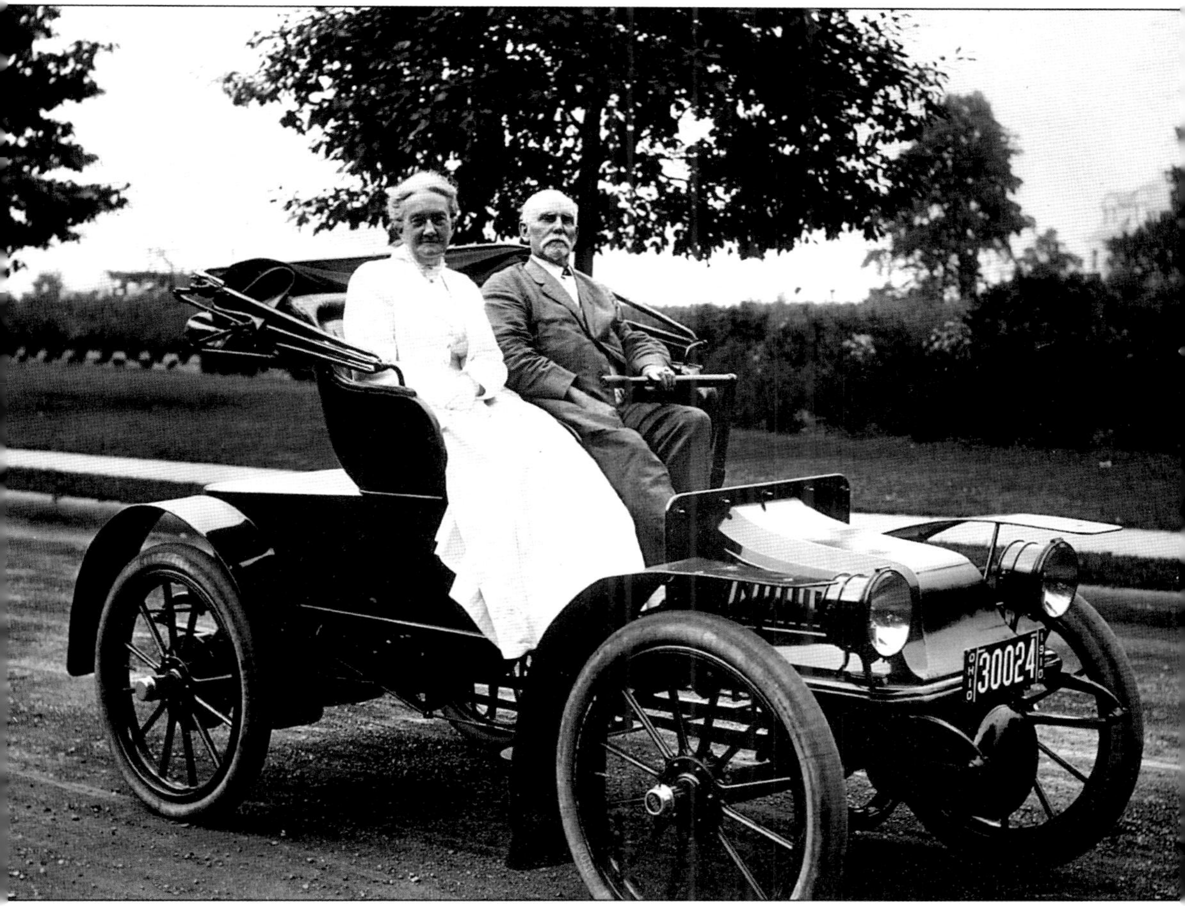

Mr. and Mrs. John Baldwin Jr. drove their 1910 Baker Electric car in a 1911 parade in Rockefeller Park on East Boulevard in Cleveland. At 10 miles per hour, the Baker's top speed, this was a lengthy drive from Berea. John Baldwin Jr. took over the running of the quarry and mill operations around the mid-1850s when his father left Berea to pursue his educational endeavors elsewhere.

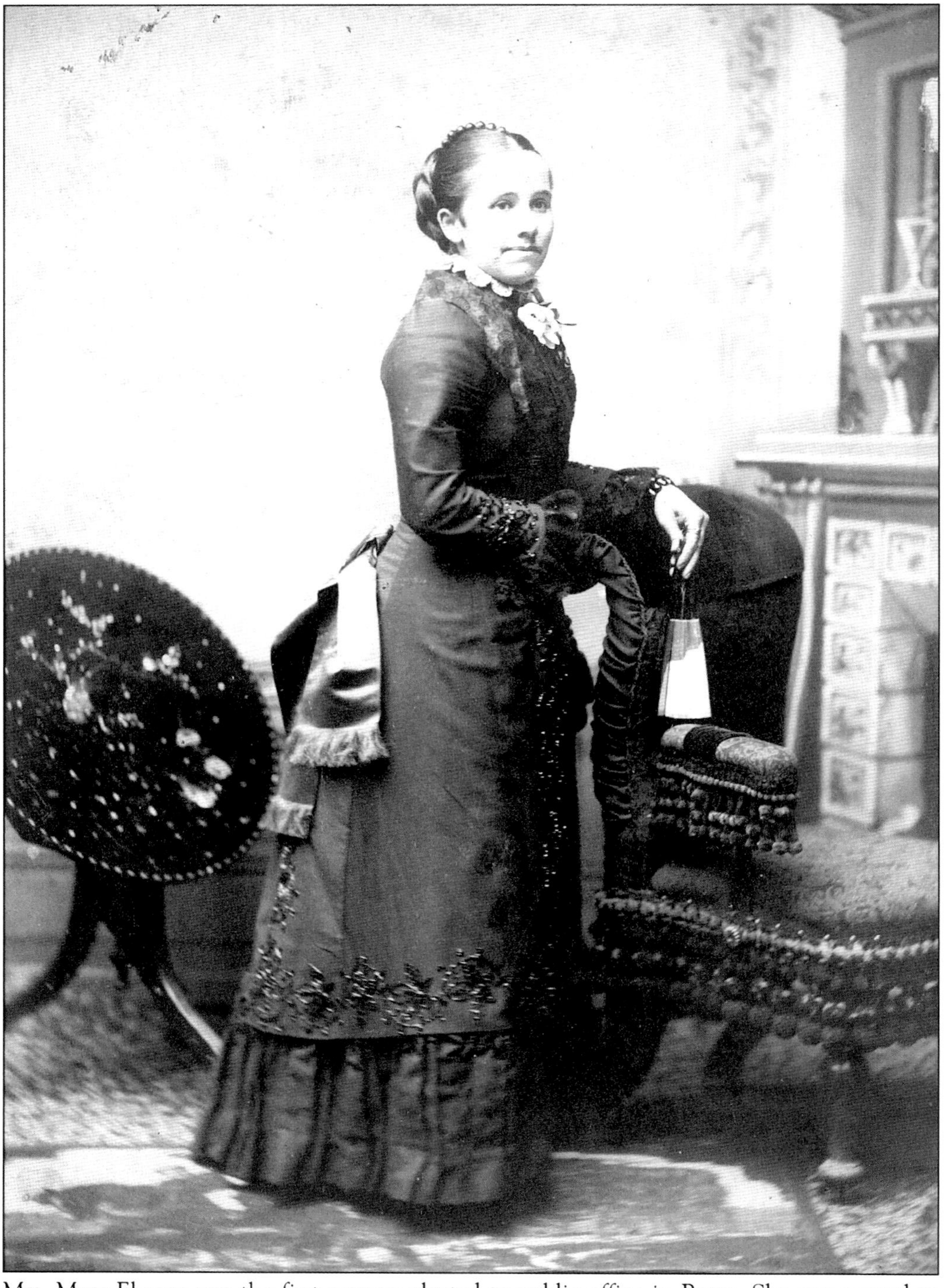

Mrs. Mary Elmore was the first woman elected to public office in Berea. She was named to the Berea School Board in 1895. Of the four leading candidates, two men and two women, Mrs. Elmore placed second with 272 votes. The Ohio Legislature gave Ohio women the right to vote in school board elections nearly 25 years before the passage of the 19th Amendment.

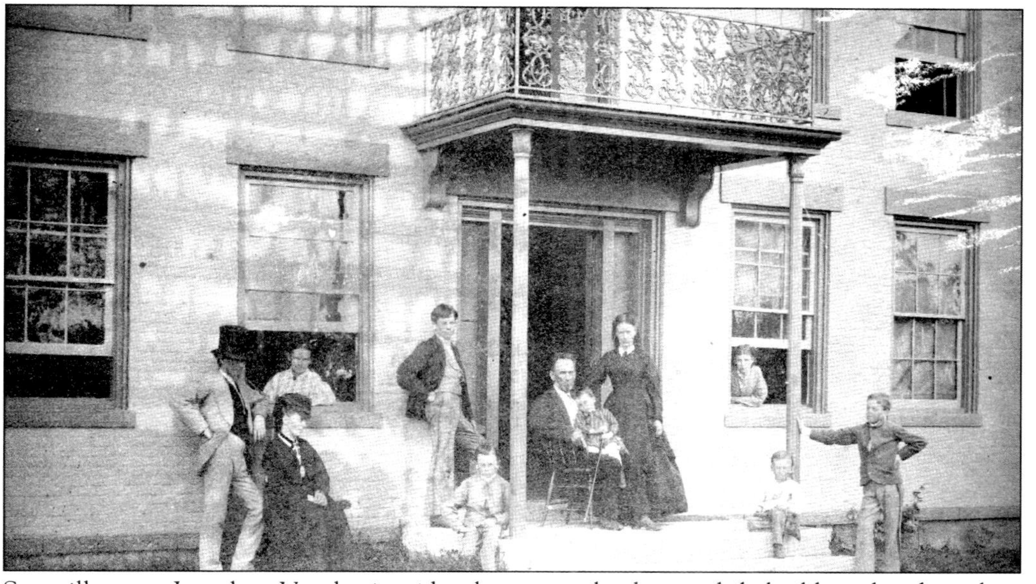

Sawmill owner Jonathan Vaughn is said to have gone bankrupt while building this showplace home in 1834 and never lived in it. Often called "the Little Hermitage," or "the Whitney House" after the first occupants, 445 South Rocky River Drive has had a succession of owners, including Baldwin University president Dr. John Wheeler from 1855–1865.

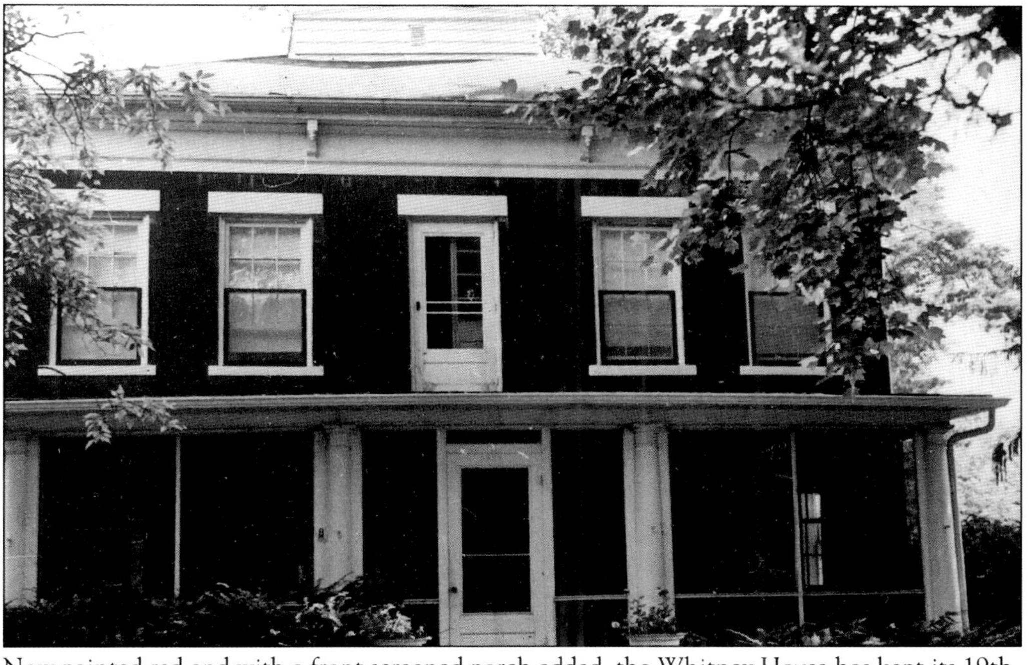

Now painted red and with a front screened porch added, the Whitney House has kept its 19th-century grandeur over the years, yet owners have added up-to-date conveniences. The stately homes on South Rocky River Drive, formerly Elm Street, caused 19th-century Bereans to refer to it as "God's side of town."

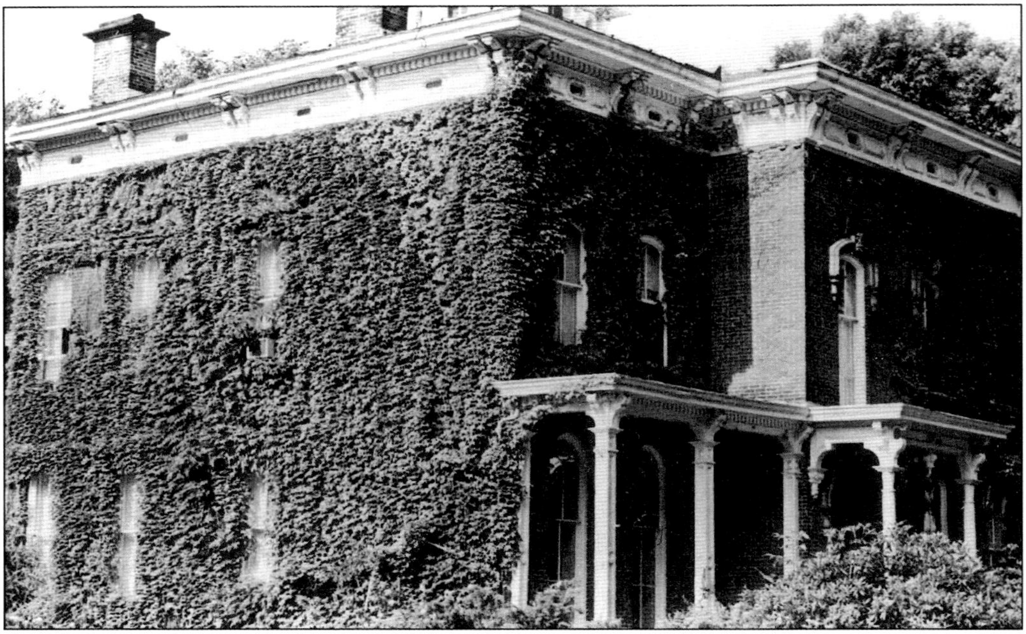

The first Berea home listed on the National Register of Historic Places, this 5,100 square-foot Italianate Revival-style mansion at 330 South Rocky River Drive boasts eight fireplaces, six chimneys, 12-foot ceilings, and a hand-carved staircase. It was the first Berea home to have a water pressure system. After a fire and a meticulous 13-year restoration by most recent owner Greg Katona, the home remains a jewel of the South Side.

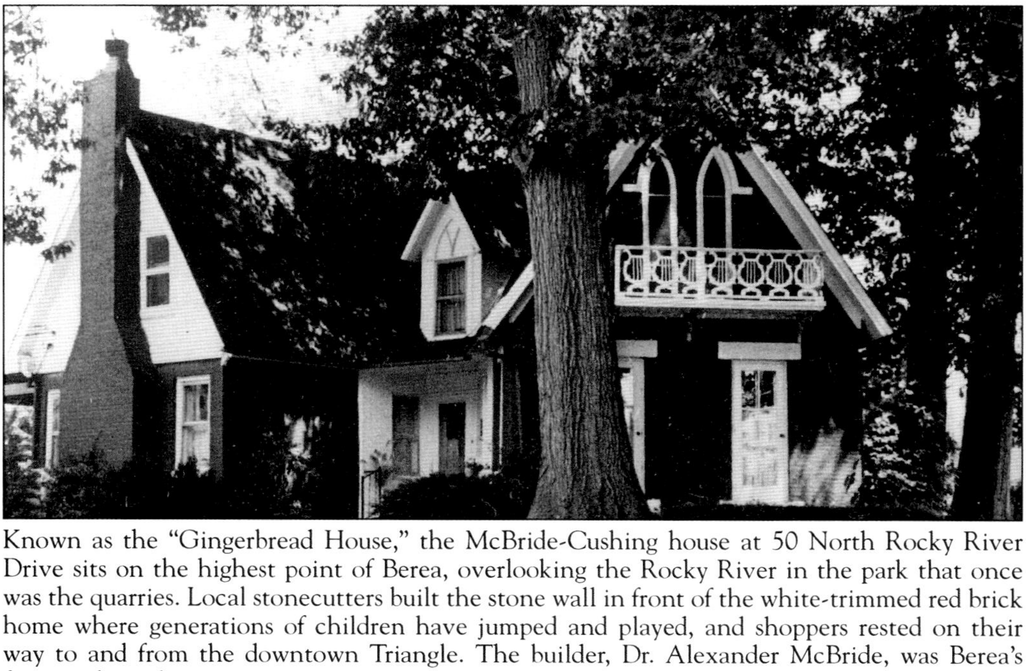

Known as the "Gingerbread House," the McBride-Cushing house at 50 North Rocky River Drive sits on the highest point of Berea, overlooking the Rocky River in the park that once was the quarries. Local stonecutters built the stone wall in front of the white-trimmed red brick home where generations of children have jumped and played, and shoppers rested on their way to and from the downtown Triangle. The builder, Dr. Alexander McBride, was Berea's first resident physician.

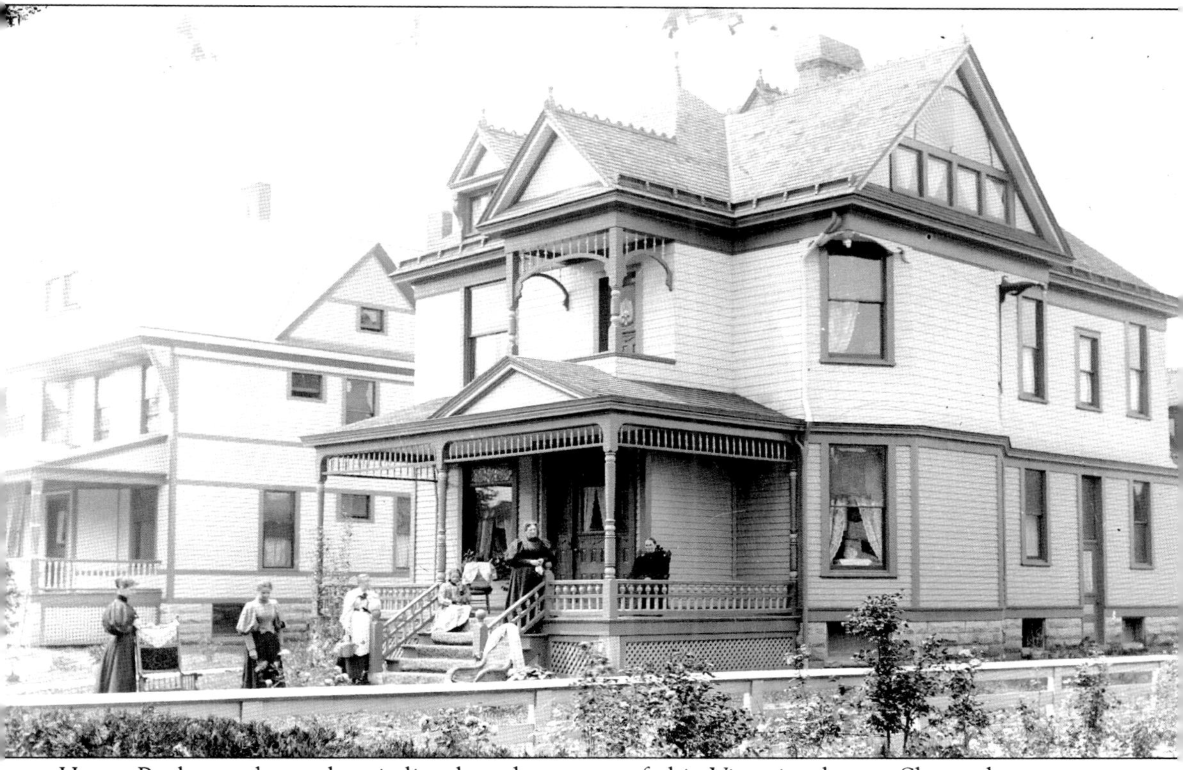

Henry Paulus, a shoemaker, is listed as the owner of this Victorian home. Shown here are members of the O.A. Kinney family.

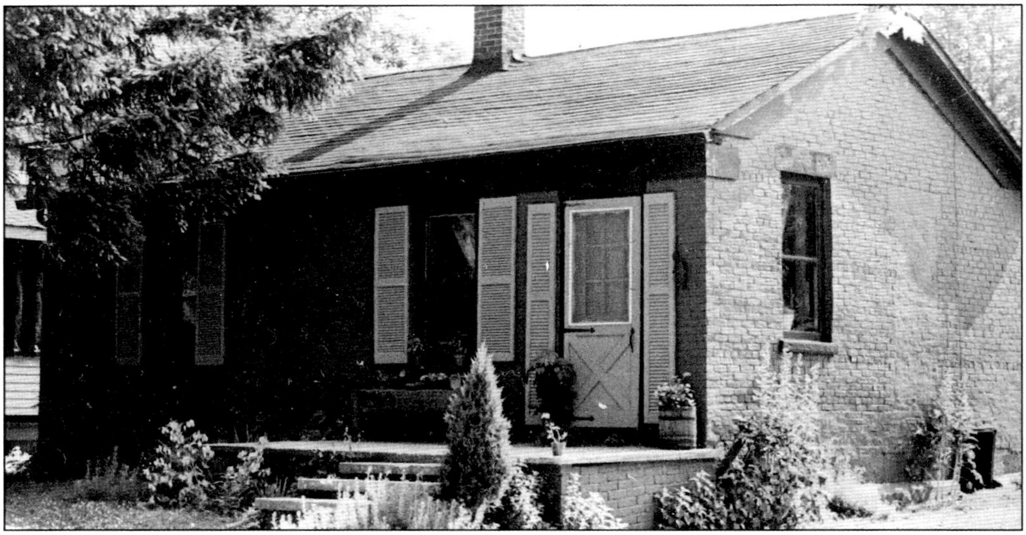

John Baldwin built this house at 197 South Rocky River Drive in 1852 and used it as a dormitory for students at the Berea Institute. When Jane Brown bought the house a few years later, she continued to offer meals, as well as lodging, to students. This part of the house, known as the "kitchen," was separate from the main house, just south of it, and has remained so; two different families occupy these homes today.

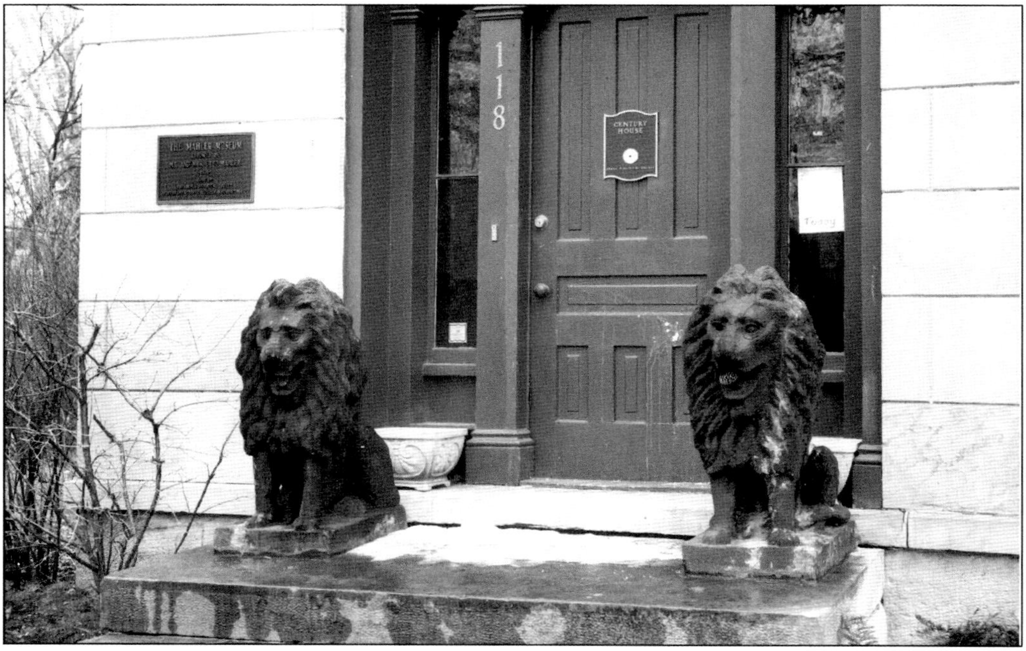

At the entrance to the Mahler Museum stand Fred and Rosie, sandstone lions that once looked down from atop the Bullinger Block on Factory Street. Bullinger's stone building was gutted in the 1899 fire, but the walls stood erect, and the lions survived. Note the "Century Home" plaque, proudly displayed on many Berea homes. The Berea Historical Society researches homes and awards these plaques to homes and buildings that have passed the 100-year mark.

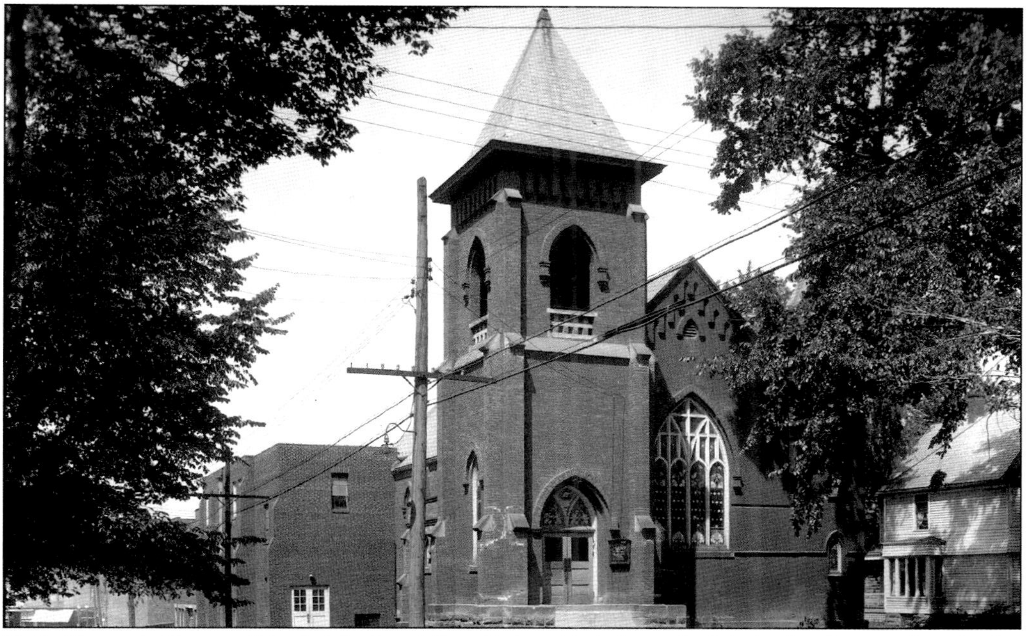

Called by early Bereans "the brick church" to distinguish it from the Methodists' stone church, the Congregational Church, built in 1855, often hosted public gatherings as well as worship services. The original sanctuary is still in use, and an education wing has been added. Erection of a 100-foot steeple marked the church's centennial. Now affiliated with the United Church of Christ, the congregation celebrates 150 years in 2005 at the corner of Seminary and Church Streets.

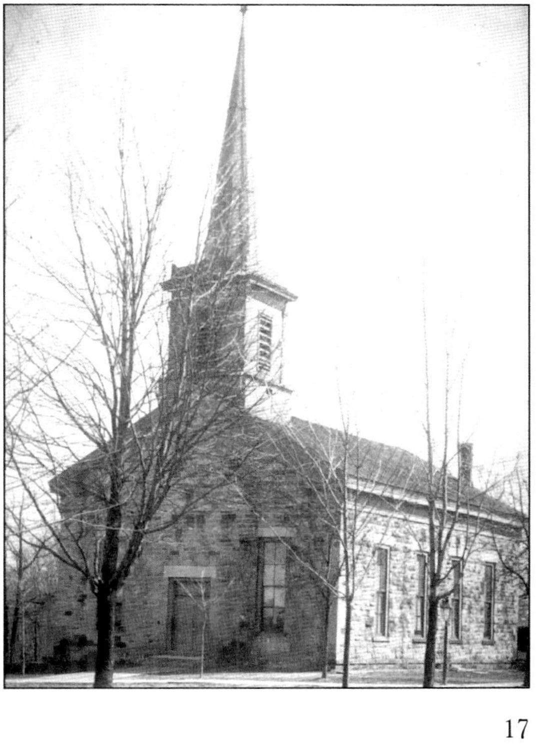

On June 5, 1899, fire destroyed the old stone Methodist Episcopal Church on the South Side. The congregation had previously obtained a site for a new church at Seminary and Spring Streets, and building plans were already underway. The cause of the fire was unknown, although arson was suspected. This fire occurred just two months before a fire that would destroy much of the business area around the Triangle.

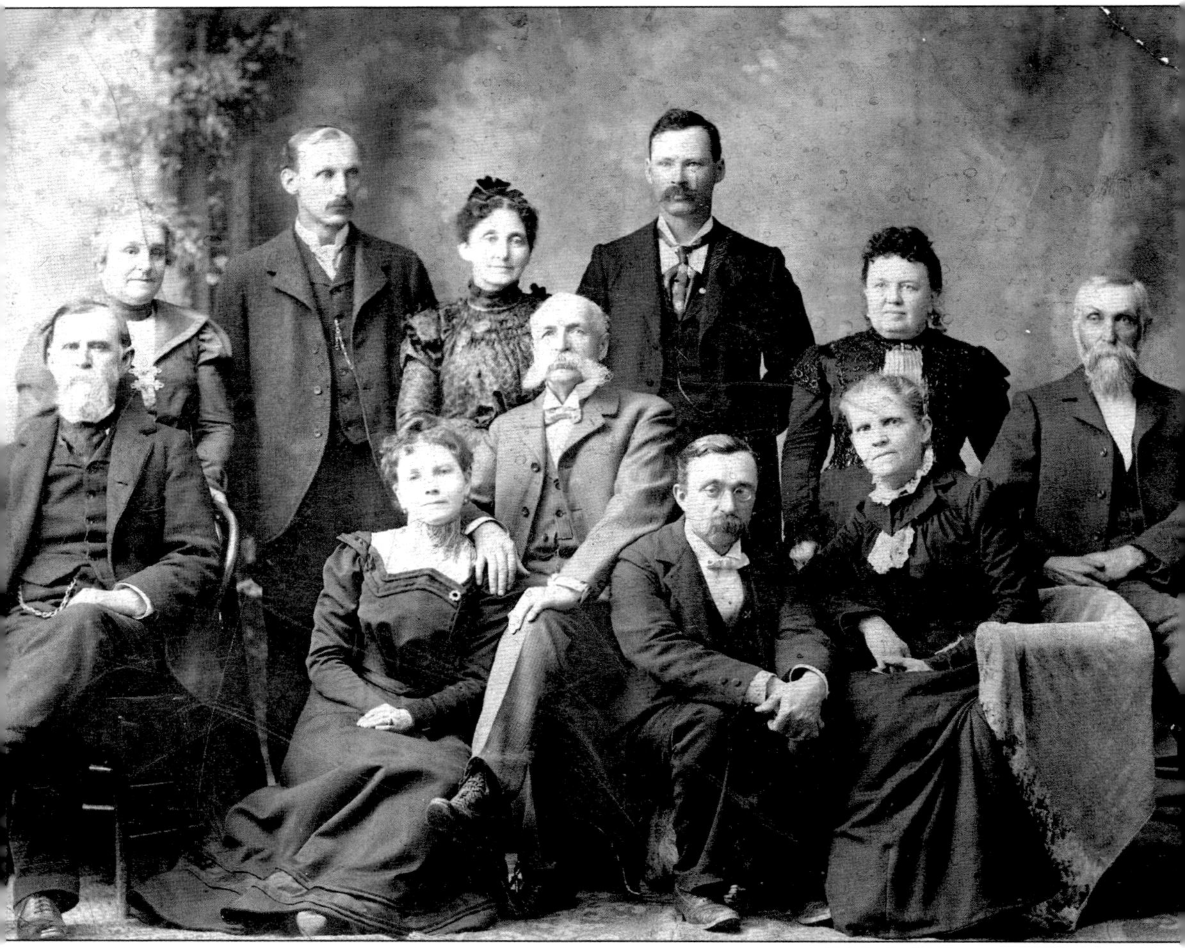

The Methodists dedicated their new building on April 29, 1900, only 10 months after the previous church burned. Members of the Building Committee of the Methodist Episcopal Church were, from left to right: (seated) W.B. Aldrich, Mrs. M.A. Sprague, M.A. Sprague, A. T. Doering, Mrs. W.J. Lawrence, and J.E. Johnson; (standing) Mrs. E.J. Kennedy, John South Simpson, Mrs. W.B. Aldrich, W.D. Gardner, and Mrs. O.A. Kinney.

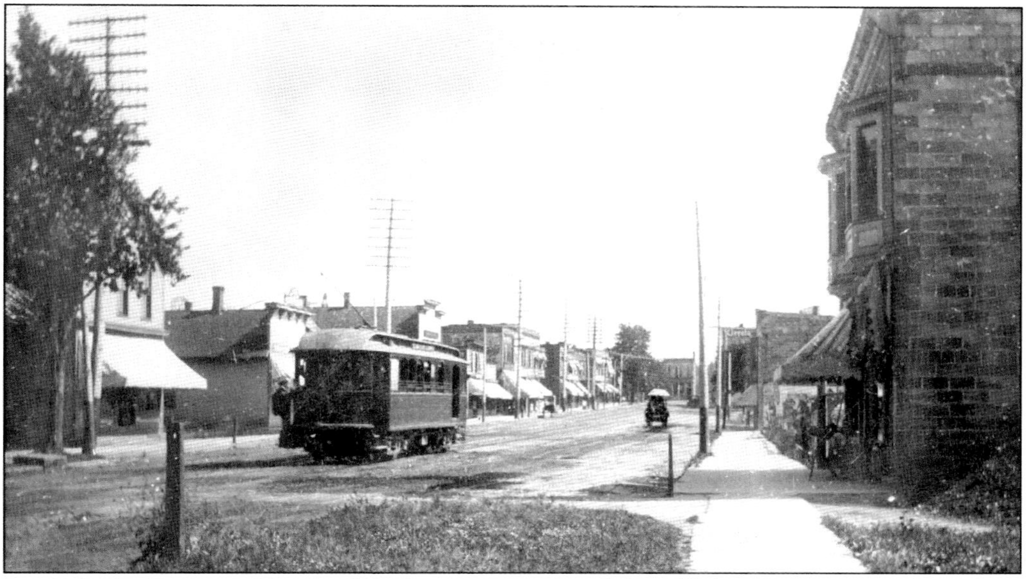

In 1893, the Berea to Cleveland Railway Line replaced the old, horse car street railway from the Triangle to Berea's Union Depot. It became the first interurban line to connect with the Cleveland Railway System. As they had done with the horse car line, Berea businessmen conceived and promoted the interurban without any city, state, or outside aid.

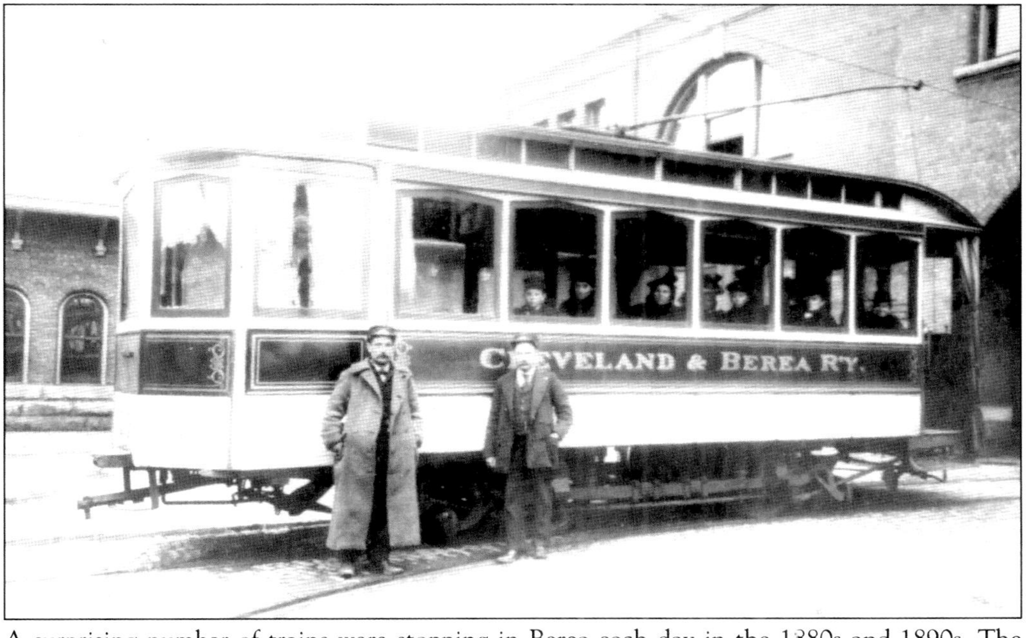

A surprising number of trains were stopping in Berea each day in the 1880s and 1890s. The Berea Street Railway offered dependable, convenient transportation from the depot for frequent visitors to the colleges, the quarries, and the grindstone factories. Front Street was an 80-foot-wide unpaved, often muddy, thoroughfare, but by taking the railway, even ladies in their bustles and long skirts could arrive at their Berea destinations in comfort.

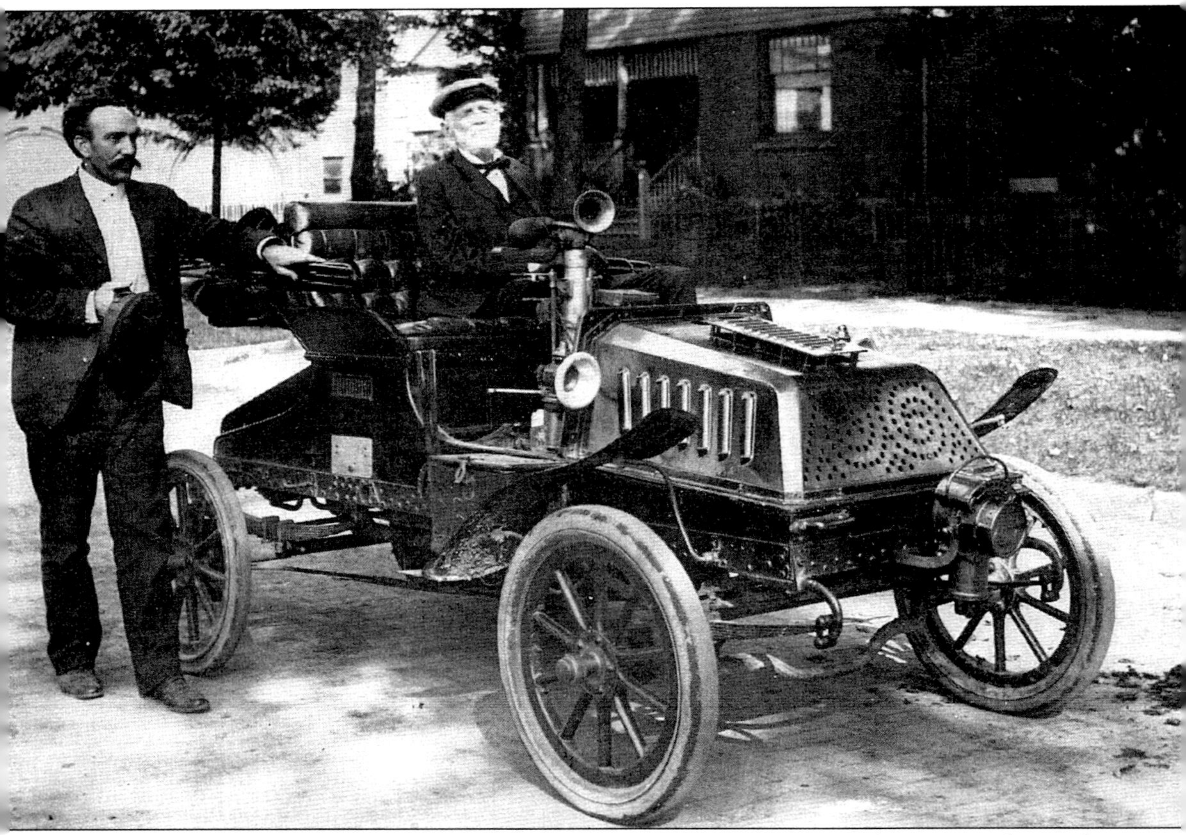

John Paul Baldwin (left), son of John Baldwin Jr., prepares to take Billy Simpson for a ride in an early automobile, probably about 1902. Although he was often the butt of community jokes, jeweler and part-time inventor Simpson had crafted the first steam-driven wagon on Berea streets in 1874. It proved impractical, but Simpson persevered, and by 1899, he produced a two-cylinder internal combustion engine to power the horseless carriage.

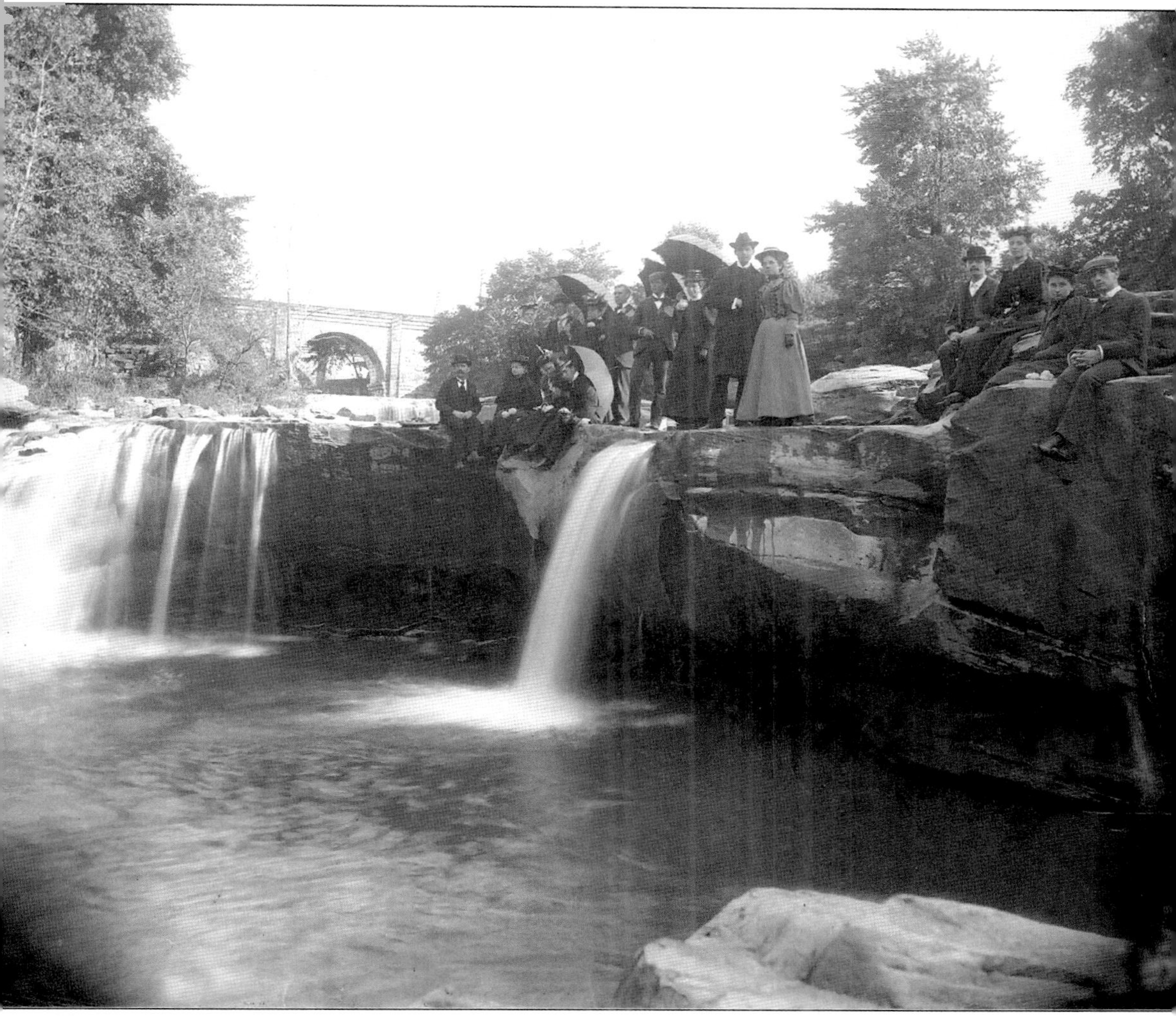

If a young Berea man was "sweet on" a young lady in the 1800s, he would hire a buggy and take her to "The Rocks" on a Sunday afternoon. Here, a rushing waterfall and cavernous rock formations offered a picturesque backdrop for games, music, and romance. The scene is virtually unchanged in the 21st century. An overlook platform now provides a favorite photograph setting and a site for an occasional wedding.

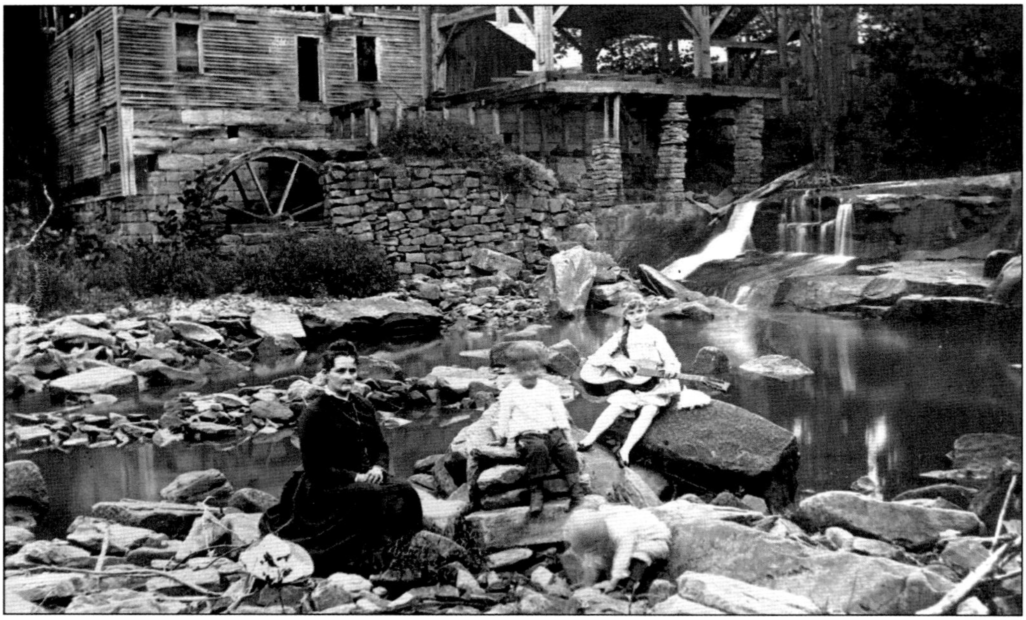

The setting at The Rocks also provides a natural echo chamber for music. Although the abandoned mill no longer stands, and clothing is more relaxed and informal, this same scene could take place today. The Rocks have delighted generations of Bereans and college students.

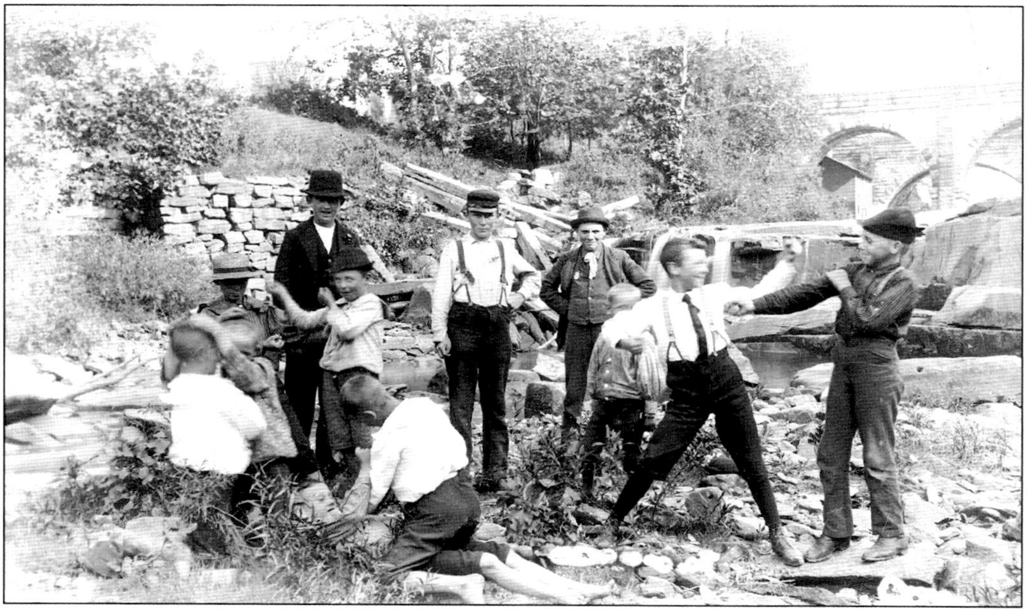

Berea quarrymen's sons, in their Sunday best at the Rocks, seem to be displaying their pugilistic abilities for a photographer, probably an unusual happening for the boys, who may also be acting out a bit for the benefit of the lone girl in the straw hat. From left to right, they are Lee Raugh, Jack Galvin, Roxie Wotalewicz, Ben Thomas, Charles Galvin, Vic Cholic, Mike Waltman, Ed Brown, George Galvin, Ed Rock, and Jim Galvin.

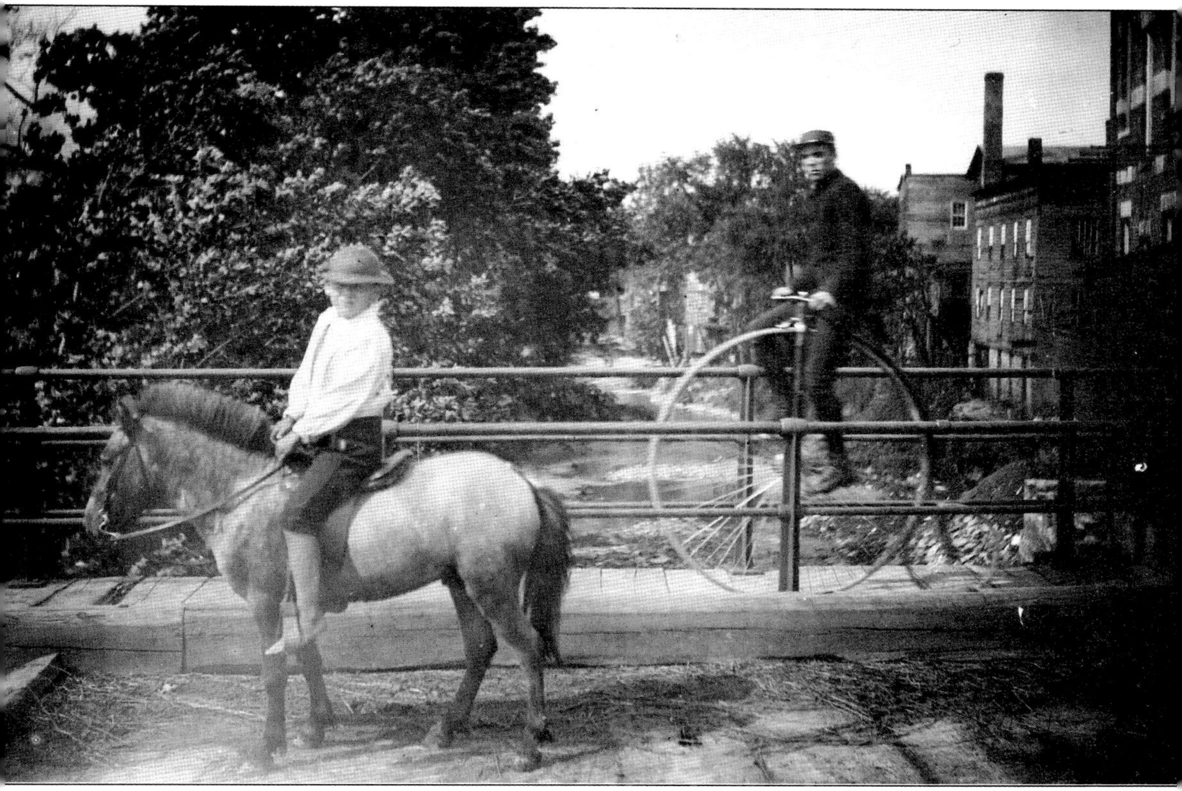

Although a few people had automobiles in 1905, these residents are shown using more common forms of transportation. They are crossing the Rocky River Bridge on West Bridge Street.

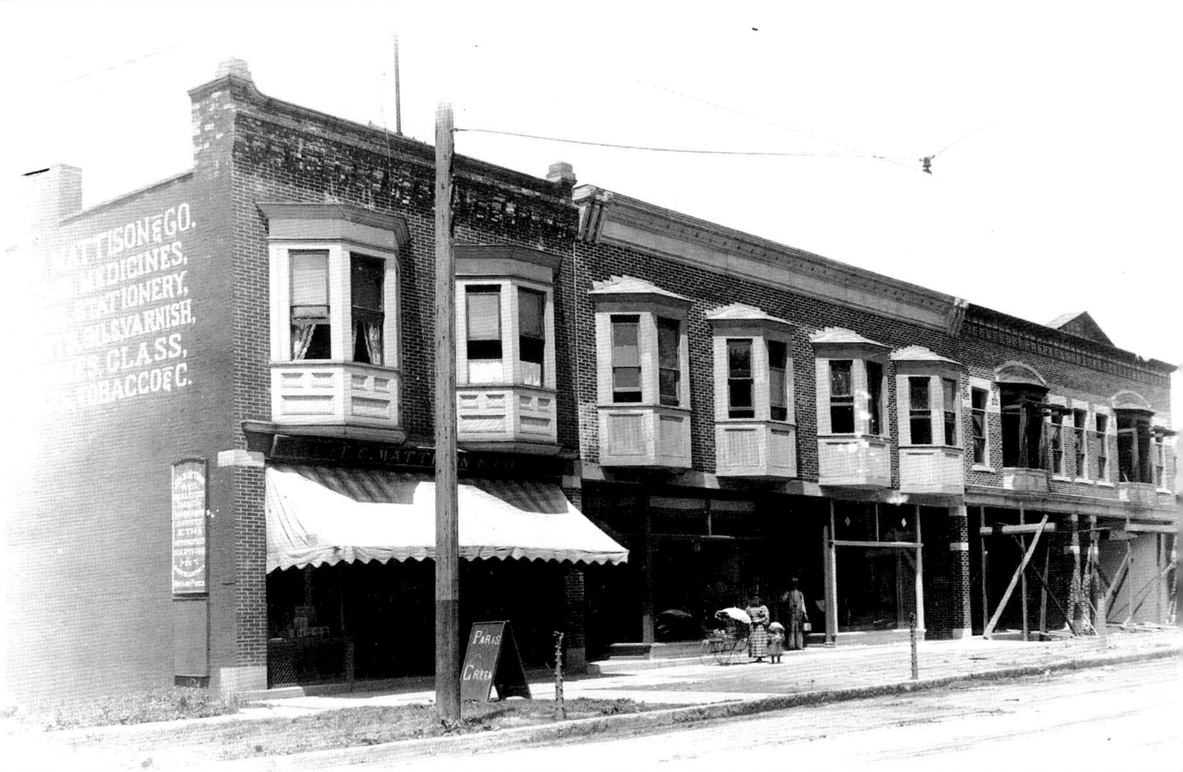

Thomas Mattison purchased E.J. Kennedy's interest in the drug store known as Kennedy & Noble and operated it for 18 years in the building known as the Neubrand Block on Front Street. In 1894, he built a two-story brick building and relocated his business. The remainder of the block was added later. Note that even in the 19th century, drug stores boasted a diverse array of merchandise. The billboard touts Paris green, a poisonous powdered insecticide.

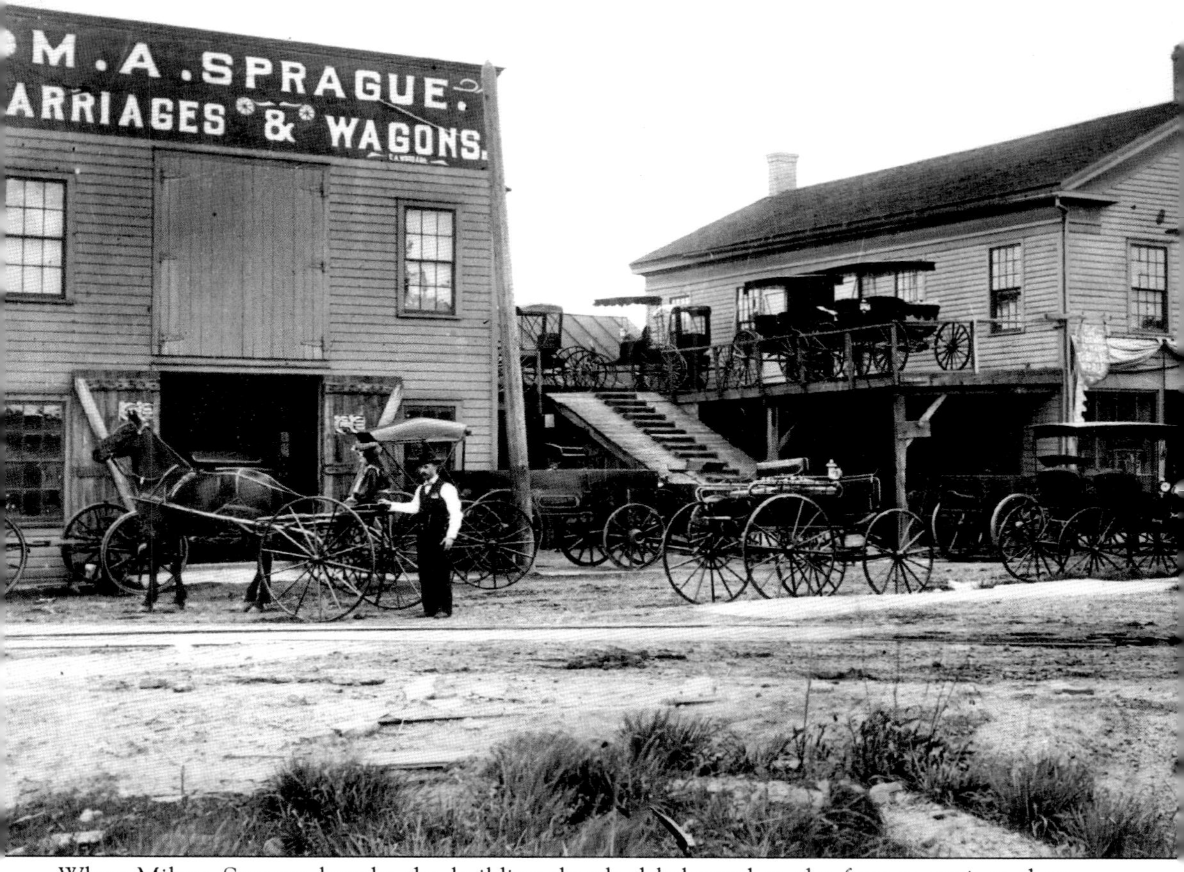

When Milton Sprague bought the building that had belonged to the former carriage shop, it was not a stranger to him. He had attended school in that building and later taught there. The M.A. Sprague Carriage & Wagon Works led southwest Cuyahoga County in the sale of carriages, wagons, and sleighs until fire destroyed it on Christmas Day 1903.

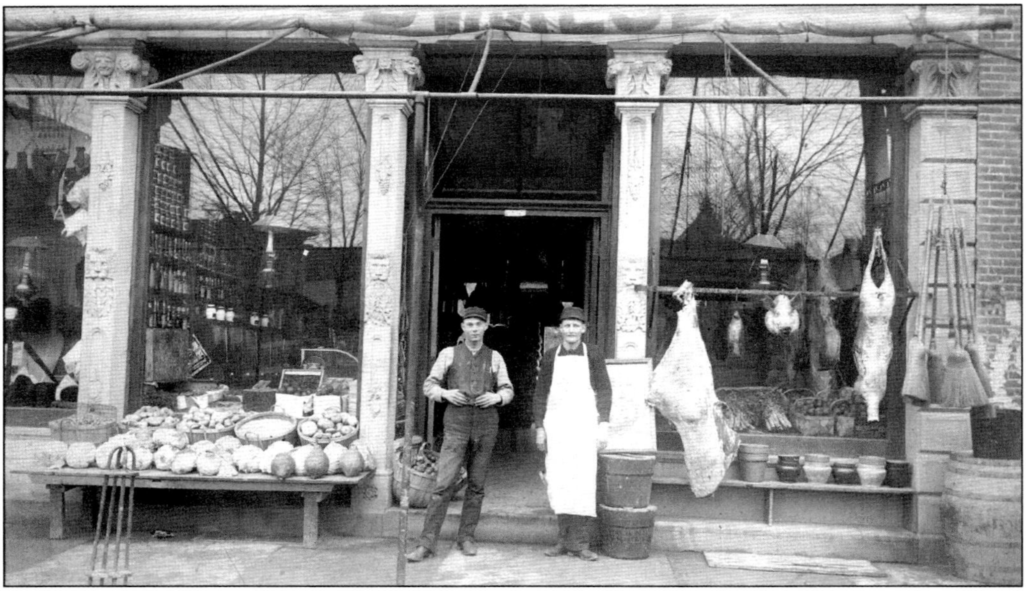

Sides of meat often hung out over the street alongside household items, such as brooms. The lions on the façade indicate this store was part of the Bullinger Block.

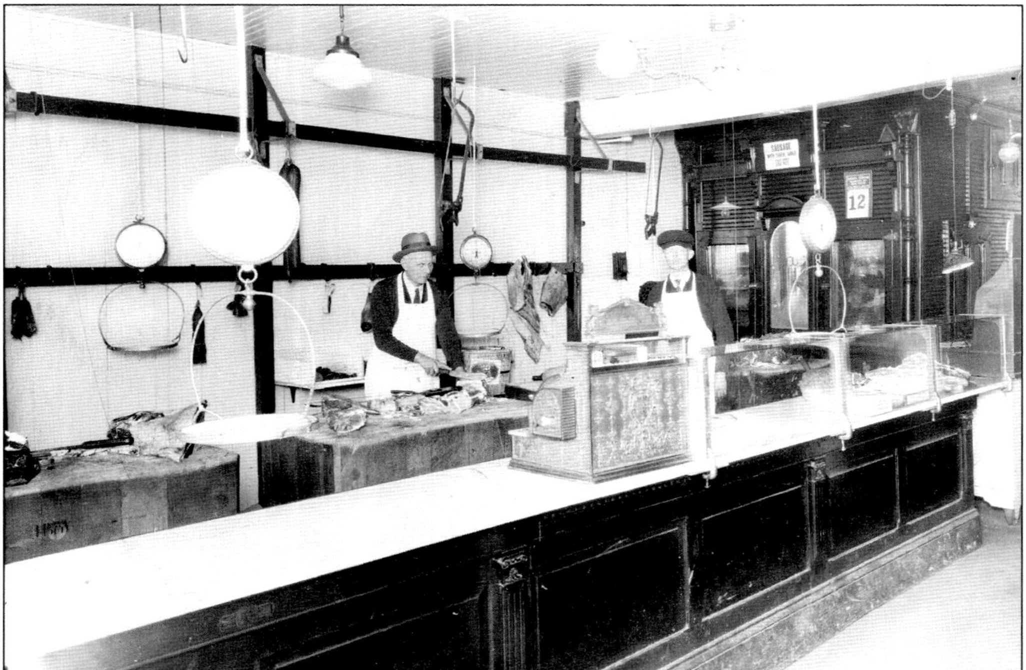

Electric lights, a walk-in cooler, and a modern cash register gave this butcher shop an up-to-date look.

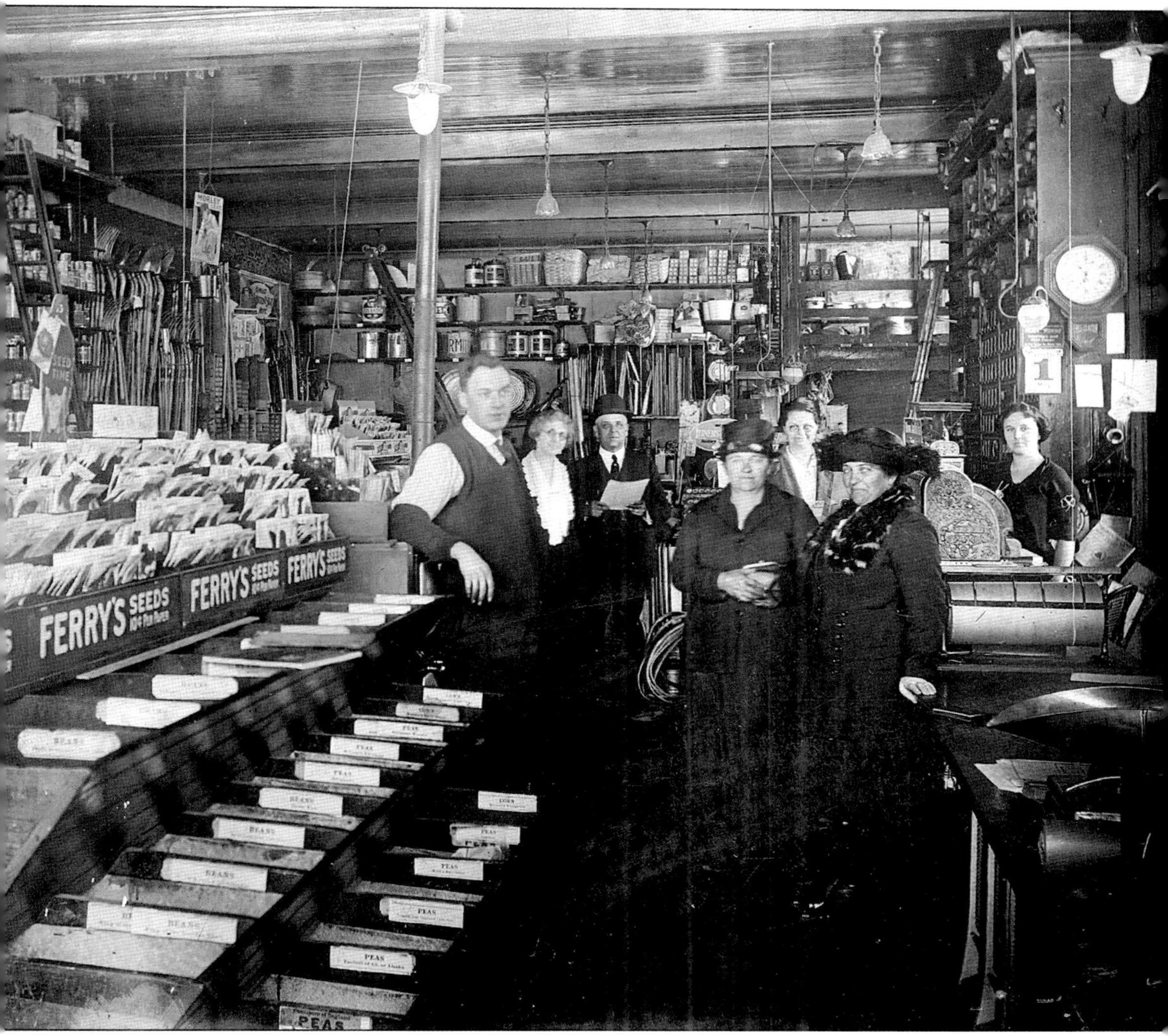

Brown Hardware Store has been a Berea institution since 1873. Cabinetmaker Godfrey Brown and his wife Esther and their seven children came to Berea from New York State in 1853. The fifth son, Fred Brown, married Irvinia Smedley. He joined his father-in-law James Smedley in a hardware business in 1873. It later became the Fred Brown Hardware Company located at the corner of Bridge and School Streets. Although Fred Brown died in 1922 and the store has since moved to another location, it still retains the name Brown Hardware.

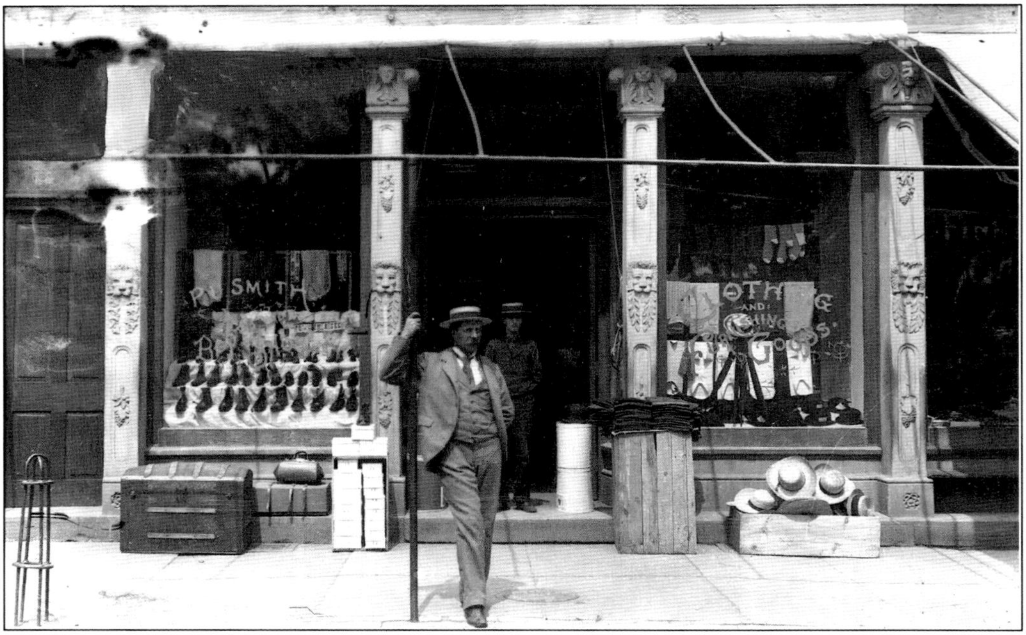

Located on the west side of the Triangle on River Street, the façade of the P.U. Smith Clothing Store displayed a lion motif, indicating that it was part of the Bullinger Block.

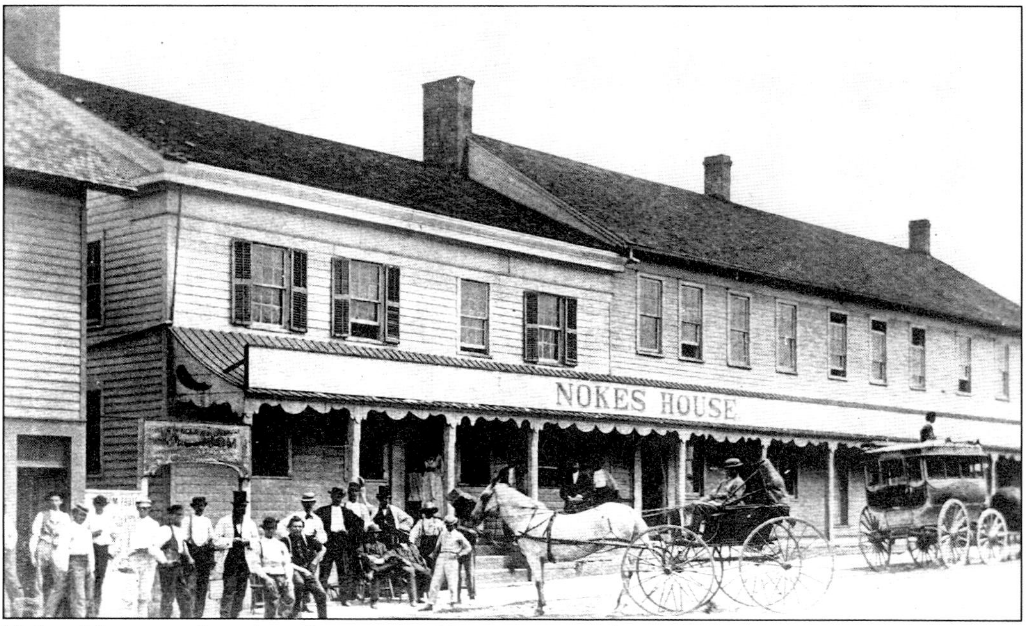

Nokes House took orders for trips to Union Depot, first by horse-drawn livery lines that competed for the jobs and later by an omnibus service started by William Brill. The fare to the depot was five rides for $1, or 11 for $2. With butter selling for 12¢ a pound and whiskey at 75¢ a gallon, this tariff might have seemed high. Yet, Bereans were proud of Brill's livery service, and the business prospered.

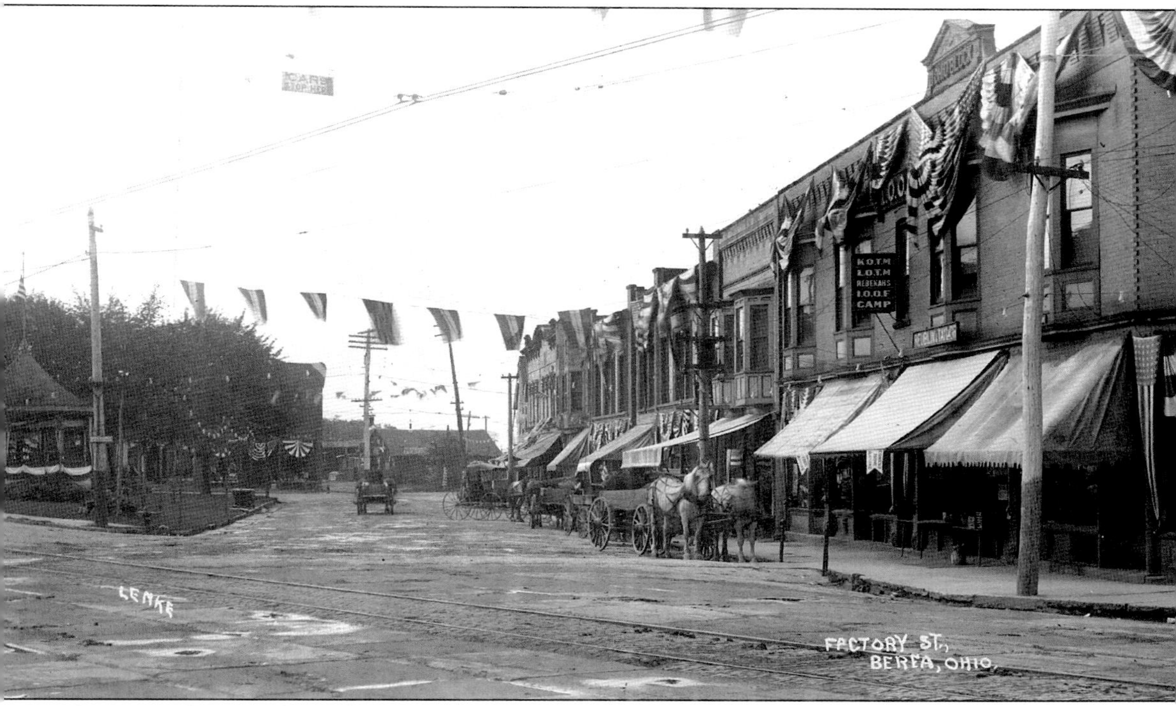

This 1910 photograph is of Factory Street looking south. The town bandstand is at left on the grassy part of the Triangle. Note the interurban tracks in the foreground on Front Street. The town appears to be decorated for a patriotic holiday or perhaps a political rally since this was a presidential election year.

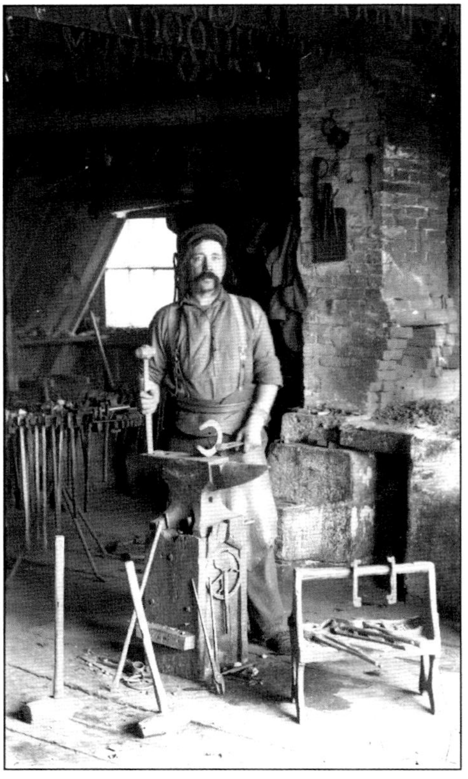

In the 1880s and 1890s, a number of blacksmiths like Louis Chevalier (above) plied their trade in Berea. The village followed a pattern for a number of years of electing or appointing them to community offices—deputy sheriff, marshal, game warden, and council. Perhaps their bulging muscles gave them extra clout as law enforcers.

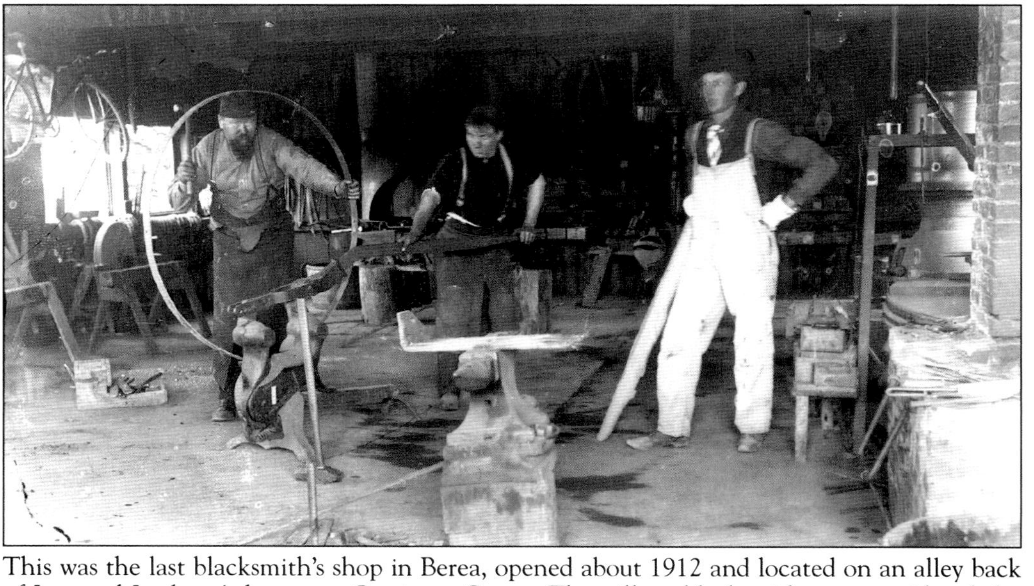

This was the last blacksmith's shop in Berea, opened about 1912 and located on an alley back of Leonard Lechner's home on Seminary Street. The village blacksmith was considered the most indispensable skilled workman in the community. With the coming of the age of the automobile, however, shoeing horses became just an occasional job. The enterprising Lechner then set up a battery sales and service center in one corner of his shop.

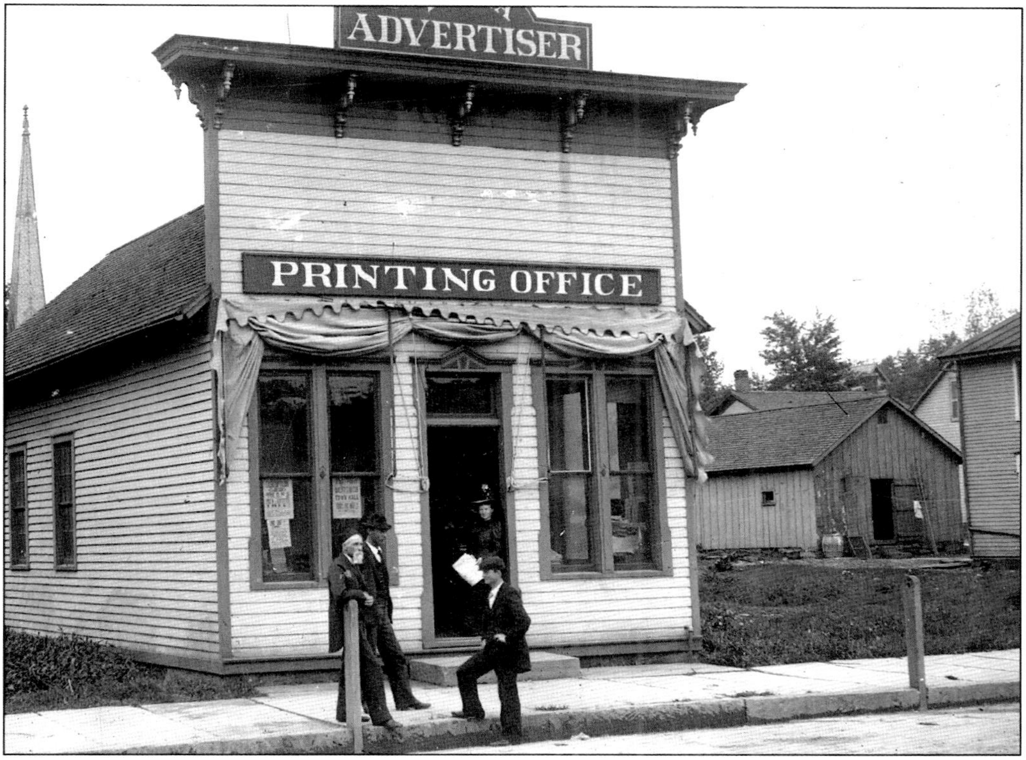

Fiery-tempered Elijah Peebles edited the *Berea Advertiser* from 1878 until his death in 1908. He lambasted editors of several competing papers, who called his paper a "smut machine" and its editor "an idiot." Nevertheless, the *Advertiser* survived, and the paper is reputed to have served the community with dignity and with a high regard for its responsibilities to subscribers.

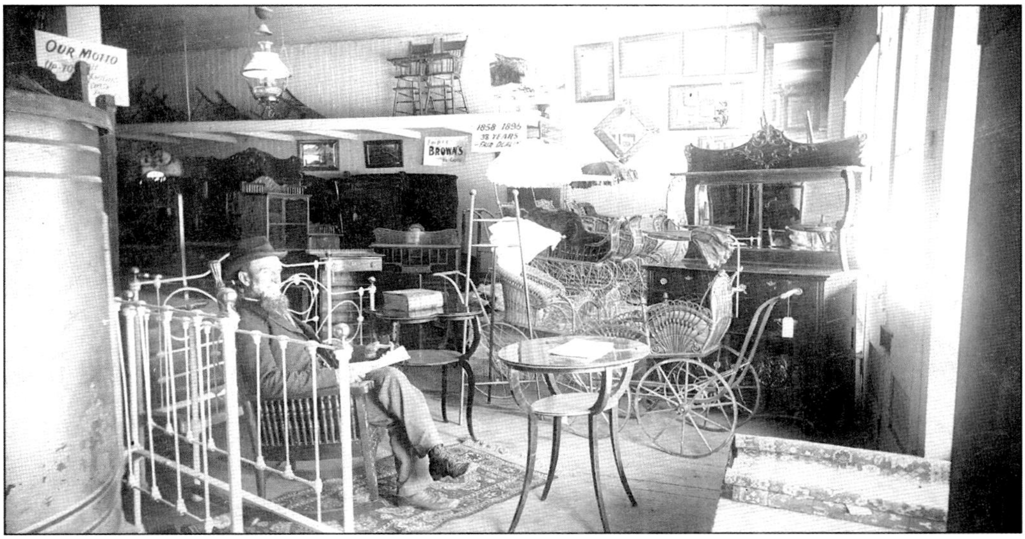

The eclectic interior of this furniture store, probably at Front and School Streets, resembles one of today's antique shops.

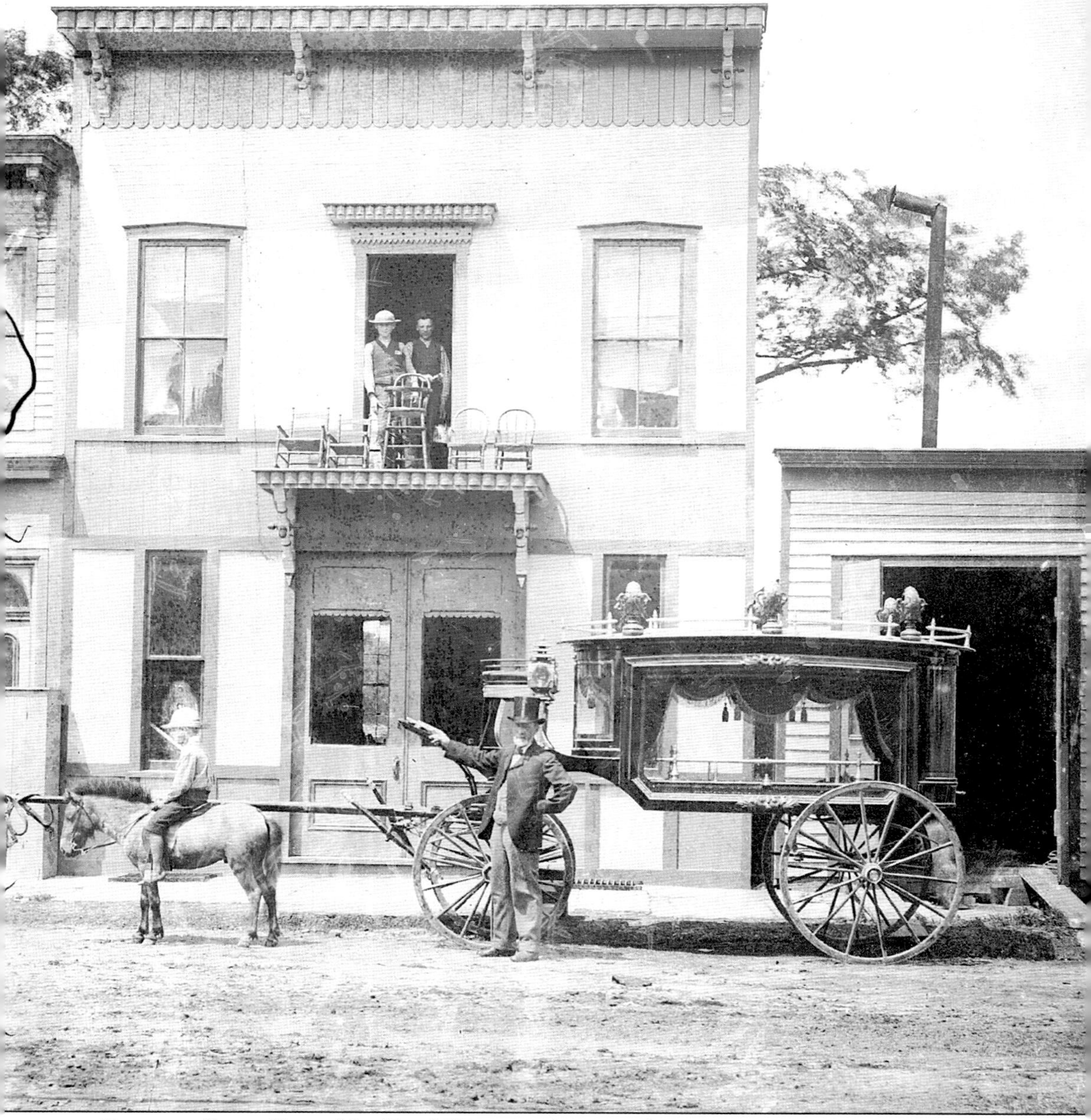

Known colloquially as "the Dead Wagon," this open hearse was a familiar sight. In 1875, a news account described the unfortunate incident of an undertaker being thrown from the seat when a wheel hit a hole on the road to the cemetery. With a sprained shoulder, the undertaker enlisted help from some of the gentlemen, dressed in their funeral-best, to help him get the coffin back onto the hearse.

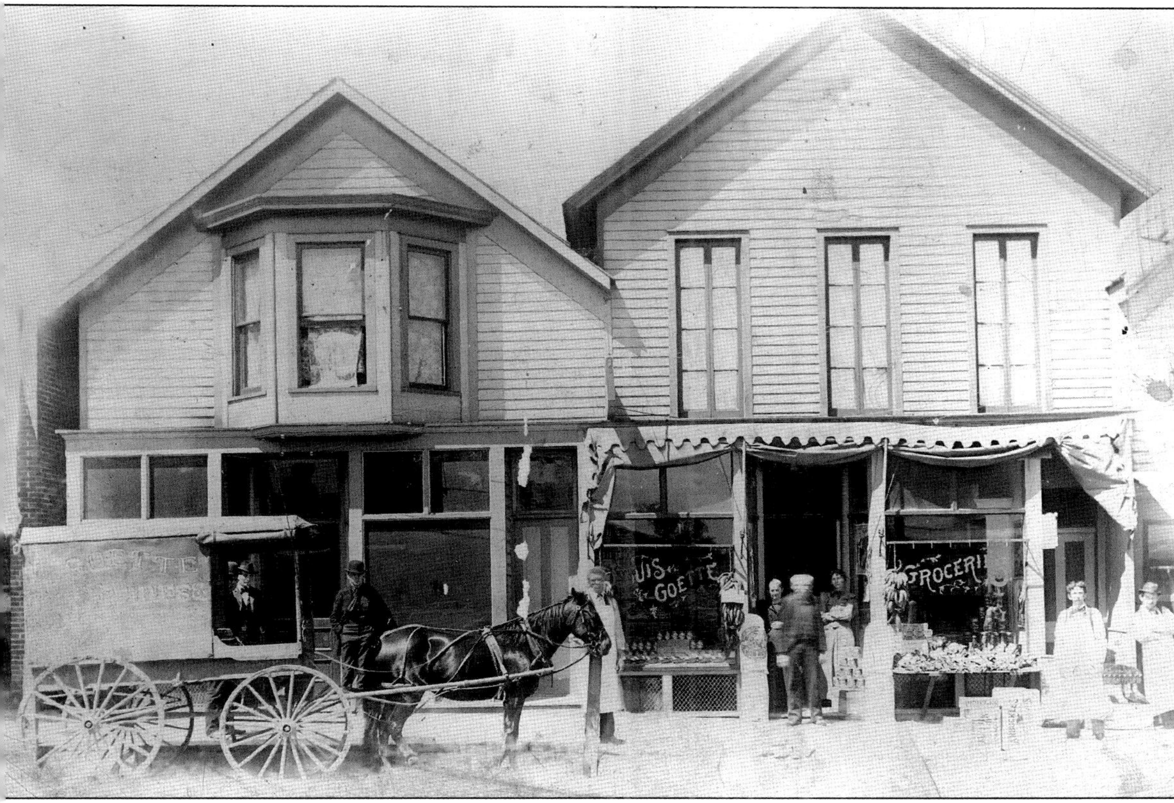

Several generations of the Goette family carried on the grocery business that Louis B. Goette established, along with a bakery, when he came to America from Germany in 1859. When Louis arrived in Cincinnati, he met Reverend William Nast, a Methodist minister well known throughout the state, who convinced him that Berea would be a good place to settle.

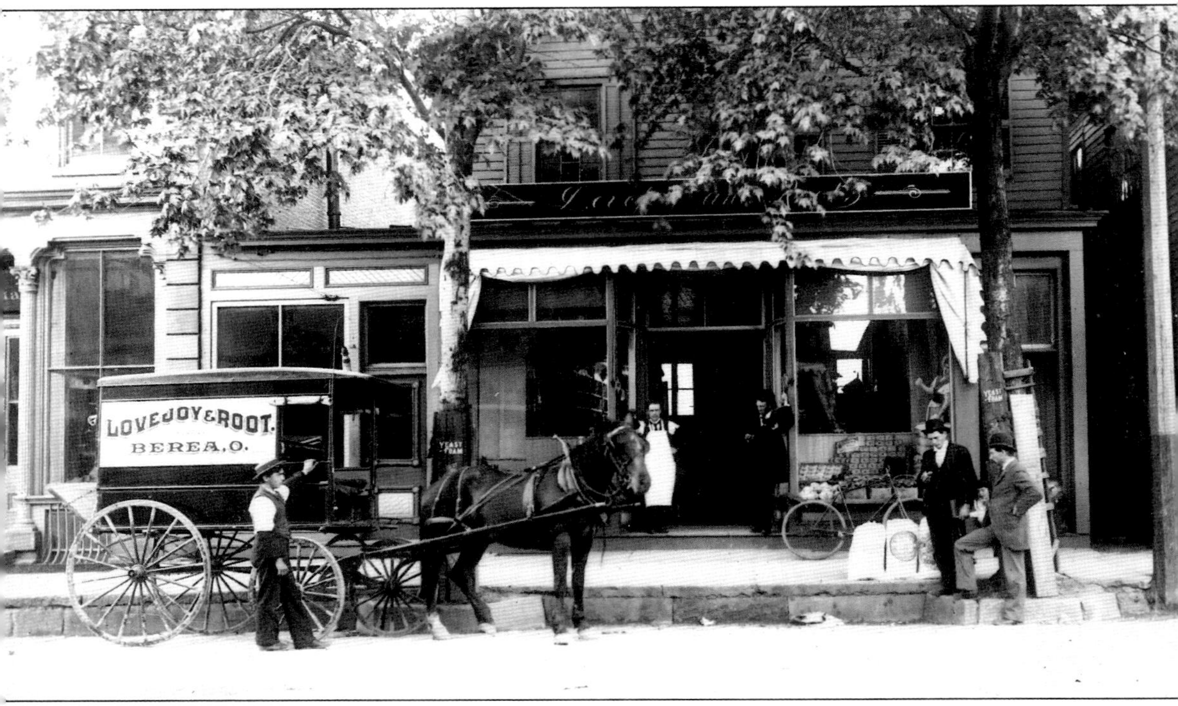

Lovejoy & Root's grocery offered shade to its customers and horse drawn delivery as well. Located on Front Street, south of East Bridge Street, it was in an area eventually taken over by the quarries.

Two

THE QUARRIES

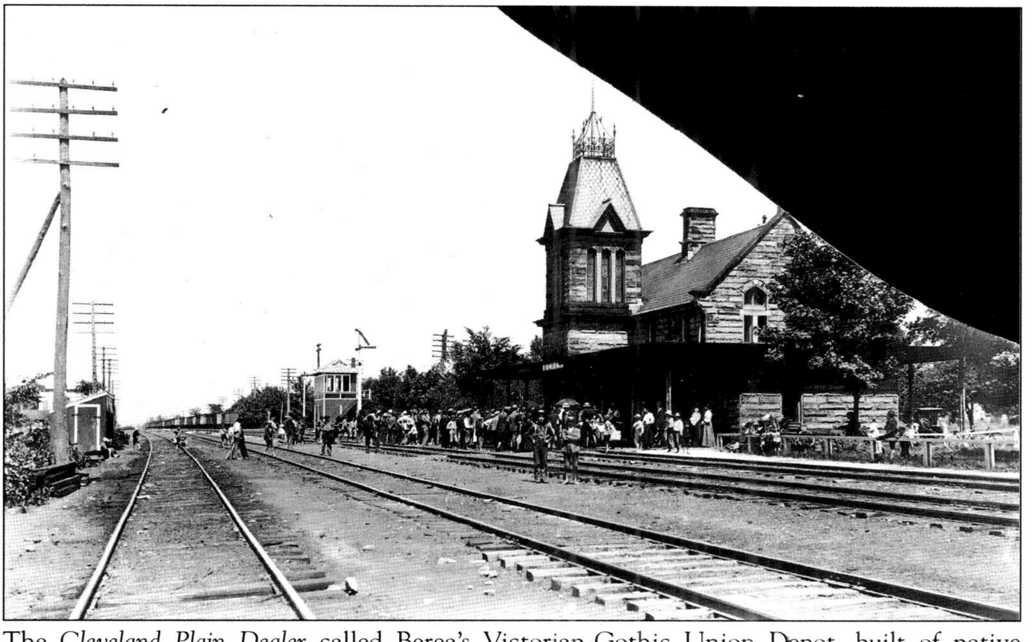

The *Cleveland Plain Dealer* called Berea's Victorian-Gothic Union Depot, built of native sandstone in 1876, "the finest passenger facility outside the big cities." As the volume of sandstone shipping increased, the old wooden depot at the end of High Street had been deemed unsuitable for freight or passenger use. At the same time the new depot was dedicated, Bereans also inaugurated a one-mile horse-drawn rail line from the center of town to Union Depot.

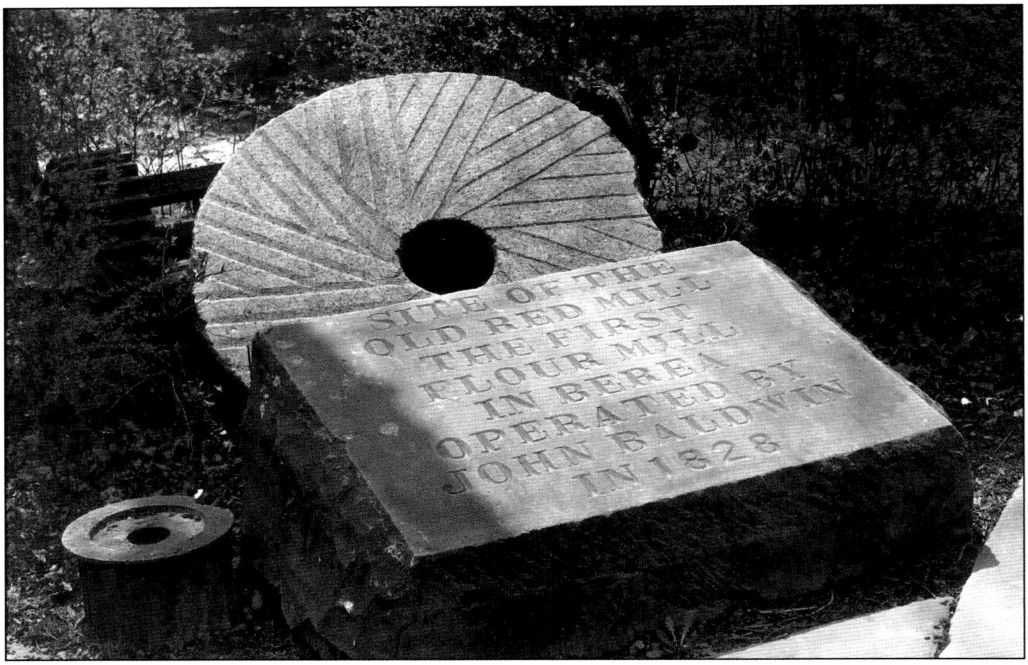

A grindstone appropriately marked the site of the grist mill that belonged to John Baldwin. It is now located at the Berea Historical Society.

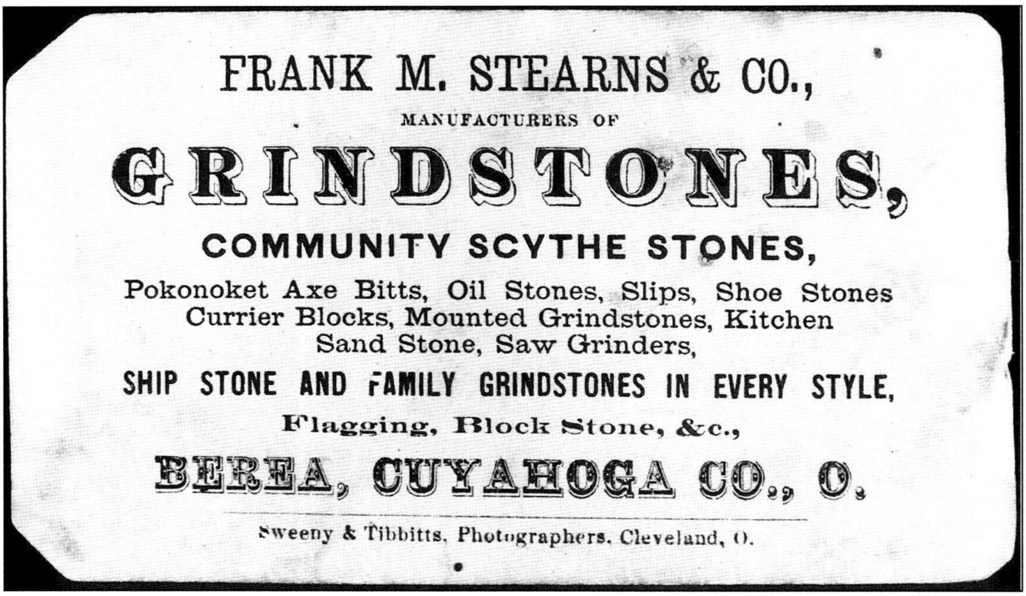

At first, John Baldwin made grindstones from thin sheets of sandstone that he found along the riverbed. He made them in the cellar of his home with a mallet and chisels and took them by oxcart and sleds to Cleveland. Eventually, others imitated Baldwin's success, and grindstone mills became prevalent. Industries used grindstones in manufacturing hundreds of articles and for keeping machinery in good condition. (Courtesy of Jim Jaworski.)

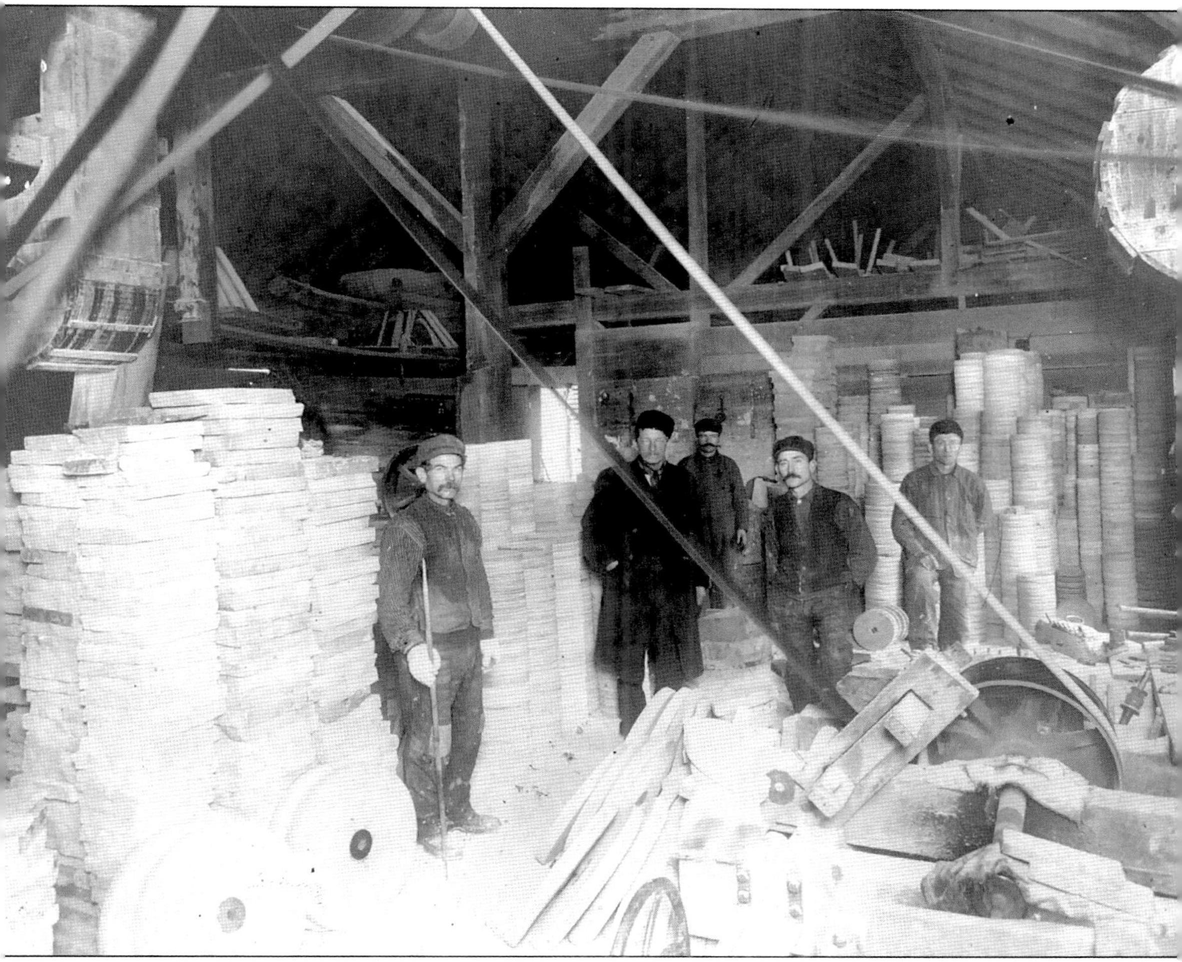

Slabs of high quality stone varying in thickness and square inches in area were hauled from the quarry to the grindstone factories. The largest factory was located in the center of Berea, not far from the Triangle, the business district. At the factory, holes were cut in the center of the slabs that were then placed on a mandrel. Turning the stone against a hardened, pointed steel bar produced a round grindstone. Thousands of rejected grindstones became sidewalks around Berea homes, and quarry workers carried discarded stones home to use in building foundations of their homes. The Stone Company used excess trimmings for filling in the quarried out pits.

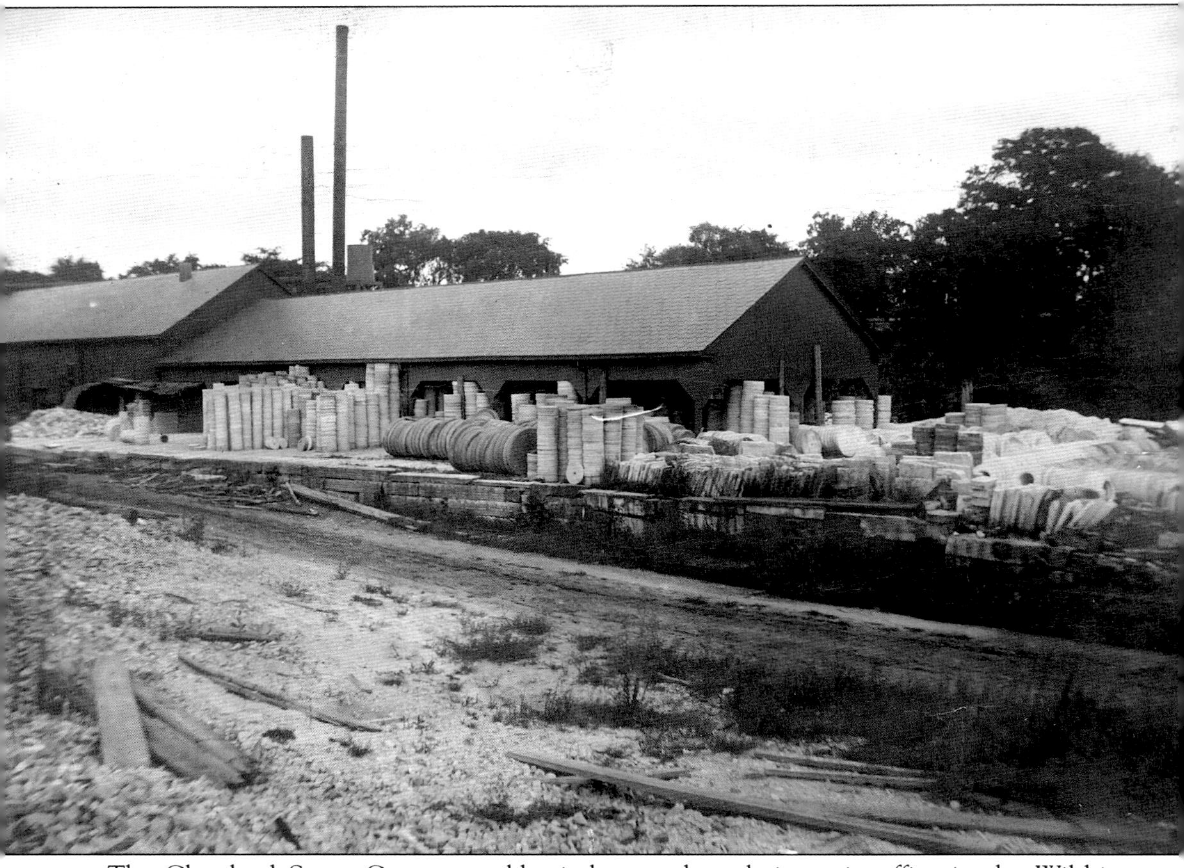

The Cleveland Stone Company sold grindstones through its main office in the Wilshire Building in Cleveland and through agencies in Chicago, Boston, New York, Philadelphia, Pittsburgh, and San Francisco. It was Berea, however, that became known as "the Grindstone City." It is believed that at one time, 93 percent of all grindstones made in the world came from Berea. In the 1860s and 1870s, the local newspaper was called the *Grindstone City Advertiser*. Today, replicas of grindstones mark the entrances to the City of Berea, and the mayor presents an annual Grindstone Award each year to an outstanding citizen.

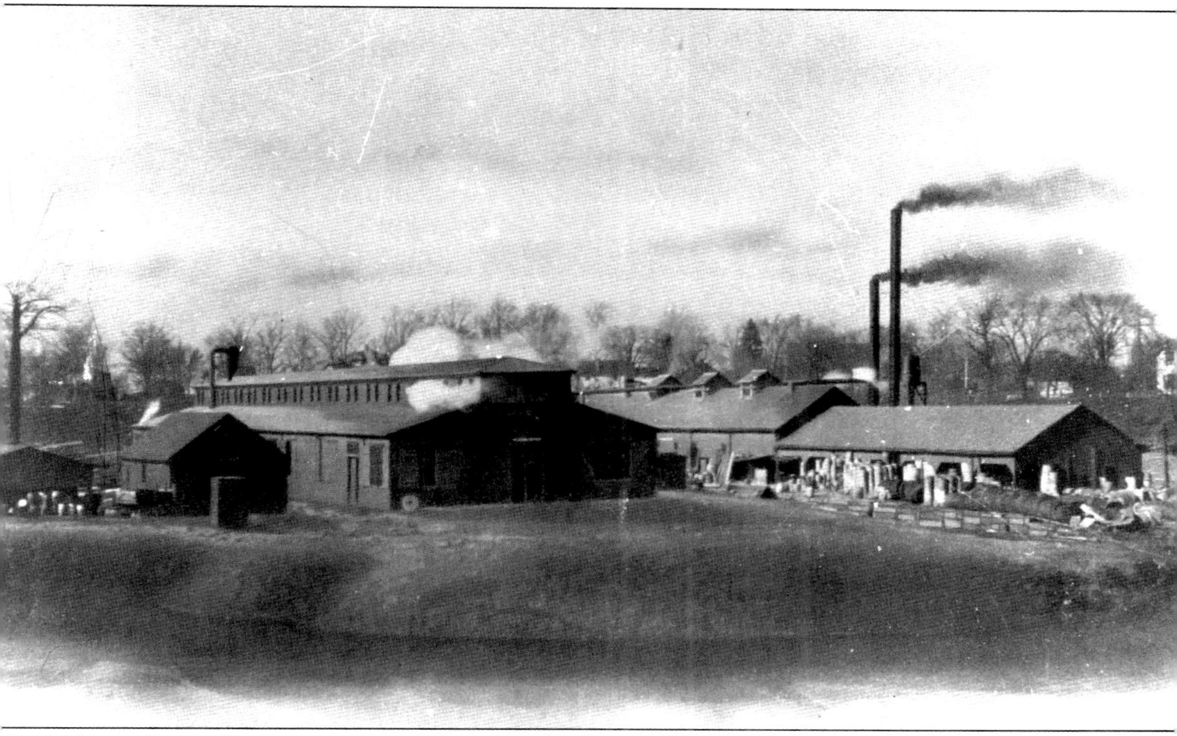

Alongside the Stearns grindstone works in the heart of Berea was the wood and iron frame factory. Dave Sterling, a chief mechanic at the quarries, invented the Sterling Grind Stone Frame, which the Cleveland Stone Company adopted to mount the grindstones. Wood frames for mounting grindstones were made of strongly braced, seasoned oak and were available for all sizes of grindstones. Iron frames could be mounted with grindstones suitable for any kind of grinding. When the stone would wear out, the hub could be returned and fitted to a new stone at a charge of $1 above the cost of the stone, according to a catalog for the Cleveland Stone Company. John Baldwin Jr. invented a blower system (at upper left) that was used in the grindstone factories to take away the dust while manufacturing grindstones.

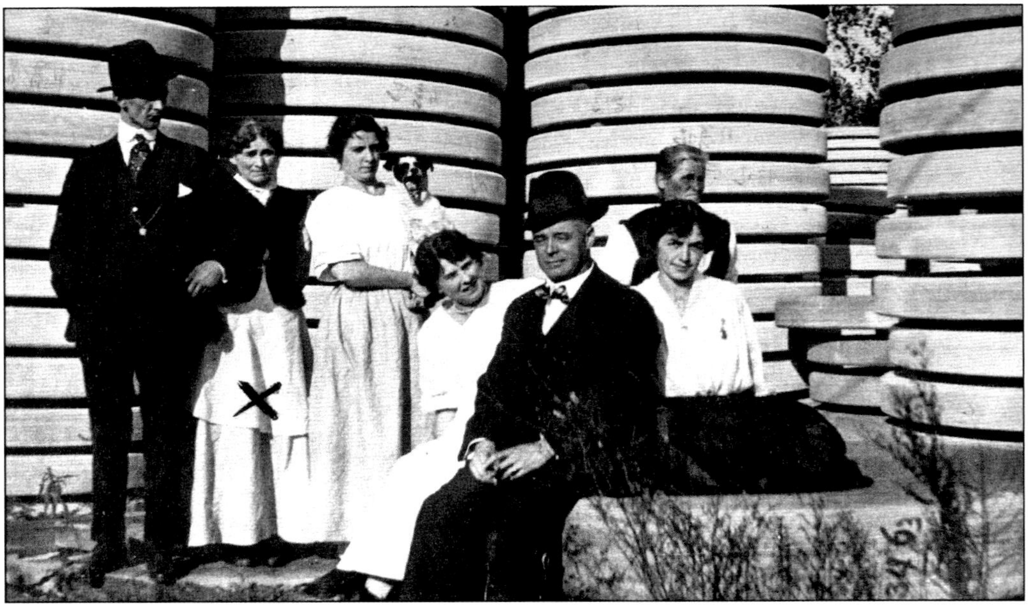

Piles of grindstones awaiting shipment were a familiar sight to residents of Berea. Grindstones were manufactured in all grades, "from the hard coarse stone required for castings (&c), to the fine soft grits adapted to cutlery and similar tools, with all intermediate grades," according to the Cleveland Stone Company's catalog. Some stones were nearly eight feet in diameter. Industries used grindstones in manufacturing hundreds of articles and for keeping machinery in good running condition. (Courtesy of Jim Jaworski.)

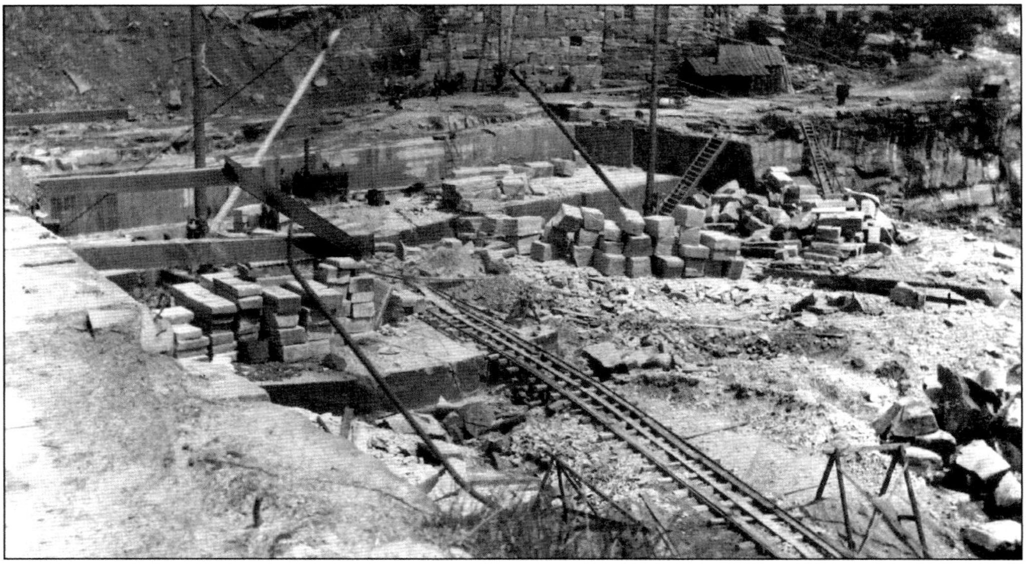

Big Quarry was near Berea's business area, the Triangle. A network of quarry-owned railroad tracks carried stone from the quarries to connect with the Big Four rail line. The quarries were required to build their tracks and maintain them to the satisfaction of the Big Four. Stretching along the Rocky River and connecting all the quarries, this stretch of the Big Four line became one of its busiest and most profitable.

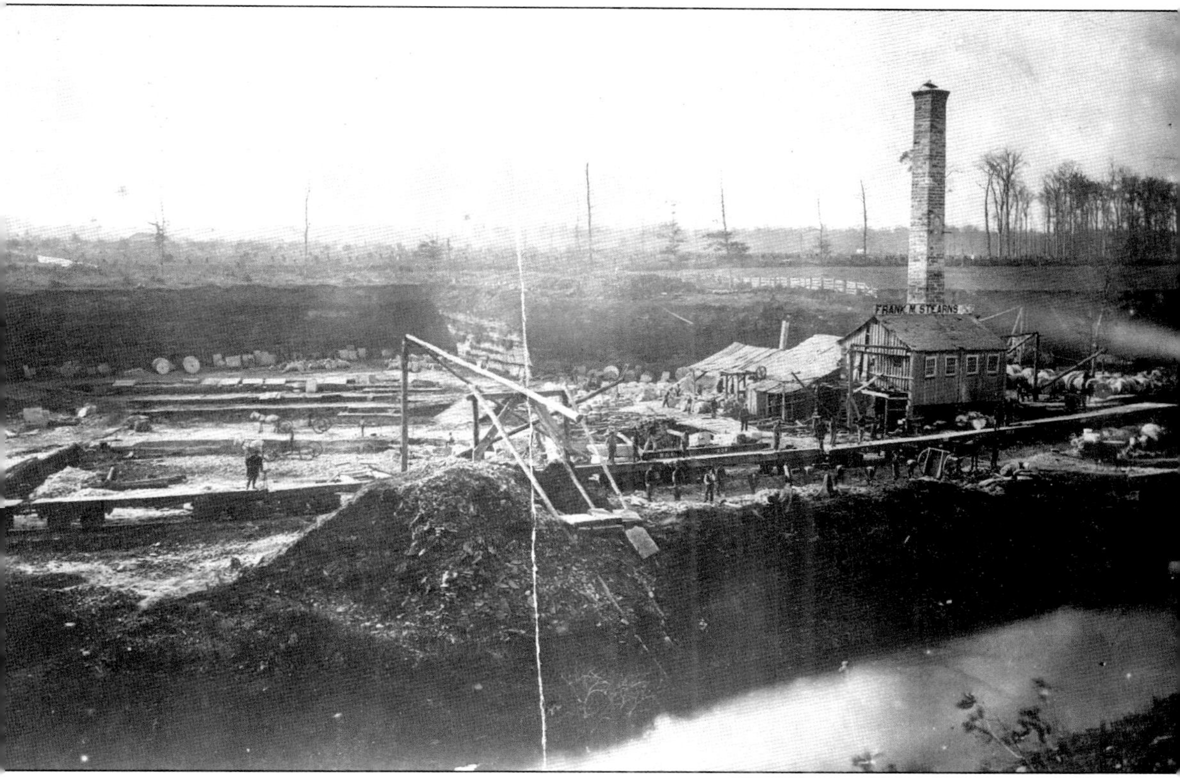

Stearns Quarry, on the west side of the Rocky River at the bend north of Center Street and near the present Parkway Shops, was a treacherous, deep swimming hole that nevertheless attracted daring swimmers. At the extreme lower right of the picture is a foot bridge across the river to Center Street. It was built for the convenience of the quarry workers.

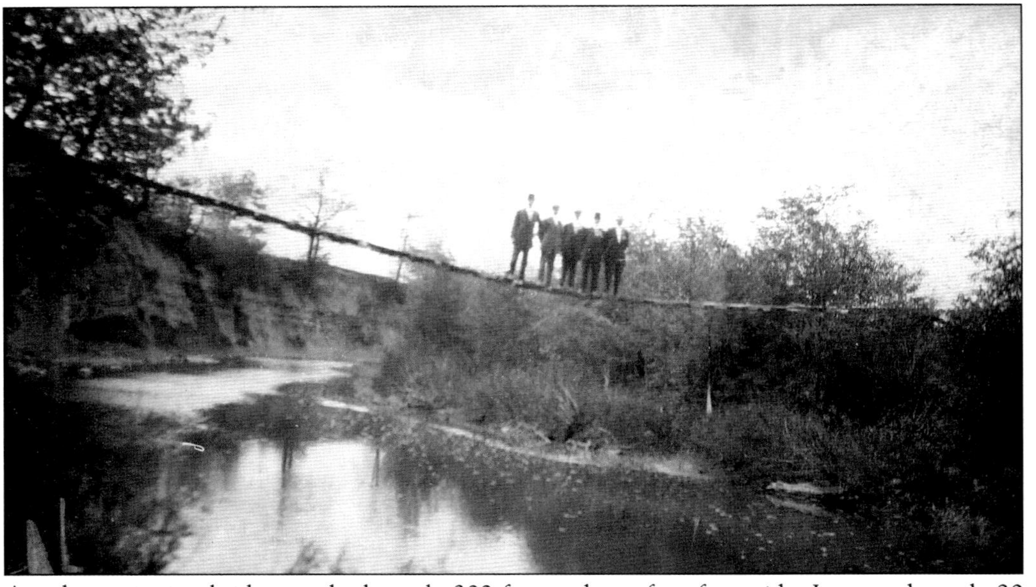

Another swinging bridge reached nearly 300 feet and was four feet wide. It swayed nearly 20 feet above the quarry railroad and Baldwin Creek to allow workers to reach Big Quarry. These bridges were hazardous, and adults as well as children who played on them, sometimes fell into the Rocky River. Drownings were not uncommon.

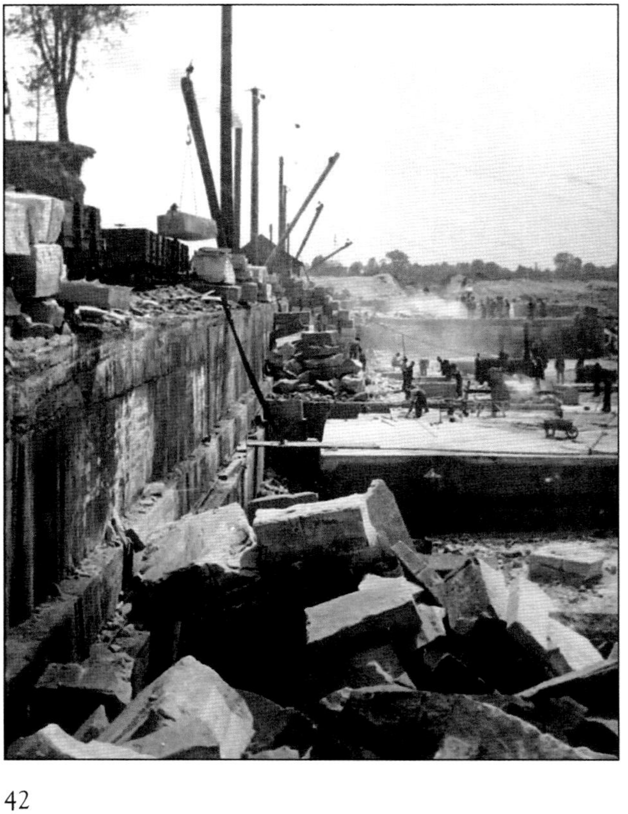

The constant specter of "grit consumption" threatened the life of every quarry worker. The fine, beige-white dust created from the constant chipping of the sandstone damaged the lungs of those who spent their lives in the quarries. Controlling the danger from quarry dust was a problem impossible to resolve. A quarry worker's only defense against this hazard was a bandana tied over his nose and mouth, which he probably removed on very warm days.

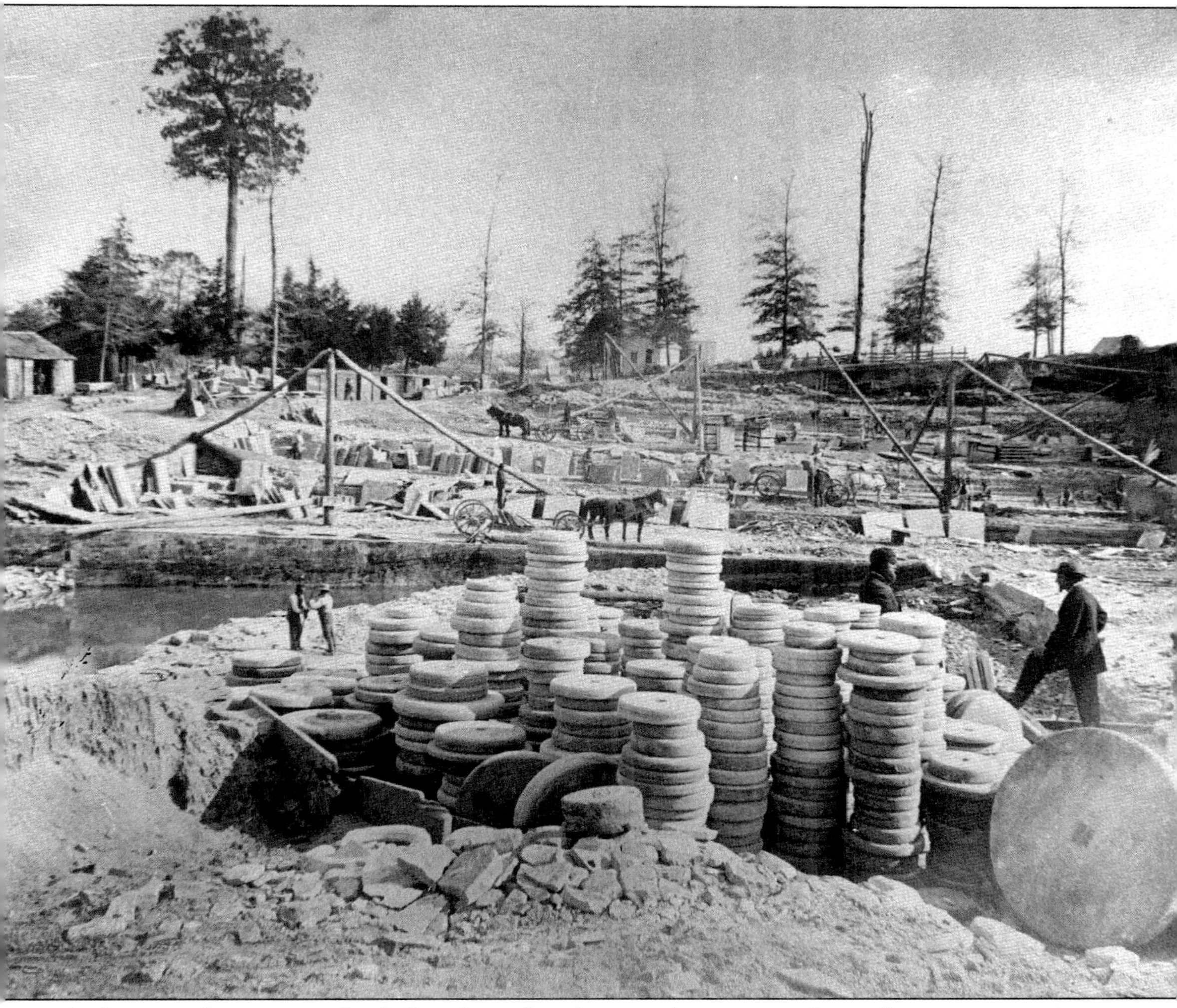

At first, grindstones were hauled to the railroad station by oxcart or horse-drawn wagons. As the demand for larger building stones increased, teams of horses often worked in the quarries. Quarrymen also moved grindstones in wheelbarrows that had leather straps harnessing the wheelbarrow to their shoulders.

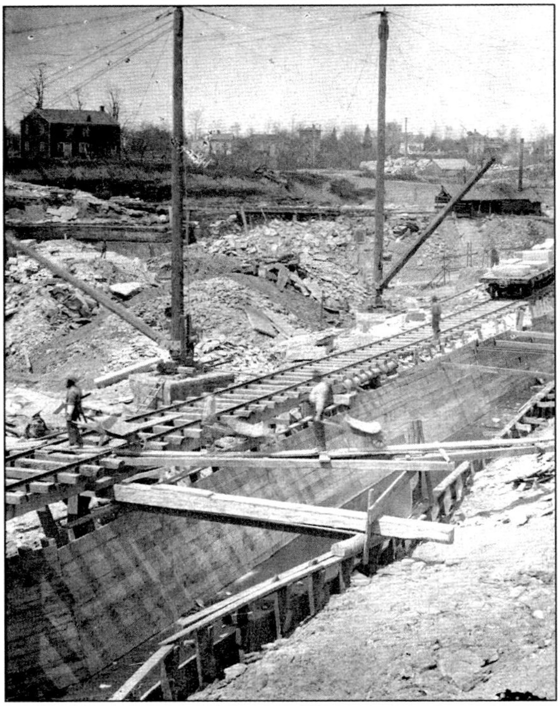

If an area contained sandstone, nothing would keep it from being quarried. Baldwin Creek was relocated by means of constructing a wooden flume. Many houses were moved from the land that was rich in the precious sandstone, and even a cemetery was desecrated. Quarrying extended up to the Adams Street Cemetery where remains of some broken tombstones can still be viewed today. The house at top left is John Baldwin's "Red House" where he made the first grindstone.

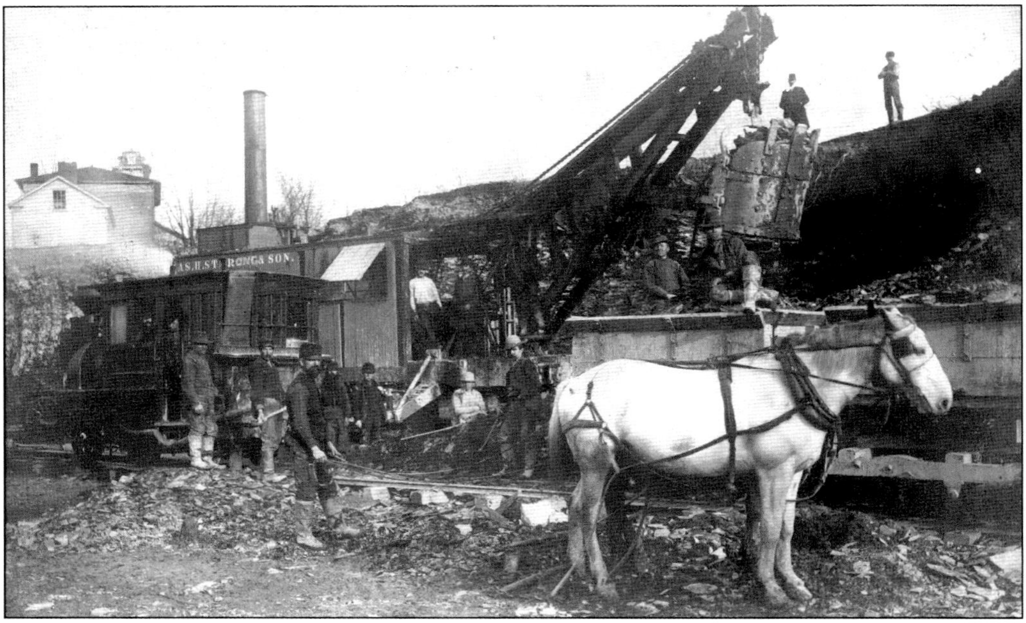

By 1900, a steam shovel removed shale and boulder clay from the layer of sandstone buried beneath. Using a steam boiler and a supply of logs and water, the steam shovel could do the work of hundreds of quarrymen in but a fraction of the time previously required. The draft horse will haul shale and clay away from the quarry site to a waiting railroad car to be used to fill in already quarried-out sites.

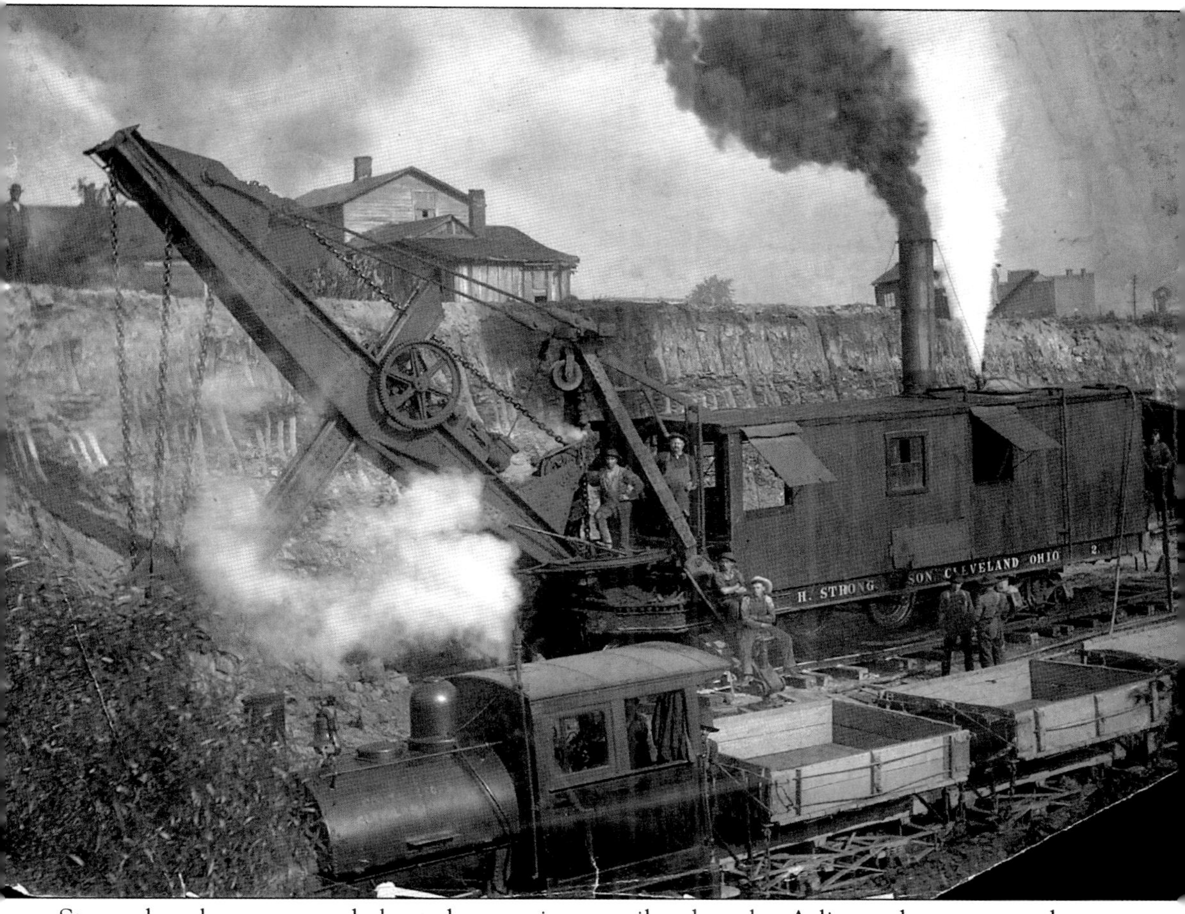

Steam shovels were moved about the quarries on railroad tracks. A licensed operator and a fireman were required for running a steam shovel. Operators had to be very skilled to manipulate the jaws of this huge piece of equipment. Because of their shape and odd balance, steam shovels could easily tip over. They also had to be very near the edge of wherever they were digging, and the ground sometimes collapsed. Fatal accidents were common, leaving quarrymen's families nearly destitute. Sometimes collections would be taken up to aid widows temporarily, but no formal program of survivors' benefits existed at that time.

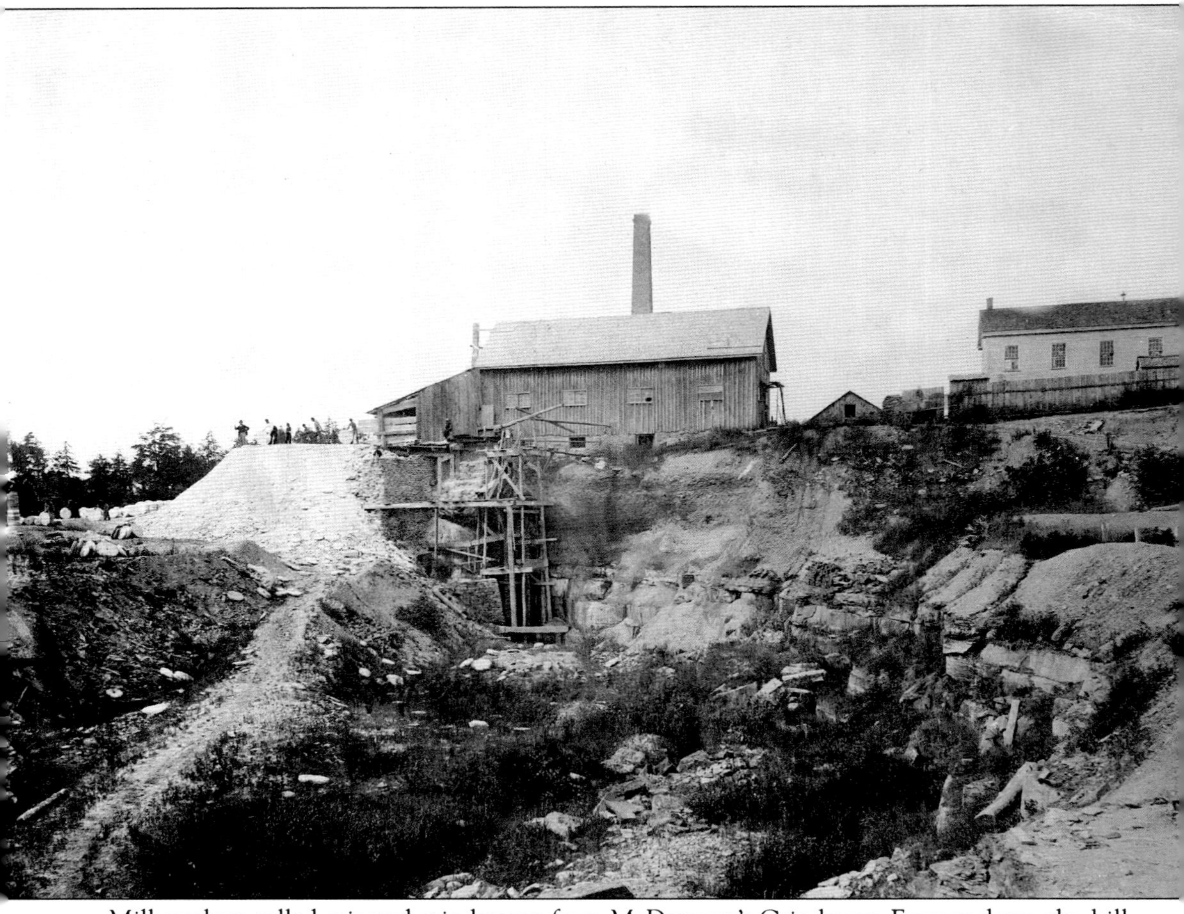

Mill workers rolled rejected grindstones from McDermott's Grindstone Factory down the hill behind the building. Today, residents of Berea can find pieces of grindstones surfacing in their gardens. At right is the old Union School on Elm Street. It was abandoned because of the noise and vibration of blasting from the quarries.

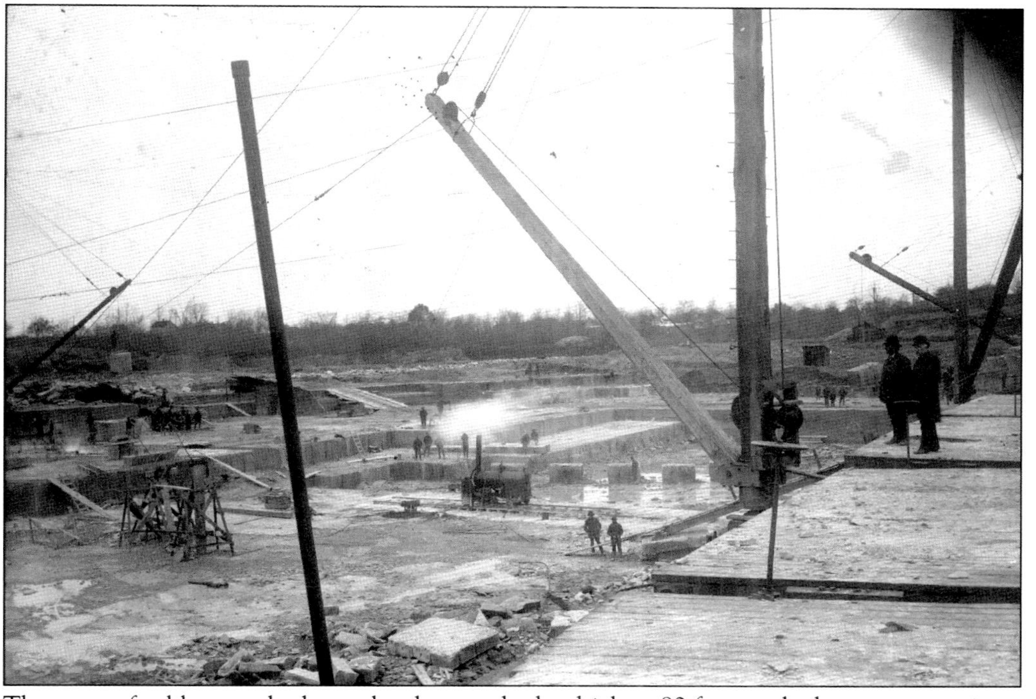

The maze of cables attached to poles that reached as high as 80 feet marked quarry operations. A second pole extended outward, connecting a series of pulleys and chains to the vertical pole. These were derricks, used for lifting huge blocks of building stone and moving them to the railroad sidings. By the turn of the century, these derricks were steam-powered, but earlier they were operated totally by the sweat and toil of the quarrymen.

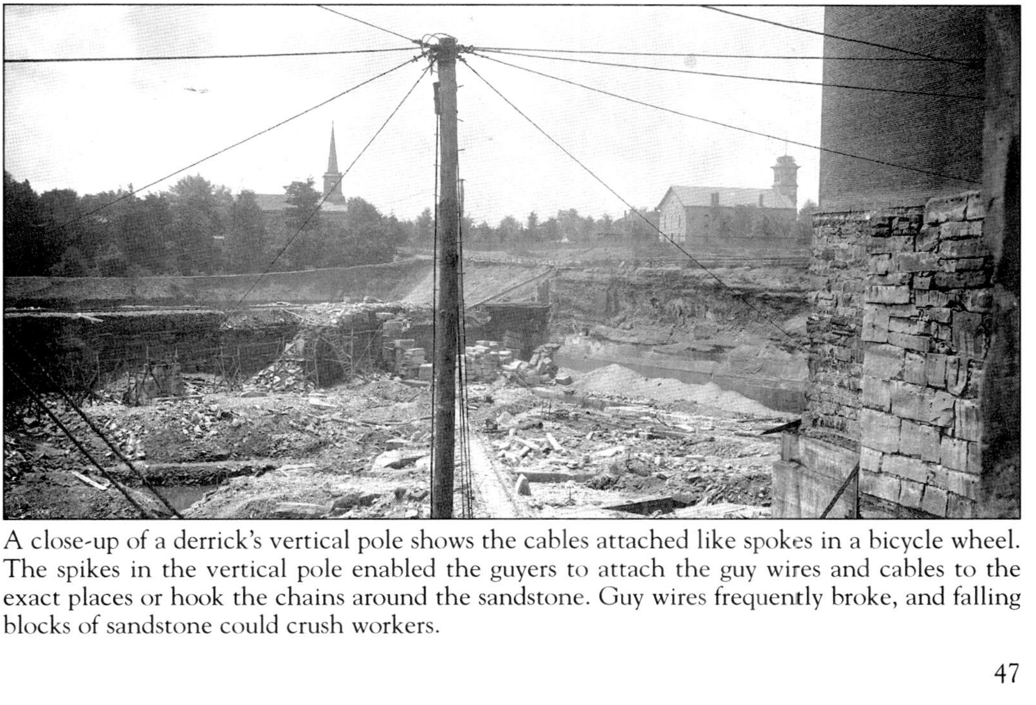

A close-up of a derrick's vertical pole shows the cables attached like spokes in a bicycle wheel. The spikes in the vertical pole enabled the guyers to attach the guy wires and cables to the exact places or hook the chains around the sandstone. Guy wires frequently broke, and falling blocks of sandstone could crush workers.

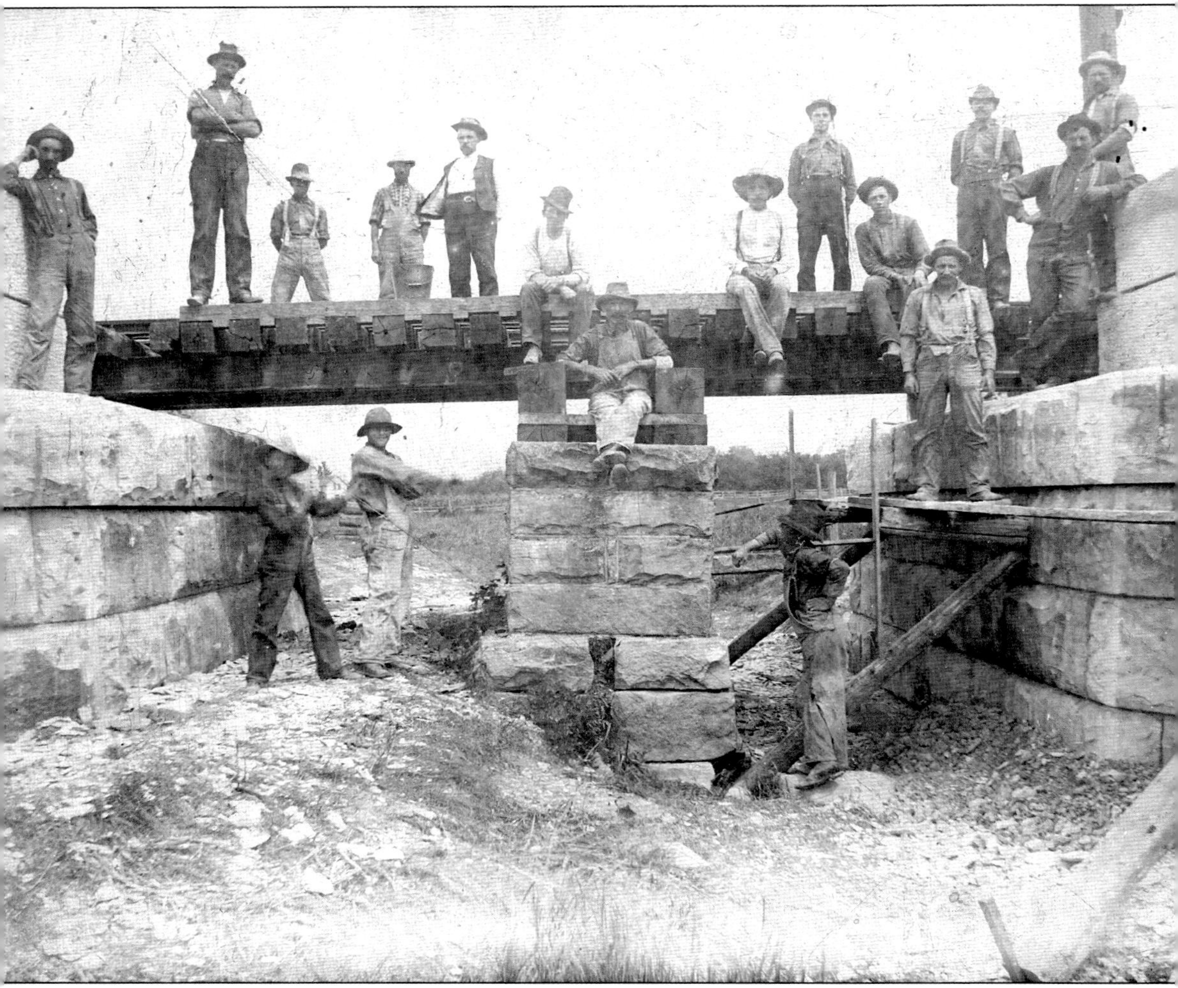

An 1890s photograph shows the building of a bridge over the Rocky River bed at Bridge and School Streets. Edward J. Kennedy, who was at that time a member of the Ohio legislature from Berea, was instrumental in obtaining state funding for this bridge.

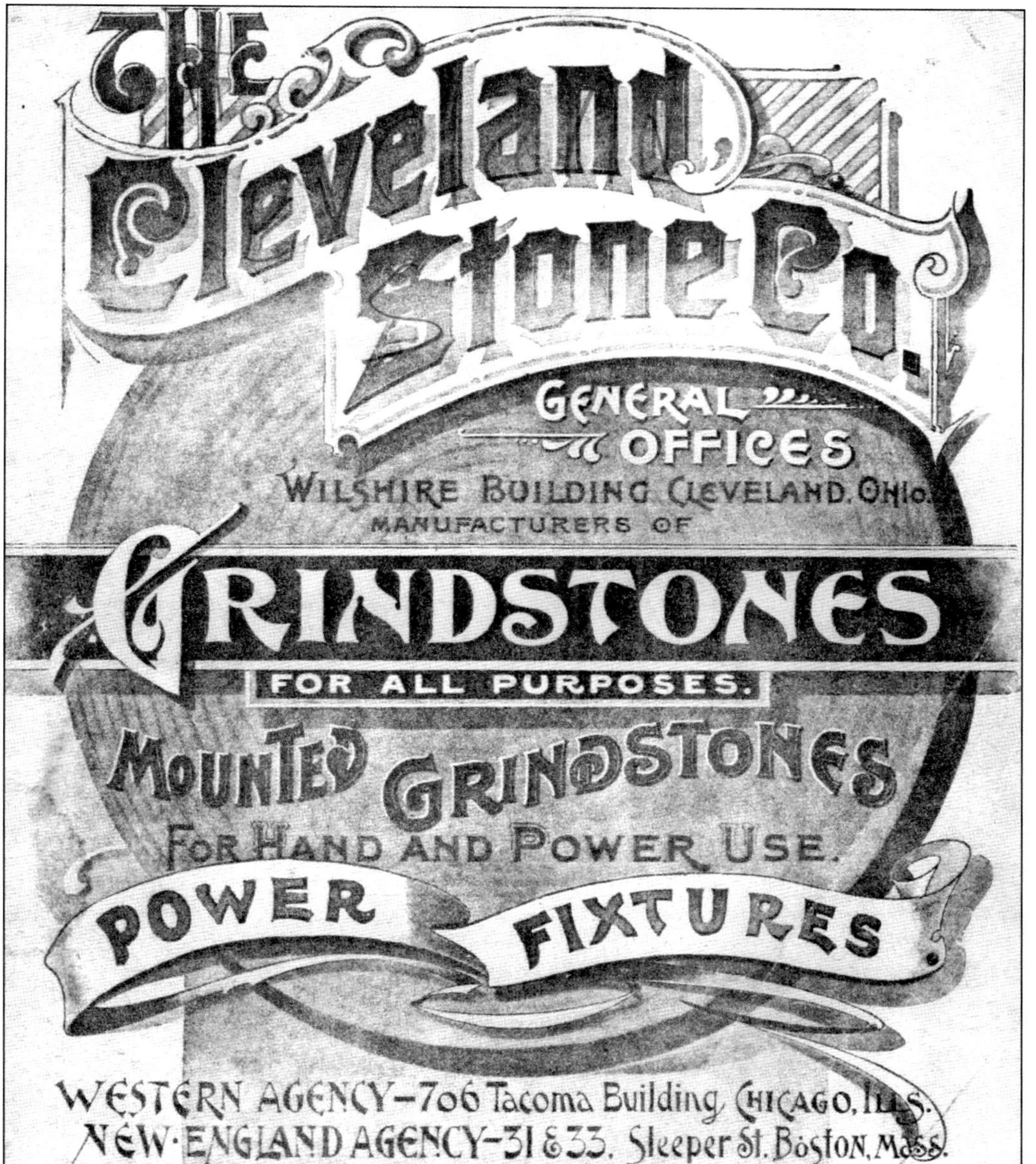

Individual quarries and even those that joined together to become the Berea Stone Company could not compete successfully with the Cleveland Stone Company that took over all of the quarries in Berea and some in Lorain County to the west in 1888. The easy sheets of stone on top of the ground were gone, and the valuable stone lay deeper underground. By the 1890s, James H. Smith, a professor of natural sciences at Baldwin University, estimated that the cost of stripping the clay and shale covering averaged between $11,000 and $12,000 an acre. Add to this the rising cost of undeveloped quarry land that by that time was $5,000 per acre, and as Professor Smith stated, "before even a stroke can be made in mining the stone. . . you have 16 or 17 thousand dollars per acre," which must be invested (from *And Then There Were None*). (Courtesy of Jim Jaworski.)

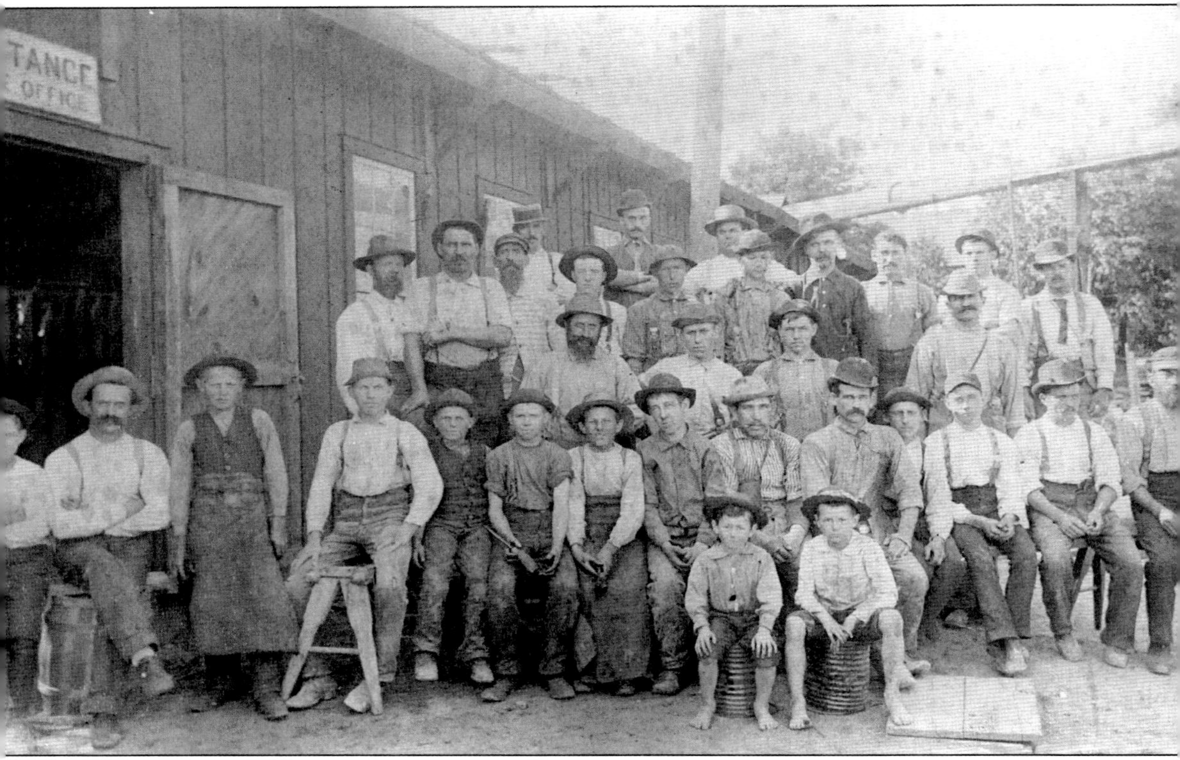

Among workers at a sawmill are many young boys who worked the 10-hour days alongside adults. The two at right front may have been water boys, who carried heavy yokes and buckets up and down 180 steps to a well that provided water to the quarry workers. Water boys earned as little as 50¢ a day for any number of trips.

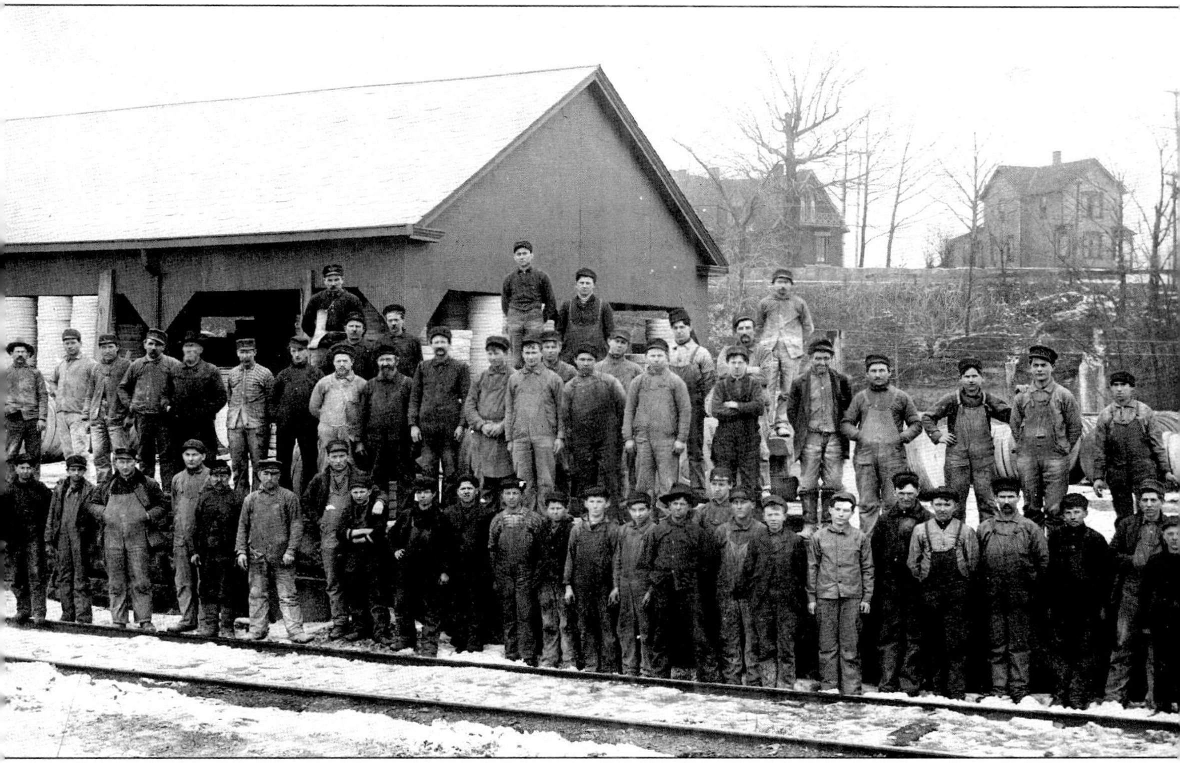

These workers at Stearns Quarry stand between Rocky River and the quarry railroad. They would have crossed the swinging bridge at Center Street to get to work.

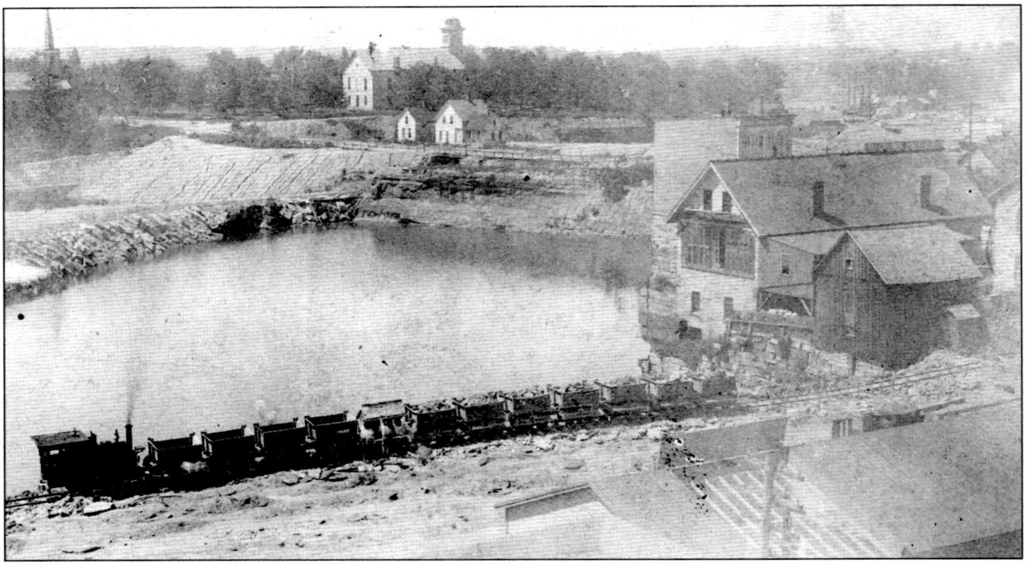

Small engines, known as "dinky" or "pony" engines, pulled strings of gondola-like cars to take quarried stone to the mills and depot. In the center of the picture is what was called "the Hog's Back" (Elm Street), a slim tract of land separating two parts of Berea. It was part of the fashionable South Side.

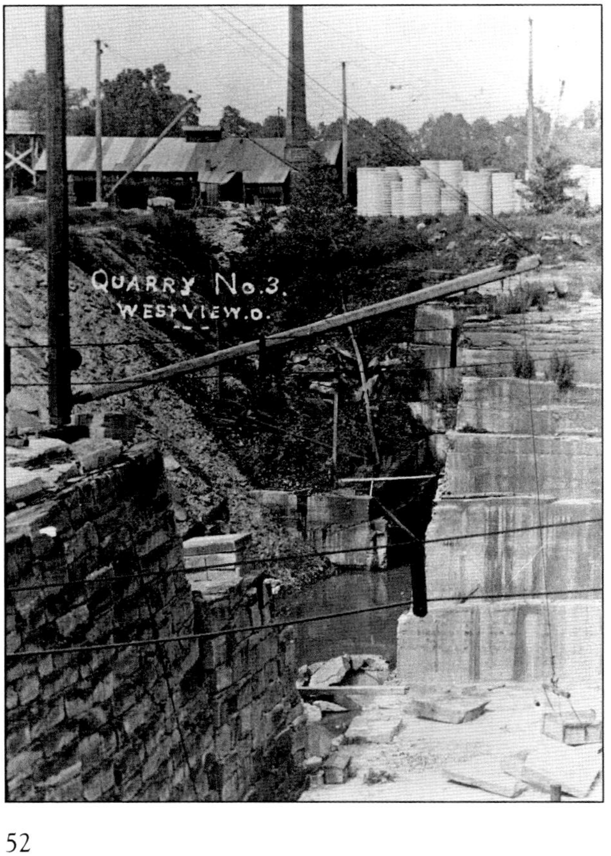

A few miles from Berea at the West View quarry and grindstone mill, the most violent action occurred during the quarrymen's strike of 1896. A striker, Vincent Marcinski, was wounded and beaten by a deputy sheriff. The strikers finally agreed to leave the West View quarry, but just then, an army of shouting, angry Polish women arrived on the scene, brandishing brooms, rakes, pitchforks, and hoes. Rather than resist the women, the lawmen retreated. (Courtesy of Jim Jaworski.)

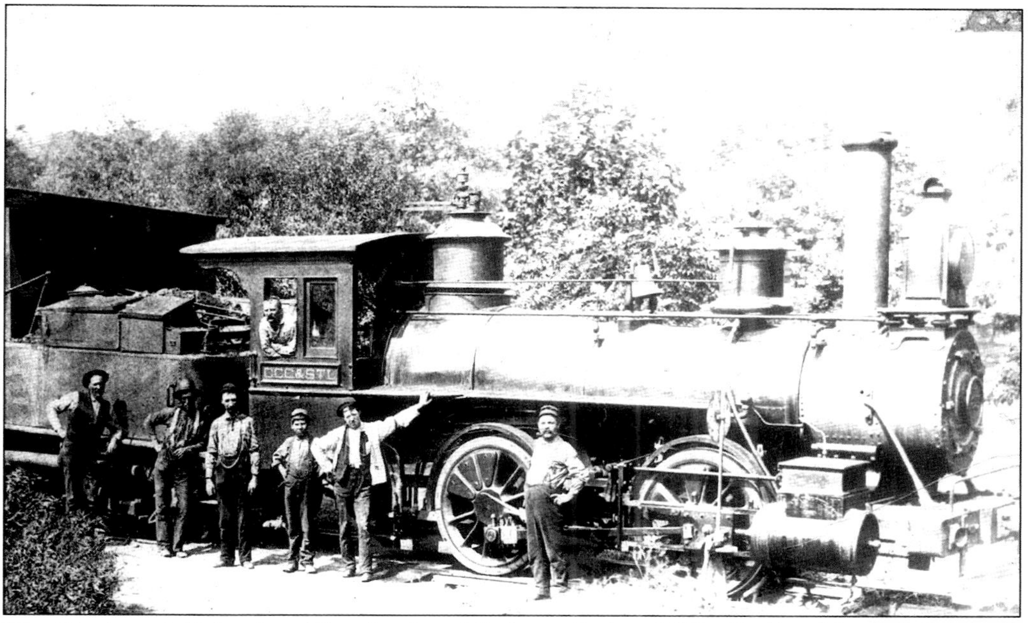

The Cincinnati, Columbus, Cleveland, and St. Louis Railroad (The Big Four) hauled thousands of carloads of stone from the Berea Quarries. In December 1878, Cleveland dedicated the 3,211-foot Superior Street Viaduct. This was the first bridge to span the Cuyahoga River to link Ohio City and Cleveland. It was built with 1,708,736 cubic feet of stone from the quarry belonging to E.W. Ensign. This would make a train about 80 miles long.

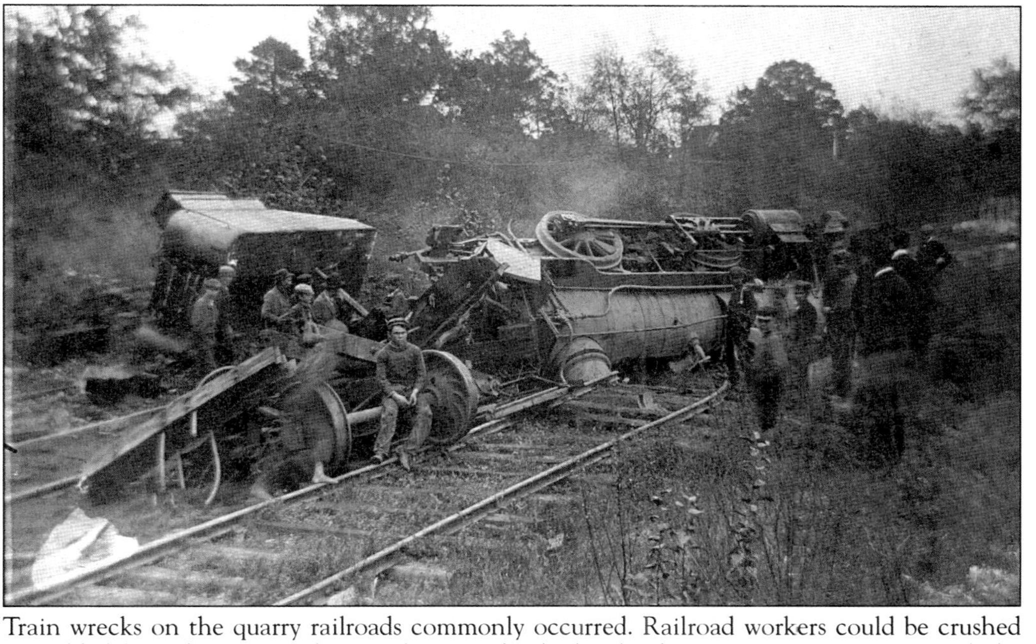

Train wrecks on the quarry railroads commonly occurred. Railroad workers could be crushed or scalded from the steam. This accident involved Cleveland Stone Company's pony or dinky engine No. 18 on October 27, 1900.

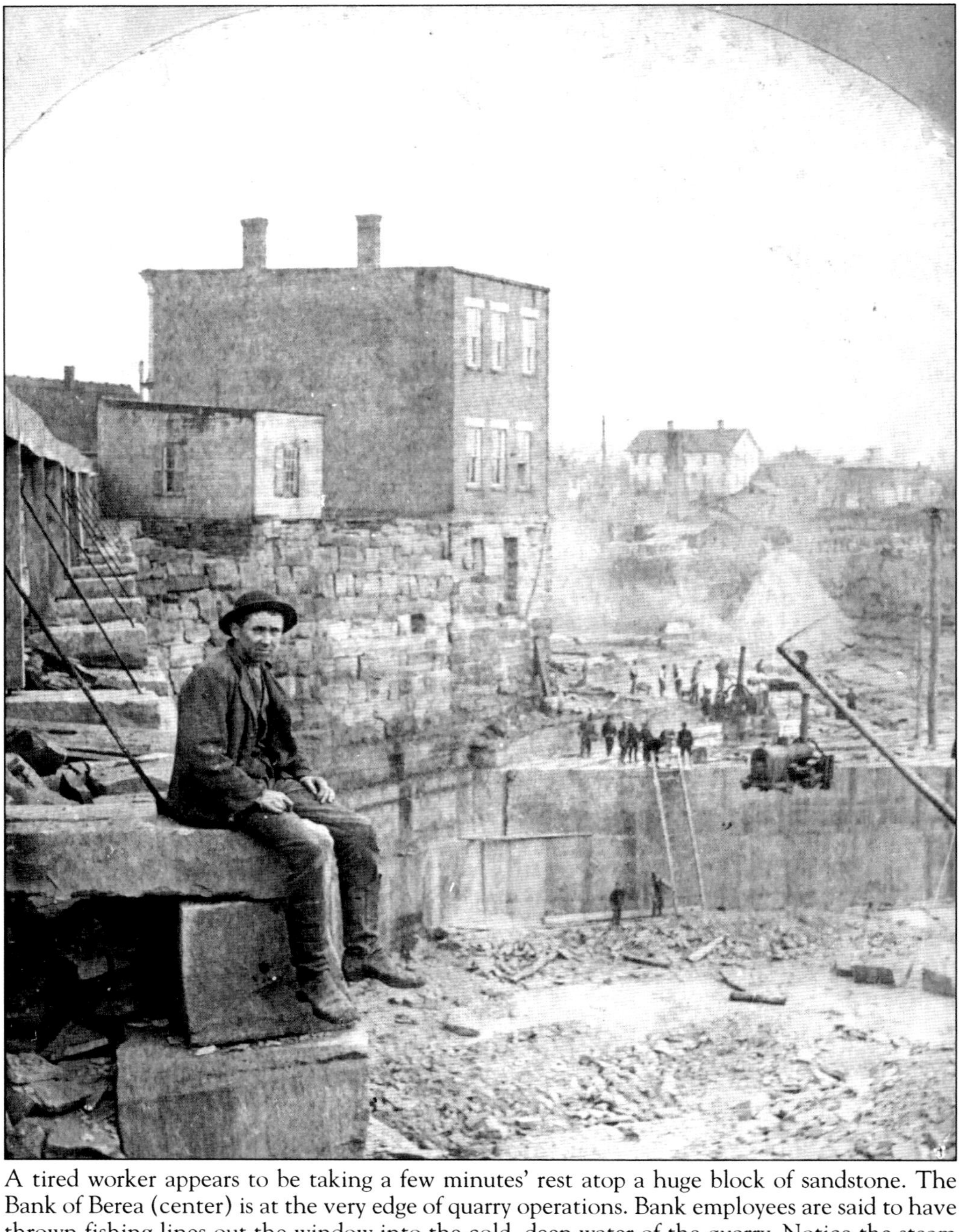

A tired worker appears to be taking a few minutes' rest atop a huge block of sandstone. The Bank of Berea (center) is at the very edge of quarry operations. Bank employees are said to have thrown fishing lines out the window into the cold, deep water of the quarry. Notice the steam engine being lifted by derrick at right. (Courtesy of Jim Jaworski.)

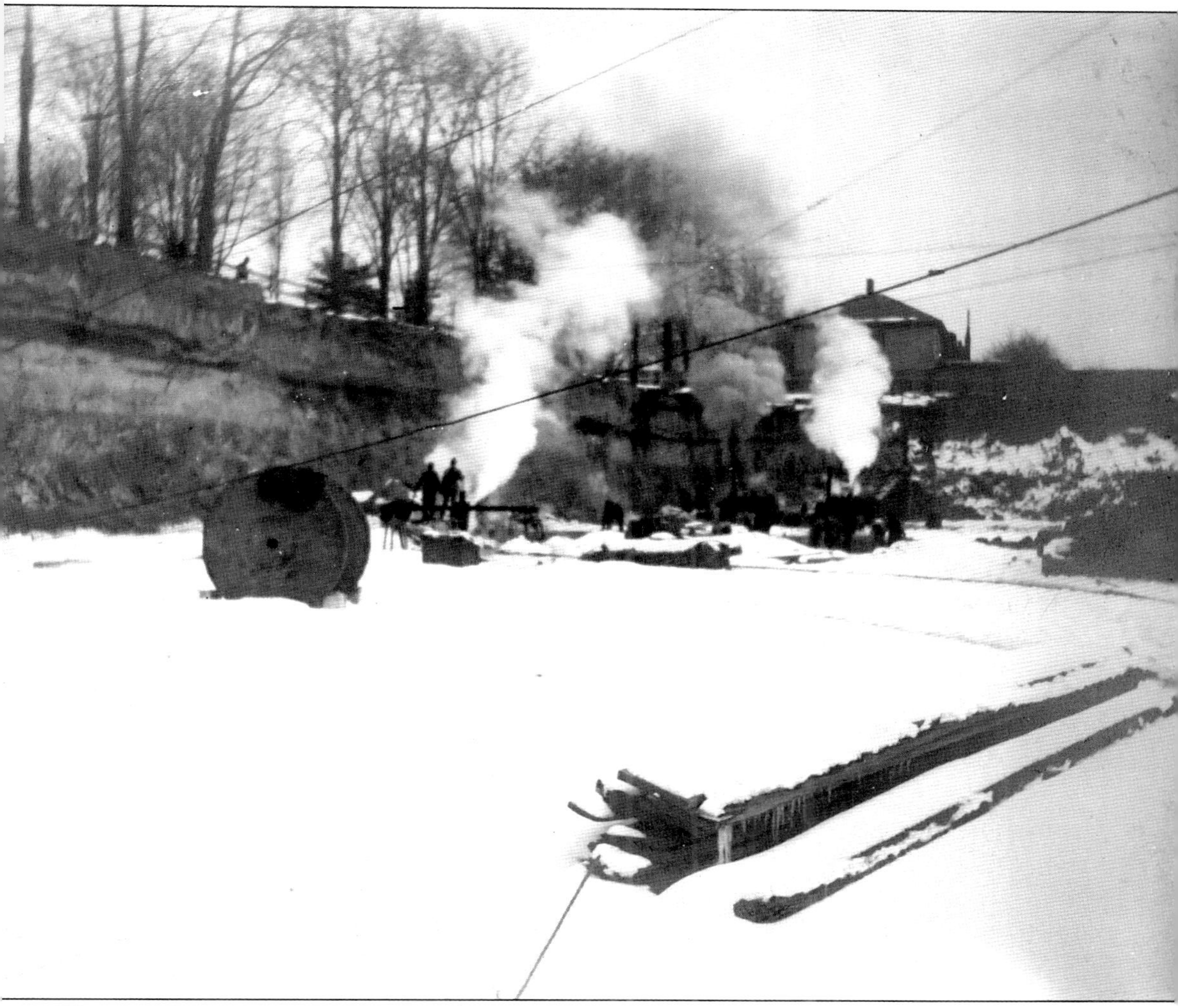

Wages in the quarries in wintertime dropped to as little as 13¢ a day, if a worker was employed at all. The sawmills employed some workers; others cleaned debris from the quarries to get ready for the next season. If weather permitted, a few might be called in to run channeling machines. Families had to put aside money and food from their gardens to live on through the winter. Wives and children of quarrymen also saved earnings from working in spring and fall in the onion fields around Lake Abram in adjoining Middleburg Township. Their daily wages amounted to nearly as much as the quarry workers.

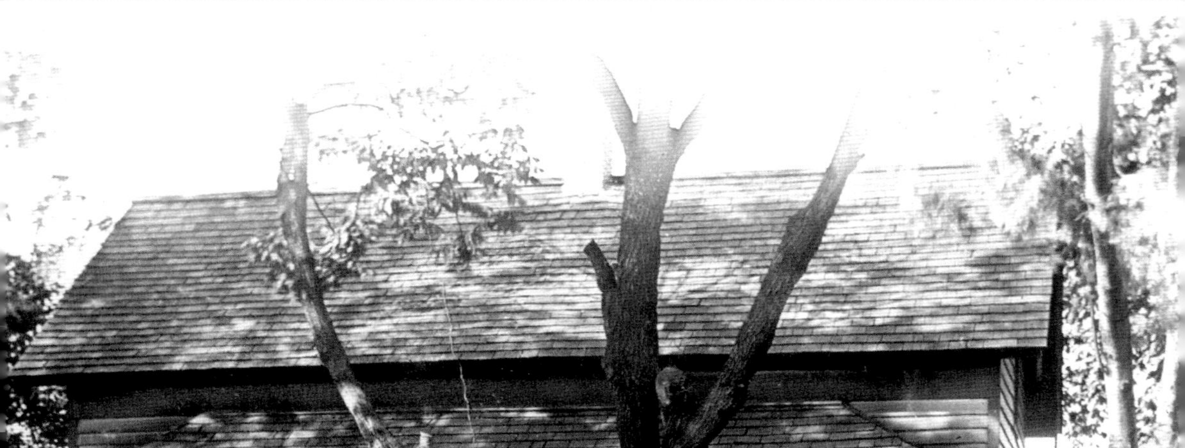

Residents of the Polish community had large families, often as many as 9 or 10 children. The original homes, built by the immigrants, were expanded by adding a more modern kitchen, bath, and additional bedrooms. Quarrymen built foundations of their homes with discarded stones they carried home from the quarry. Many of these homes have been further modernized and are still occupied.

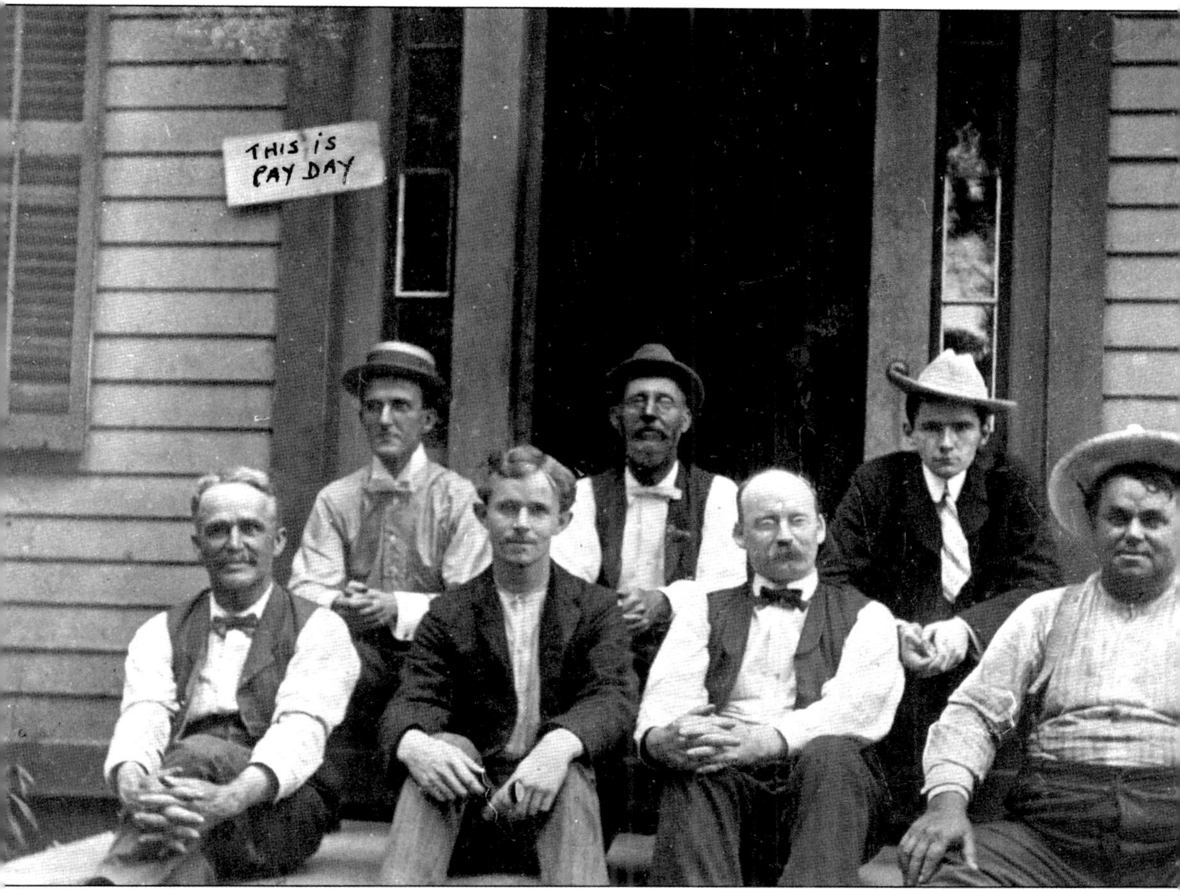

The Berea office of the Cleveland Stone Company faced Bridge Street at the edge of Big Quarry. In later years, it became the law office of Elmer Barnum, a leading Berea citizen whose father Thomas Barnum had succeeded P.J. Morrissey as general superintendent of the Cleveland Stone Company. The Stone Company employees in this 1900 photograph are, from left to right: (front row) S. Crocker, E. Cash, L. Maher, and E.J. Cash; (back row) C.F. Searles, P.J. Morrissey (superintendent of the quarries), and E.A. Burr.

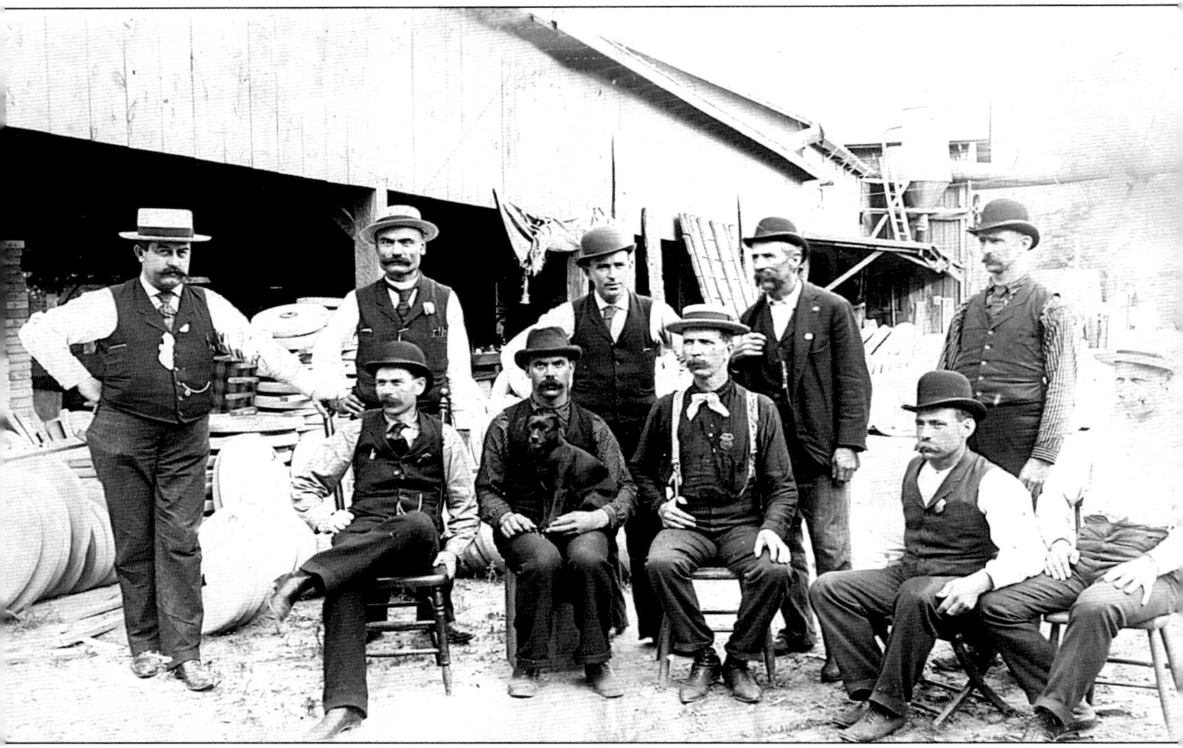

In 1896, a six-week-long strike crippled the sandstone quarry operations. Quarrymen's wages averaged only $1.50 per week, a cut from $1.75 that had occurred during the Panic of 1873. The Knights of Labor had made inroads toward unionizing some Cleveland industries, and many quarrymen saw this as a way to gain safer working conditions and higher wages. During the strike, Mayor E. Christian appointed a strong force of deputies to assist Sheriff Leek (on left) to protect the lives and property of citizens. Eventually, 115 men were deputized and two units of the National Guard, Company D were assigned to Berea by the governor. The Cleveland Stone Company issued an injunction against all trespassers and held the Village of Berea responsible for any damage that might occur to its property. The strike brought attention to the quarry workers' plight, but the Cleveland Stone Company refused to recognize their union as a bargaining agent.

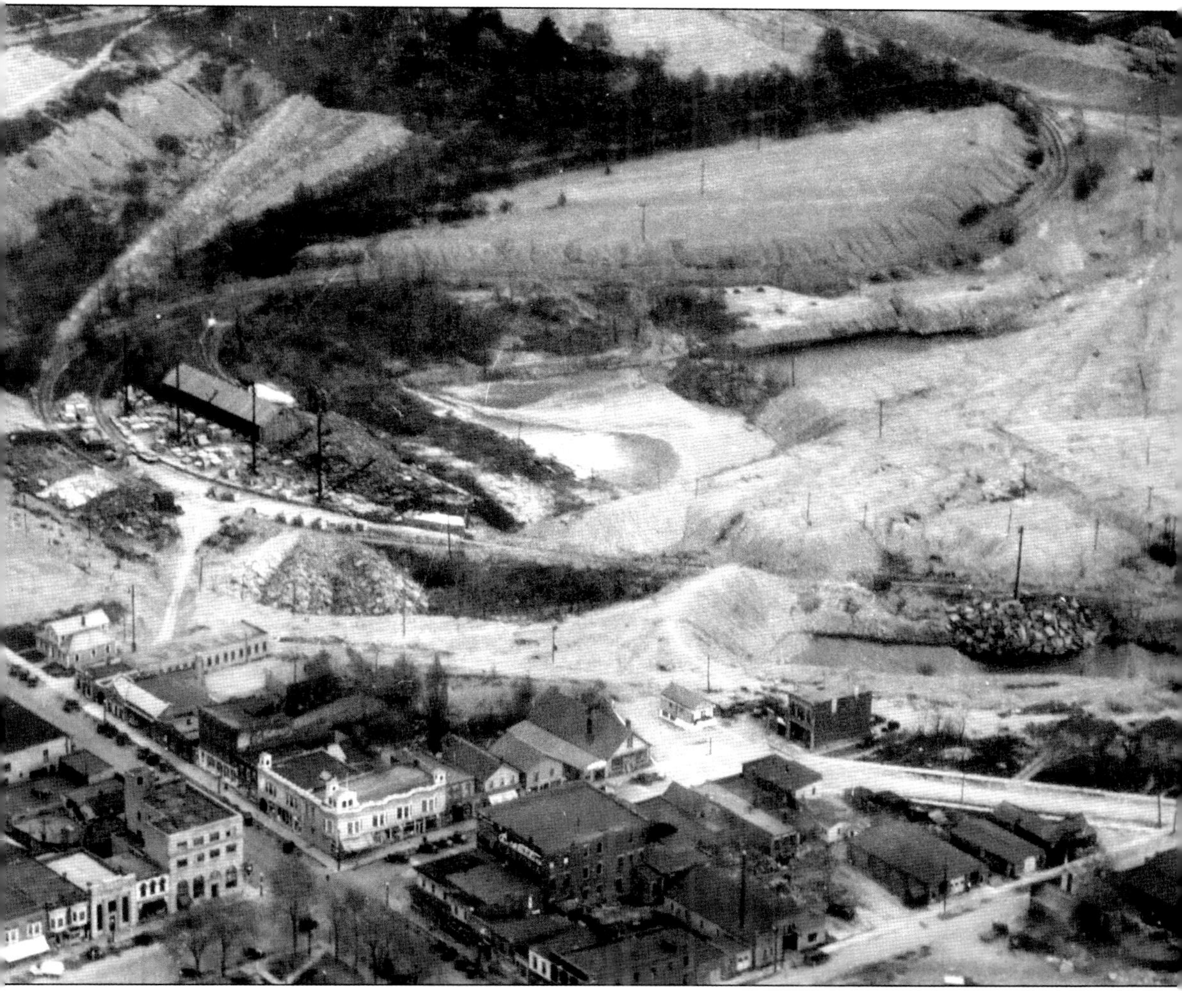

By the 1930s, quarrying had consumed much of the south part of town. The popularity of limestone as a building material and the effects of the Great Depression gradually diminished the numbers of quarrymen who would trudge to and from the quarries each day. Old Jumbo sounded for the last time in 1936. An estimated 2,000 WPA (Work Projects Administration) workers began the task of developing the former quarry areas into a recreational area. The Cleveland Stone Company donated the land to the Cleveland Metropolitan Park Board. Today, it is a pleasant area of lakes, picnic areas, trails, and park roads. The Big Quarry area that bordered downtown Berea (in photograph) is now a city-owned park known as Coe Lake where a gazebo, picnic pavilion, and well-stocked lake attract residents for concerts, art fairs, and family recreation. (Courtesy of Jim Jaworski.)

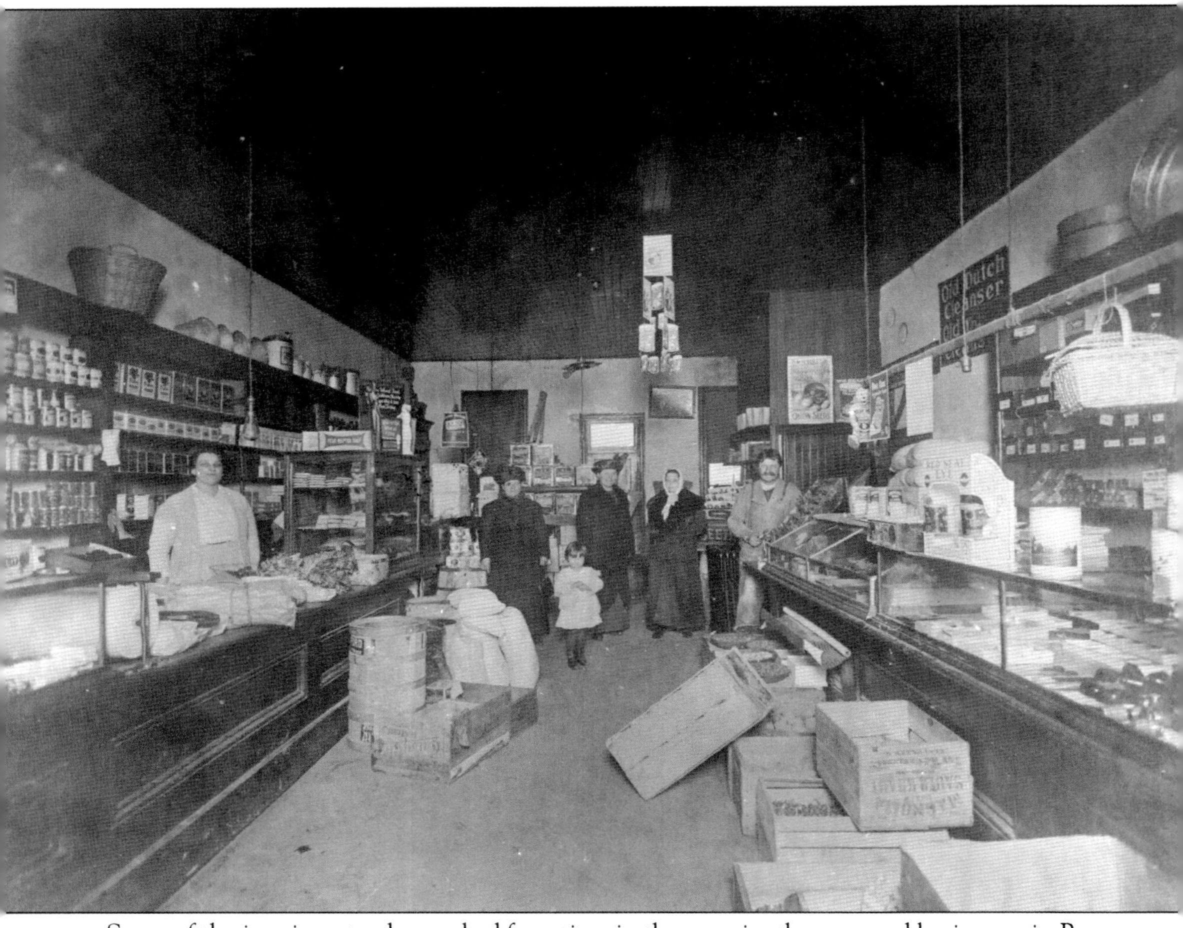

Some of the immigrants who worked for a time in the quarries then opened businesses in Berea. In 1892, the Dziedzikowski family started the first Polish-operated grocery store on Front Street in downtown Berea. By 1900, a clothier, tailor, shoe repairman, cabinetmaker, a photographer, and a funeral director and licensed embalmer—all Polish entrepreneurs—had joined the ranks of Berea businesses.

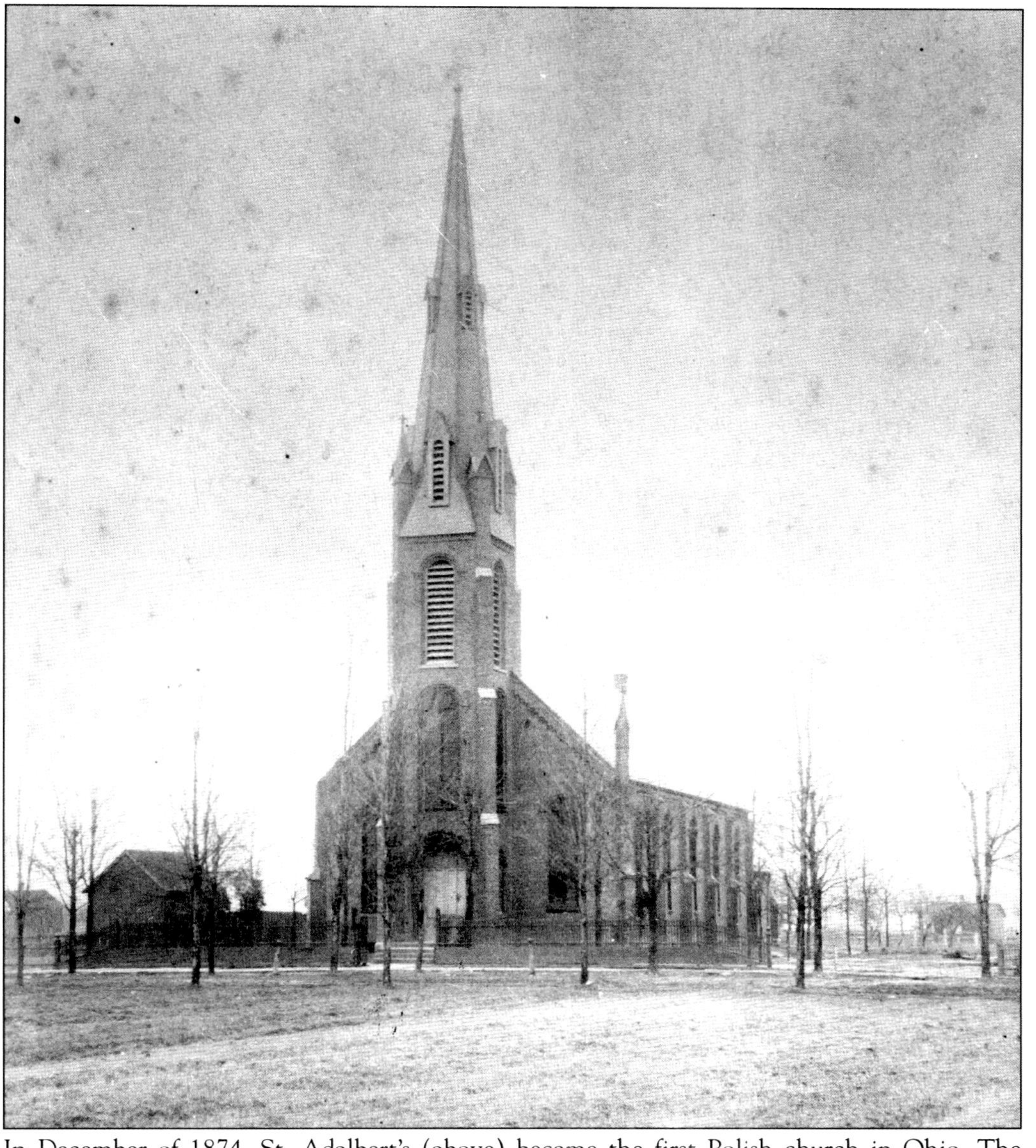

In December of 1874, St. Adalbert's (above) became the first Polish church in Ohio. The first immigrants who came to Berea to work in the quarries were English, Irish, and German. They established St. Mary's Catholic Church, and their homes clustered about that church. With the influx of immigration from Eastern Europe following the War Between the States, many Polish arrived. At first, they worshiped at St. Mary's, but by 1873, the Polish community numbered about 100 families. They longed to hear the Mass and the Gospel in their native Polish. Residents petitioned for their own church. Upon its completion, school classes were started at once in the choir loft; a school building was constructed two years later. The beautiful altars, hand-carved in Poland and shipped to Berea piece by piece, are still in use in a newer St. Adalbert's Church that replaced the original one in 1938.

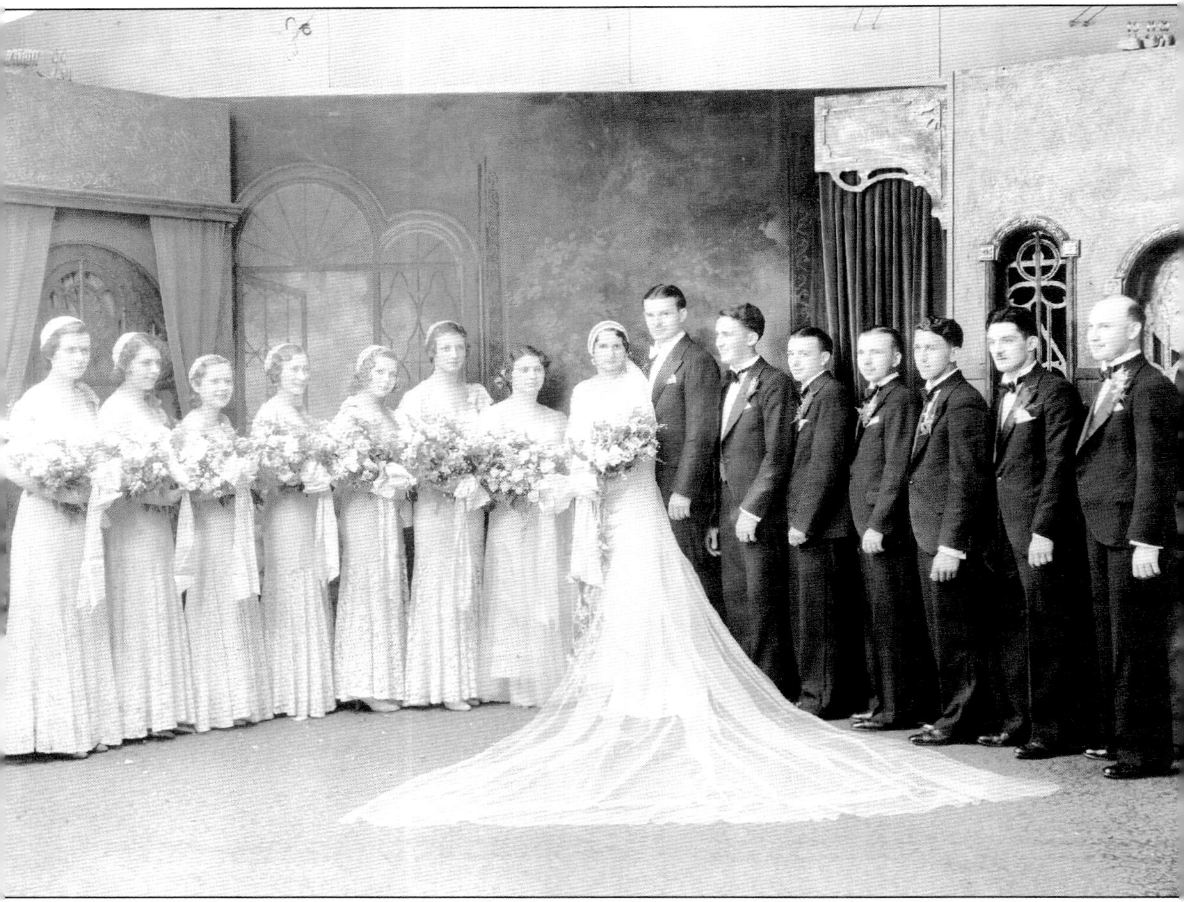

The elaborate wedding of John and Anna Toranski in the early 1930s indicates the success and prosperity achieved by many second generation Polish-Americans. John's family owned and operated Johnny's Florist on West 71st Street in Cleveland. One of the bridesmaids (fourth from left) is Josephine Pauline Zahzycka (Jaworski), whose son Jim Jaworski contributed to this book. (Courtesy of Jim Jaworski.)

Three

The Colleges

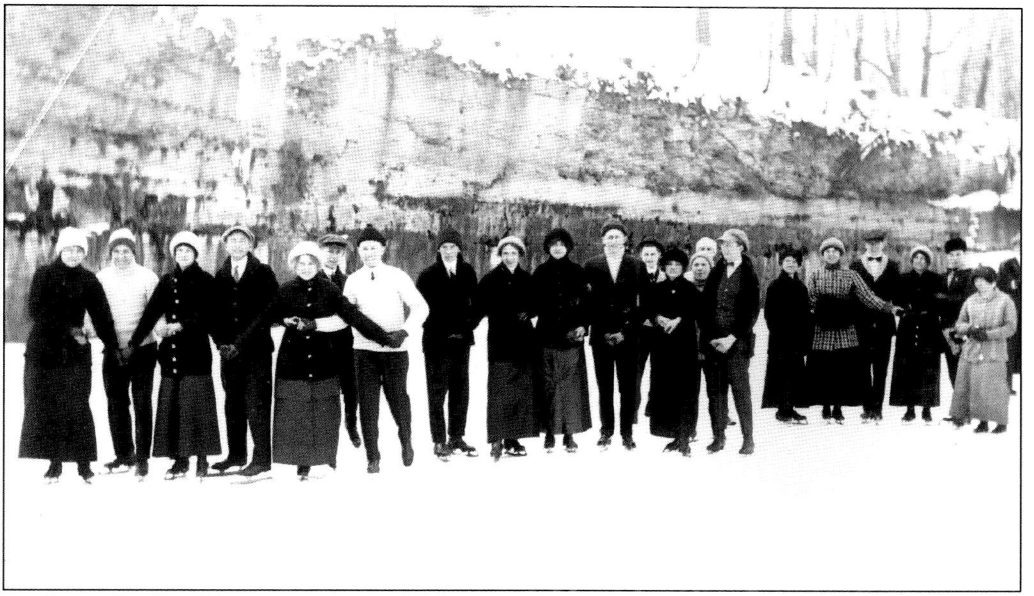

Students from Baldwin-Wallace College enjoyed a skating party in the Stearns Quarry in 1914, the first year after the merger of Baldwin University and German Wallace College. This merger united the dreams and determination of John and Mary Baldwin that youth should not be denied opportunities for education because of race, nationality, creed, or gender. In these years just prior to World War I, students came to Baldwin-Wallace from Germany, England, Scotland, Russia, and Lithuania.

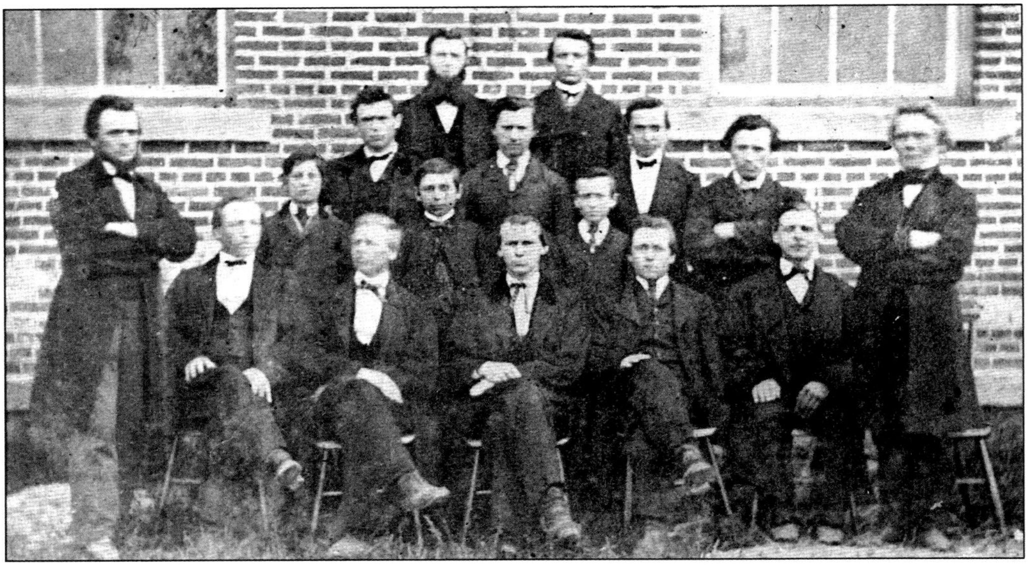

This was the first graduating class of German Wallace College in 1864. The lone woman (second row, far left) presumably is William and Margaret Nast's daughter, Fanny, whom records show was a member of the class. She later married into the Gamble family of Cincinnati's Procter and Gamble Company. With a gift of $20,000, she established the Nast Theological Professorship and also gave $5,000 to endow a professorship in practical theology

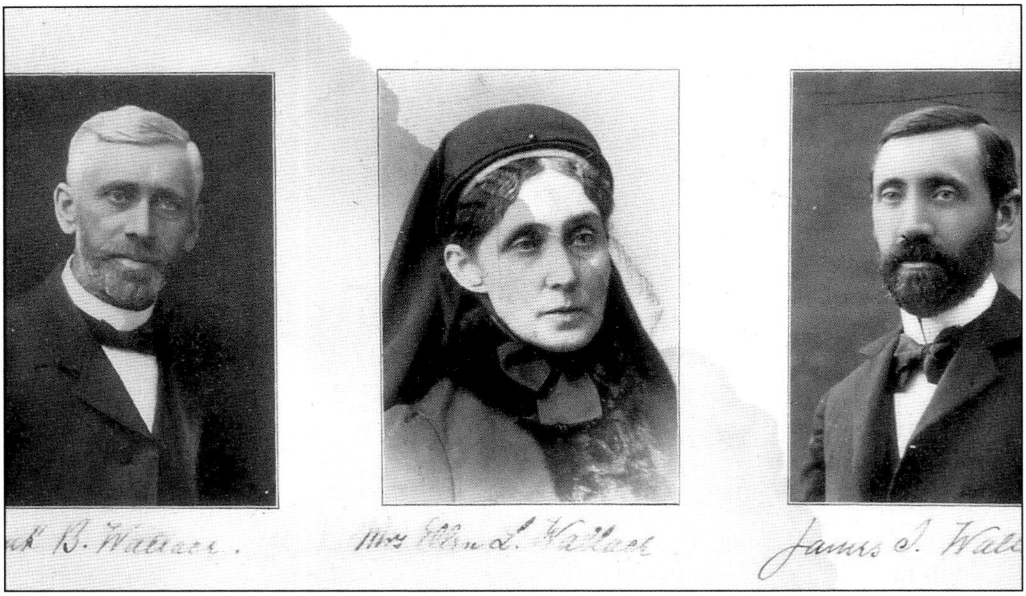

James I. Wallace (right), a wealthy quarry operator, and his wife Ellen donated the land, stone, and funds to assist in the establishment of German Wallace College, an outgrowth of the German Department of Baldwin University. Agreeing not to duplicate courses, the two schools set up a reciprocal agreement for students in both colleges. James Wallace was mayor of Berea in 1853–1854. Robert Wallace (left), brother of James, became a member of the first fraternal lodge in Berea, the Odd Fellows, in 1854.

William Nast, a prominent leader of the German Methodist movement in America, pictured with his wife Margaret Eliza Nast, traveled widely, always promoting Berea as a desirable place to settle. He was connected with the German department of the Baldwin Institute, forerunner of Baldwin University, and later became the first president of German Wallace College when it separated as an independent institution for German studies, a post he held for nearly 30 years.

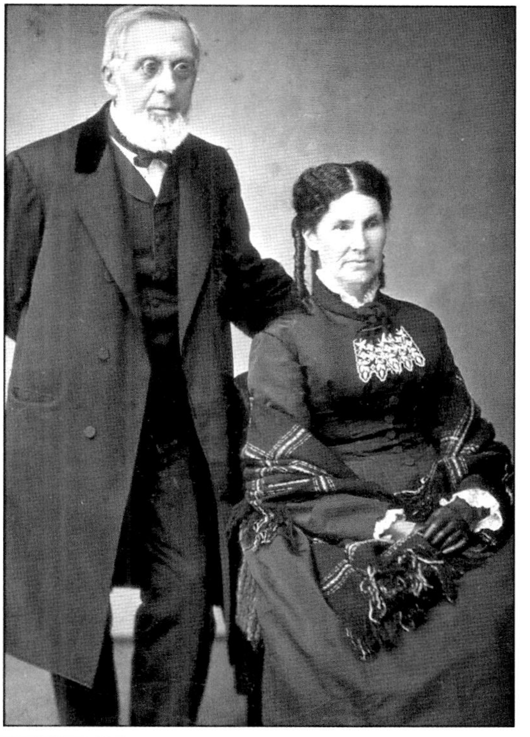

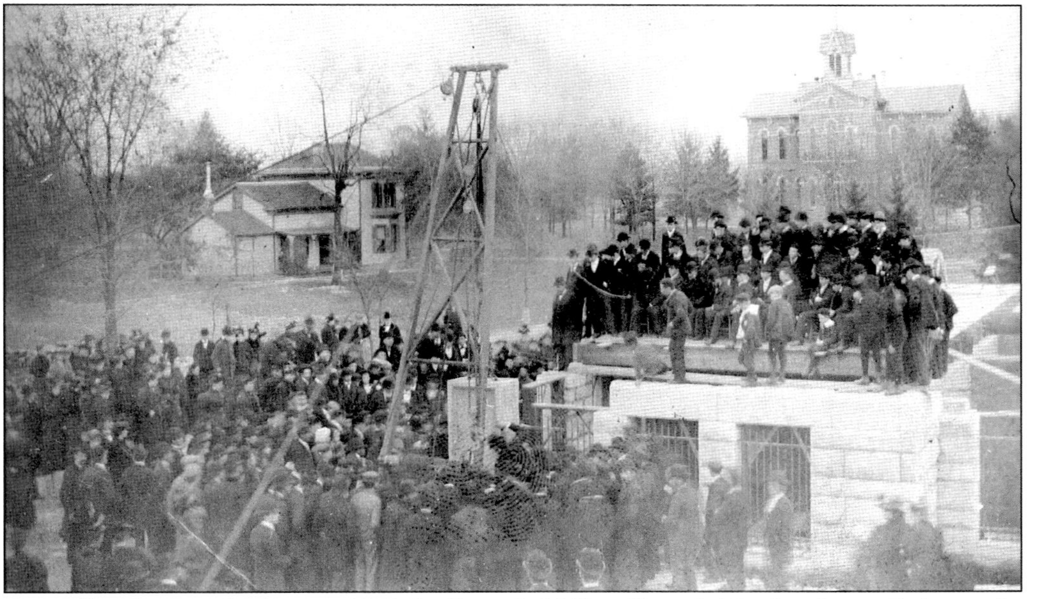

Groundbreaking took place in 1889 for Dietsch Hall or Dietsch Toechterheim, "a home for daughters," on the German Wallace campus. The hall was the gift of a German farm family in western Ohio. The story goes that when John C. Marting, treasurer of German Wallace College, paid a visit to the Dietsch farm in northwestern Ohio, he and the farmer knelt down to pray in the fields. The farmer is said to have prayed for favorable crops, while treasurer Marting prayed for Farmer Dietsch's largesse.

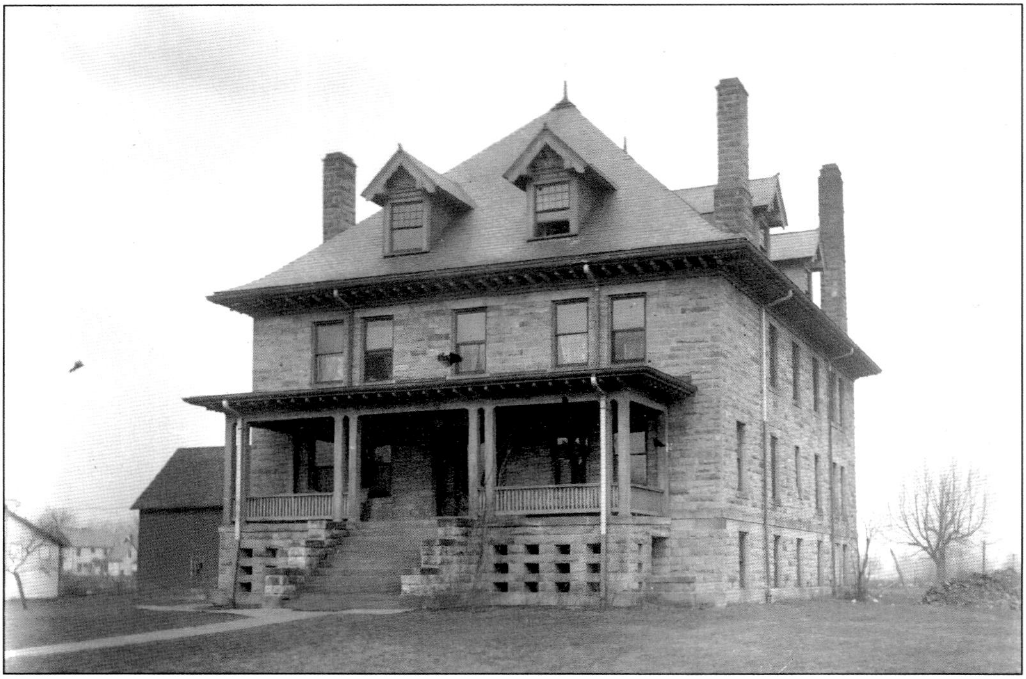

Quarrying was creeping so close to the Baldwin University campus by the 1890s that a new campus site was chosen on the north side of town. Hulet Hall (above), built in 1868, was moved, stone by stone, to the new location at the northwest corner of Bagley and Beech Streets. As a residence hall for women, it took on a completely different architectural style than the previous structure.

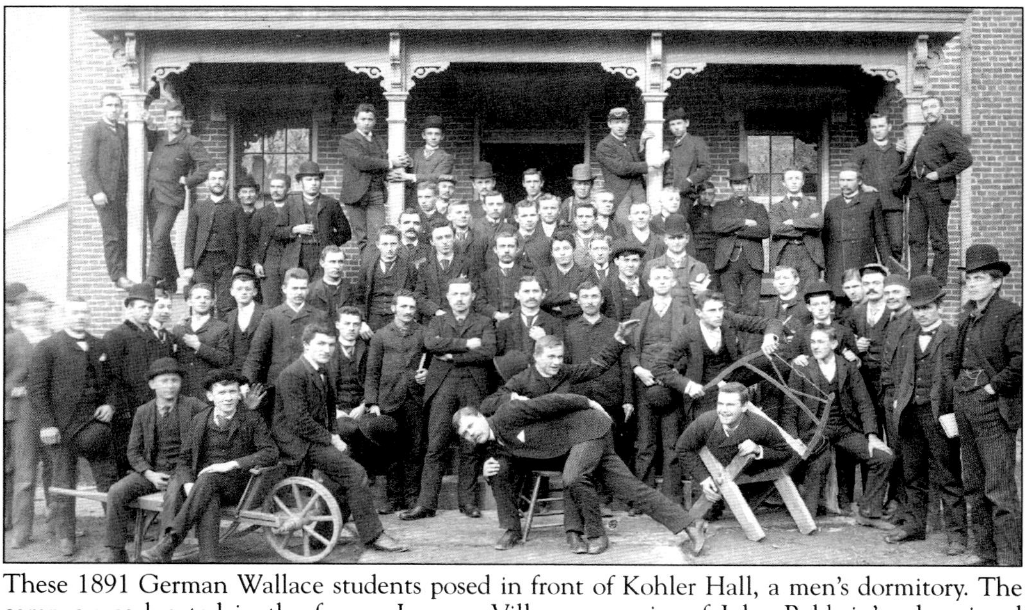

These 1891 German Wallace students posed in front of Kohler Hall, a men's dormitory. The campus was located in the former Lyceum Village area, site of John Baldwin's educational experiment that had failed in 1842. (Courtesy of Baldwin-Wallace College.)

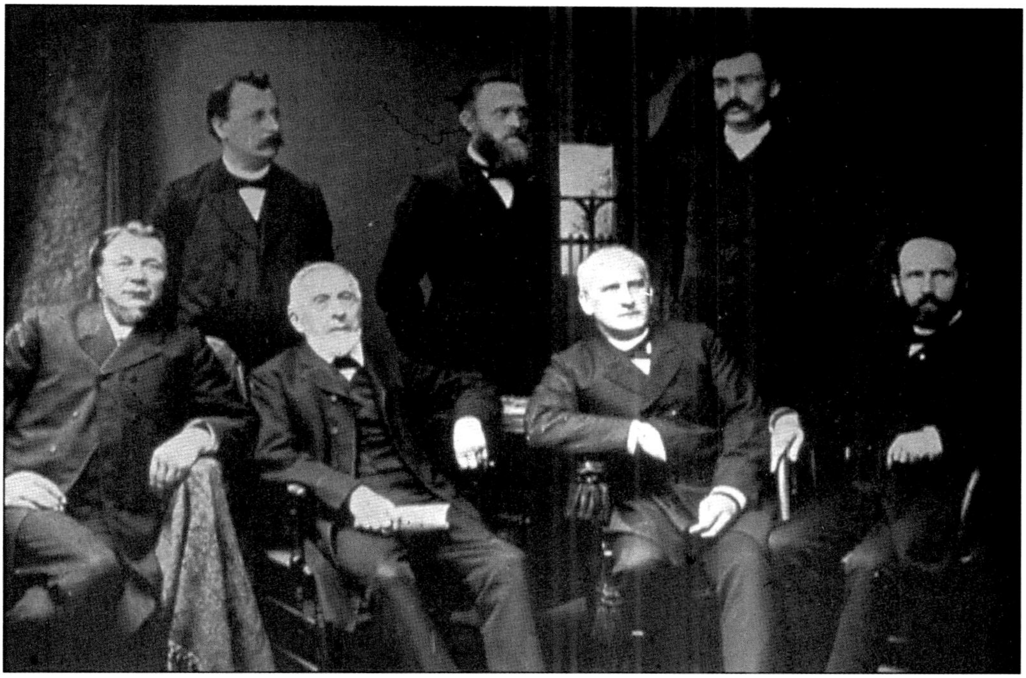

William Nast (second from left), first president of German Wallace College, is seated with other members of the original faculty. He was president from 1864 until 1893. His successors were Karl Riemenschneider, Edwin S. Havighurst, and Arthur L. Breslich. Breslich became the first president of the merged Baldwin-Wallace College in 1913.

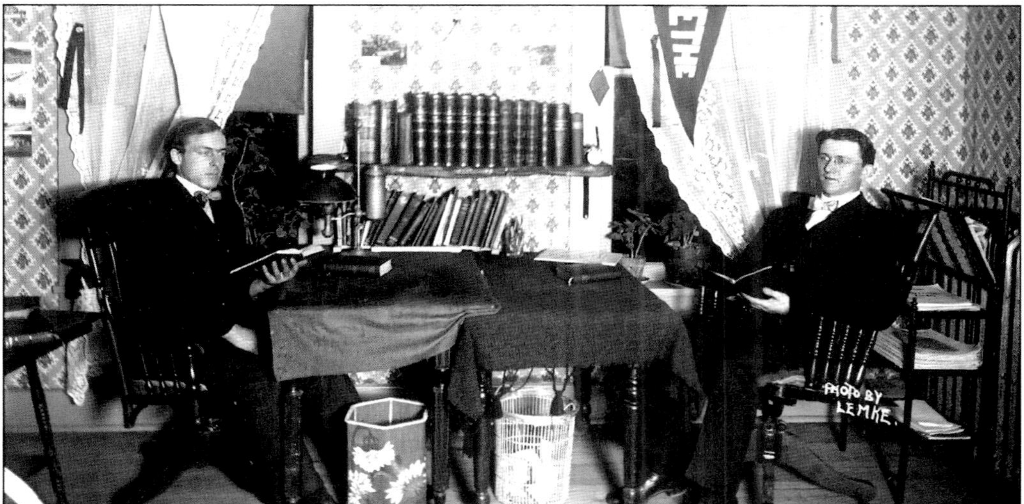

Both the Goethe and Schiller literary societies were social as well as academic groups. They sponsored dramatic and musical events on the campus. The literary societies in the 1890s and early 1900s became local fraternities and sororities and affiliated with national Greek letter organizations in the 1930s. (Courtesy of Baldwin-Wallace College.)

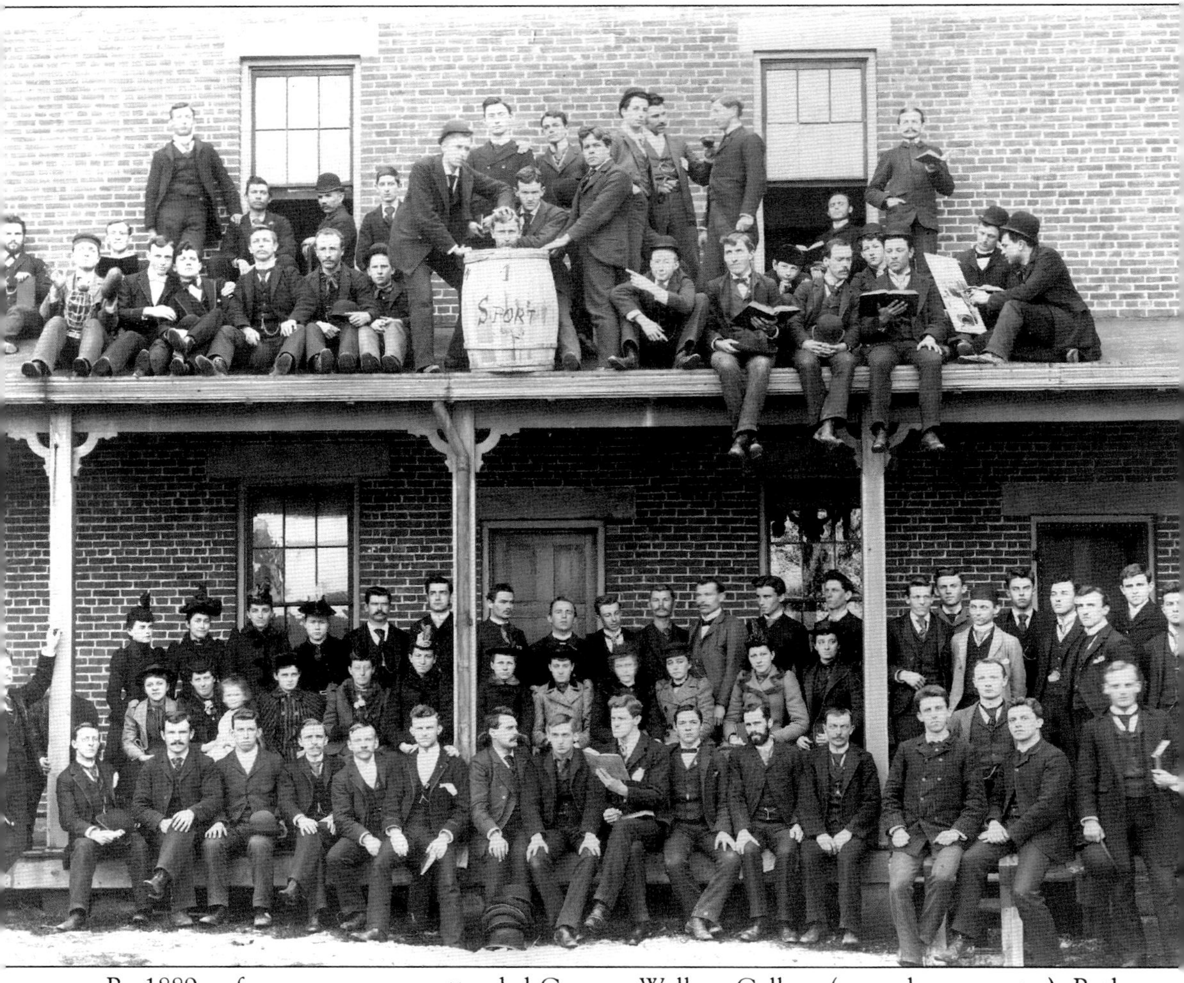

By 1889, a few more women attended German Wallace College (second row, center). Both schools held fast to John Baldwin's original premise—equal opportunity for education for all—combined with hard work. (Courtesy of Baldwin-Wallace College.)

By the late 1890s, Kohler Hall (above), Dietsch Hall, Memorial Hall, and the college chapel, the former Emmanuel Methodist Church, comprised the German Wallace College campus. (Courtesy of Baldwin-Wallace College.)

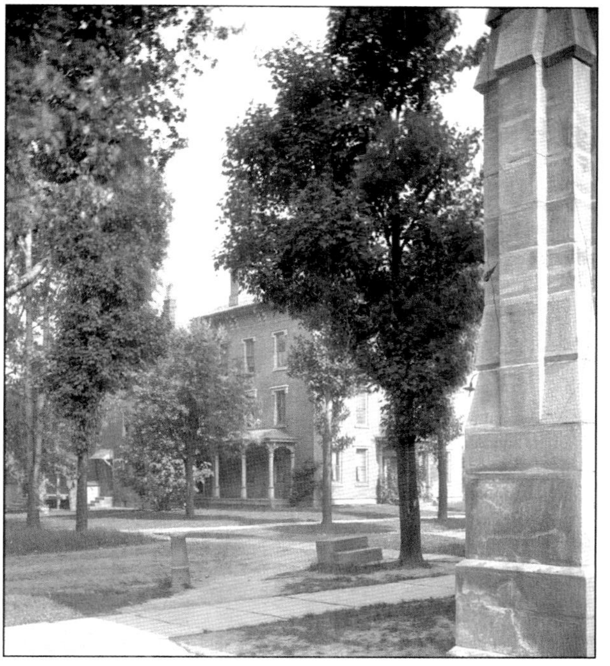

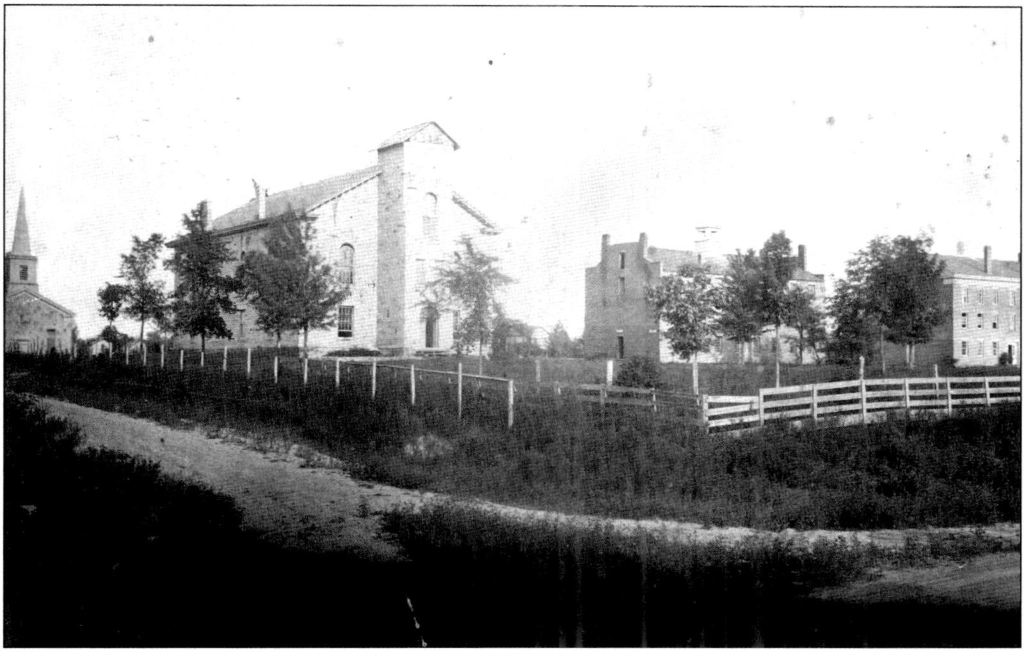

The first Baldwin University campus was on the South Side of town near the quarries. From left to right are the Methodist Church, Hulet Hall, North Hall, and South Hall. In 1888, the university sold its sandstone-rich campus to the Cleveland Stone Company for $100,000 in cash and began relocating to the north side of town.

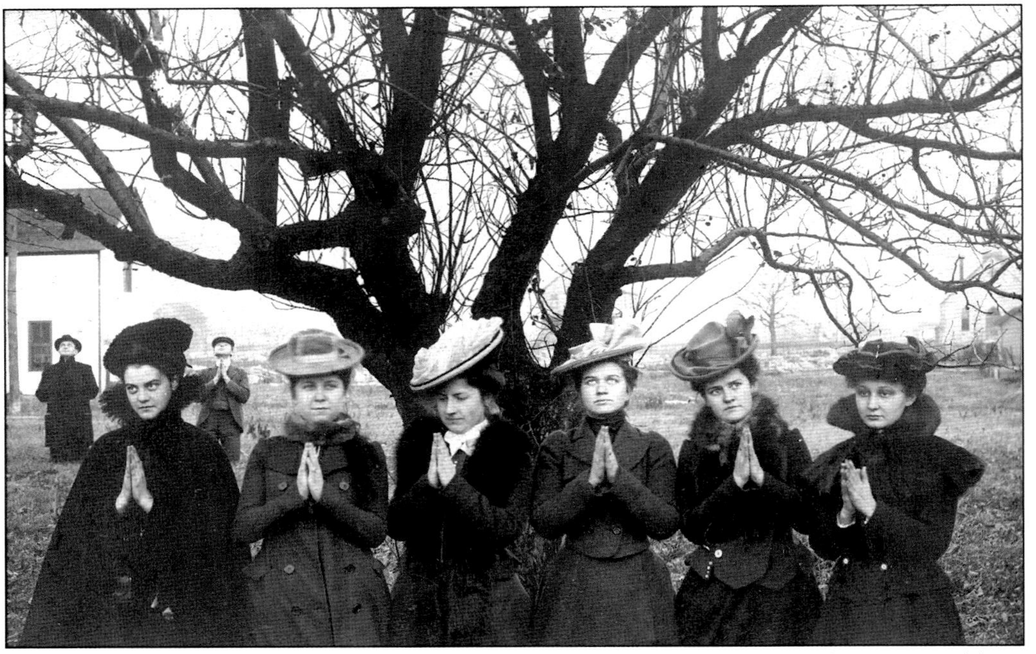

Religion was of paramount importance at both colleges. These students at Baldwin University in the early 1900s could be having a prayer vigil—or are they fearfully waiting for Halley's Comet?

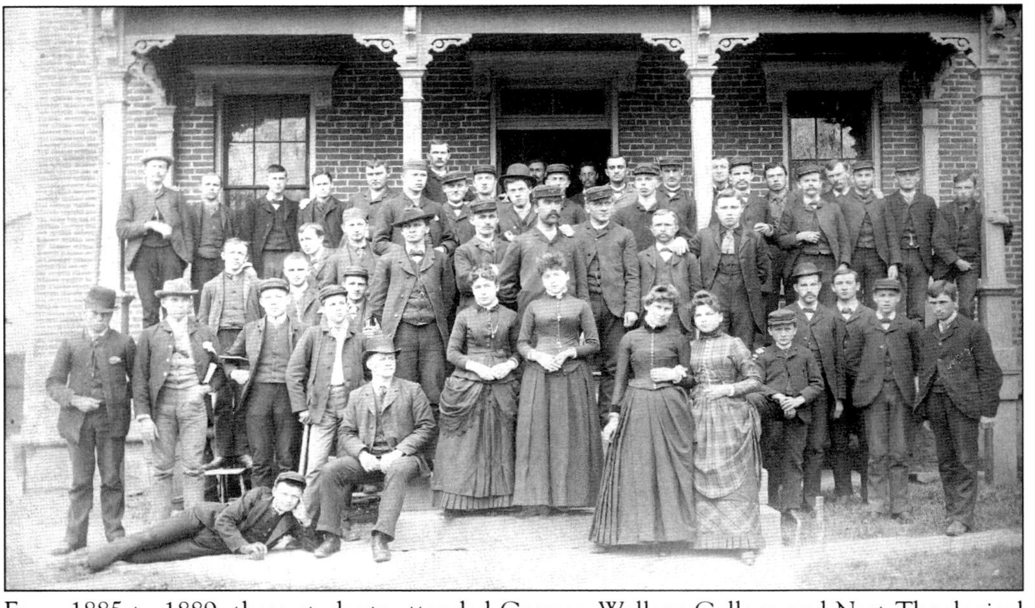

From 1885 to 1889, these students attended German Wallace College and Nast Theological Seminary. The school trained workers for all fields of Christian activity and teachers for public schools, high schools, and colleges. Students who desired to enter agriculture, engineering, law, or medicine could obtain strong two-year courses at German Wallace. (Courtesy of Baldwin-Wallace College.)

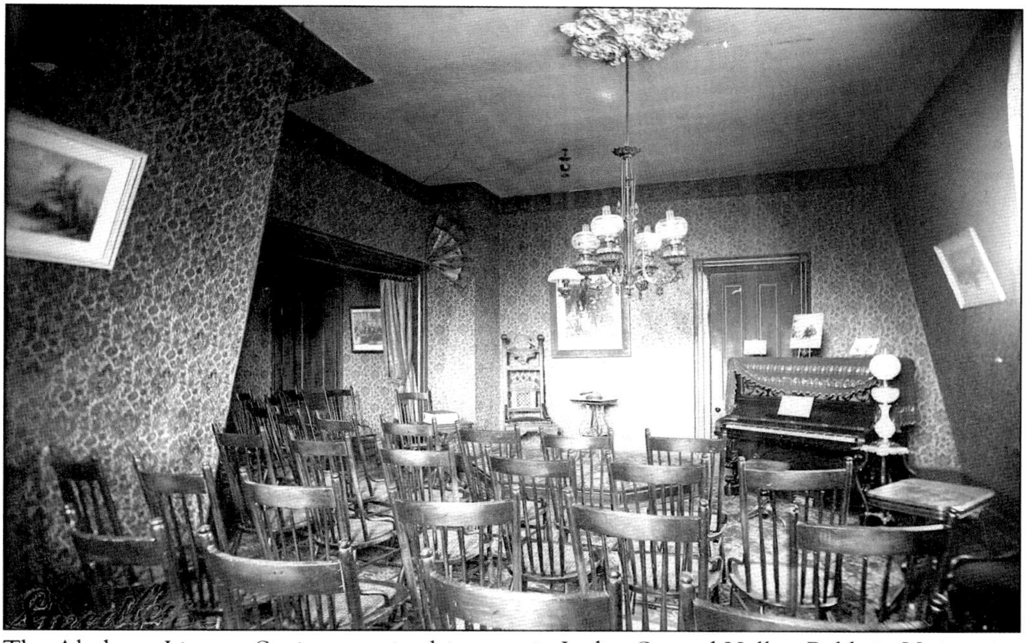

The Alethean Literary Society met in this room in Ladies Second Hall at Baldwin University. The First Ladies Hall was destroyed by fire on May 31, 1899. Built by J.V. Larkin for John Baldwin, who gifted it to the university, it had stood as a landmark for a half-century but was marked for removal after the Cleveland Stone Company purchased the property.

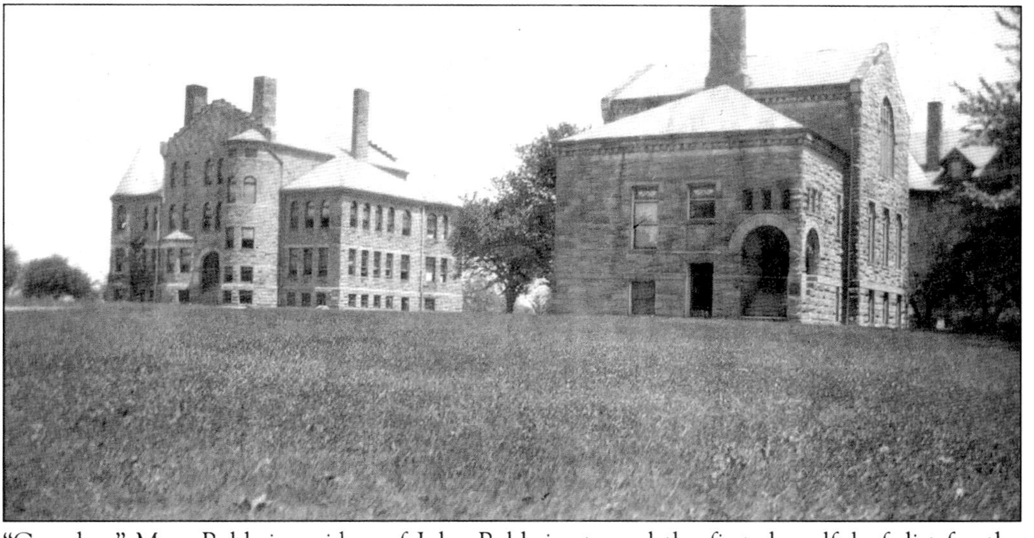

"Grandma" Mary Baldwin, widow of John Baldwin, turned the first shovelful of dirt for the groundbreaking for Wheeler Hall (left), originally Recitation Hall, in 1892. In 1894, John Baldwin Jr. and his wife Lury gave the Philura Gould Baldwin Library (right) in memory of their daughter. Philura had organized the first library for Baldwin University and was a highly respected young woman. She died at age 27. First floor classrooms still have stained glass windows honoring early leaders of the college.

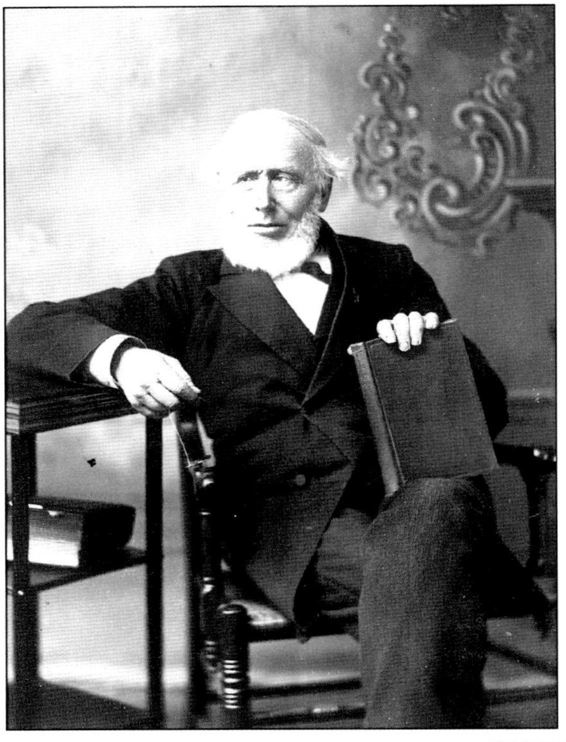

Dr. William Pierce, a veteran in Methodism for many years, became the first resident pastor in Berea. He came to Berea in 1846, at the beginning of the Institute. He was connected with the college, as trustee or teacher, all of his active life. He was regarded as "a man of an unusual degree of taste and culture and gave the stamp of culture to the community."

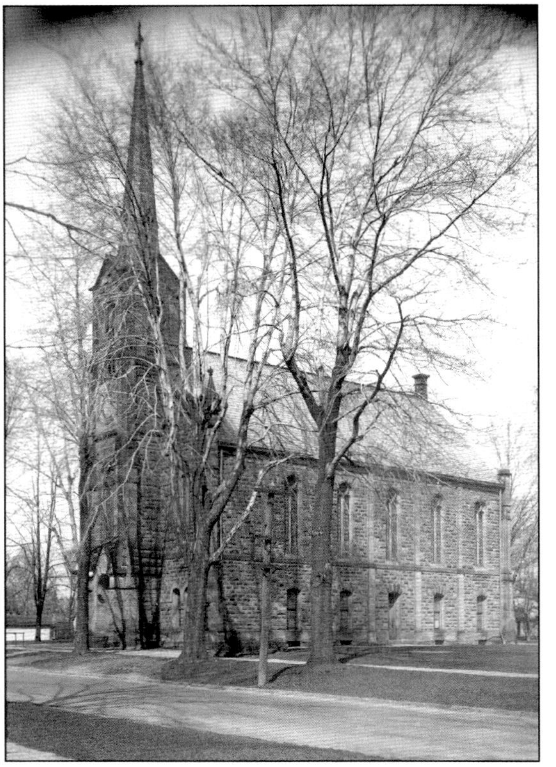

German Methodists who settled in Berea erected the former Emmanuel Methodist Episcopal Church of native sandstone in 1872 to serve Berea's college and community. The Emmanuel Methodists eventually merged with the nearby Methodist Episcopal Church, and the building now is known as Lindsay-Crossman Chapel of Baldwin-Wallace College, named for two former college trustees. Its spire and that of the neighboring Congregational Church (UCC) mark the Berea skyline.

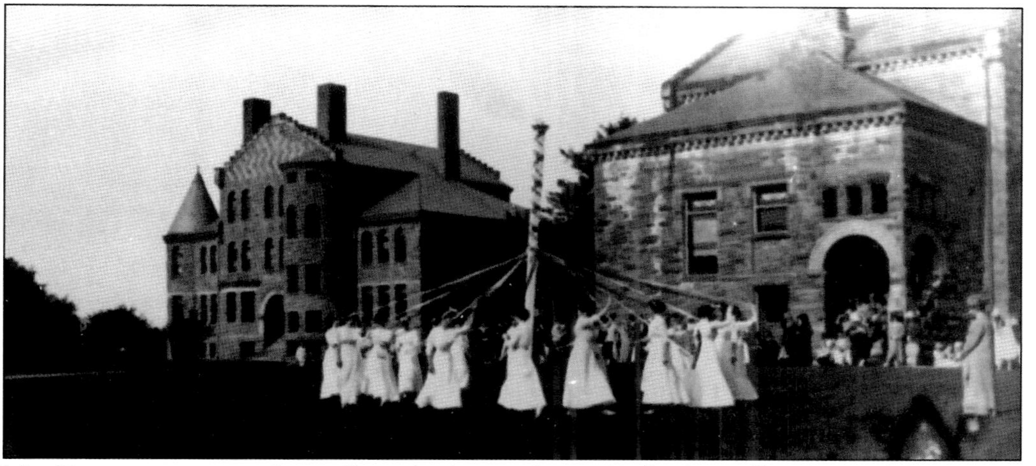

May Day ceremonies traditionally took place in front of Wheeler Hall and the Philura Gould Baldwin Library as shown here in 1914. To celebrate the college's sesquicentennial in 1996, the coronation of the May Queen and the May Pole Dance were re-staged here. Traditions of other years re-enacted were chariot races, the tug of war, breakfast at The Rocks, and weekly all-college assemblies.

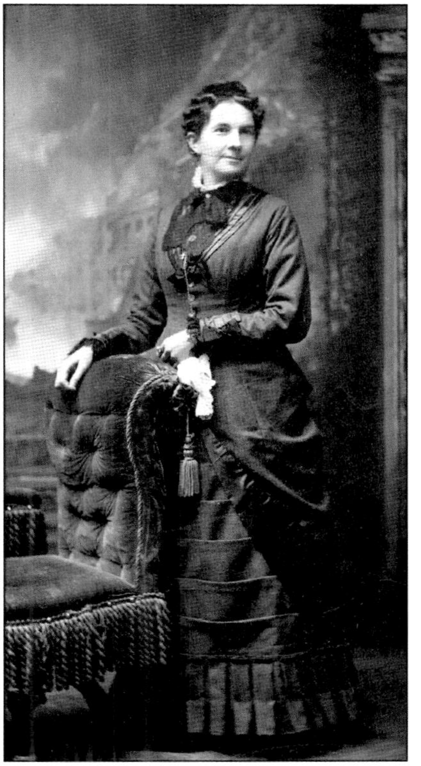

Lury Ann (Gould) Baldwin (Mrs. John Baldwin Jr.), regarded as a perfect lady and a tireless worker and leader in any worthy cause, lived to be 83. She was a versatile writer whose articles and recollections of Berea people and college life in Berea became invaluable in preserving the town's history. Lury Ann and John Jr. had three children: John Paul, Philura, and Milton. The latter two died as young adults within four years of each other.

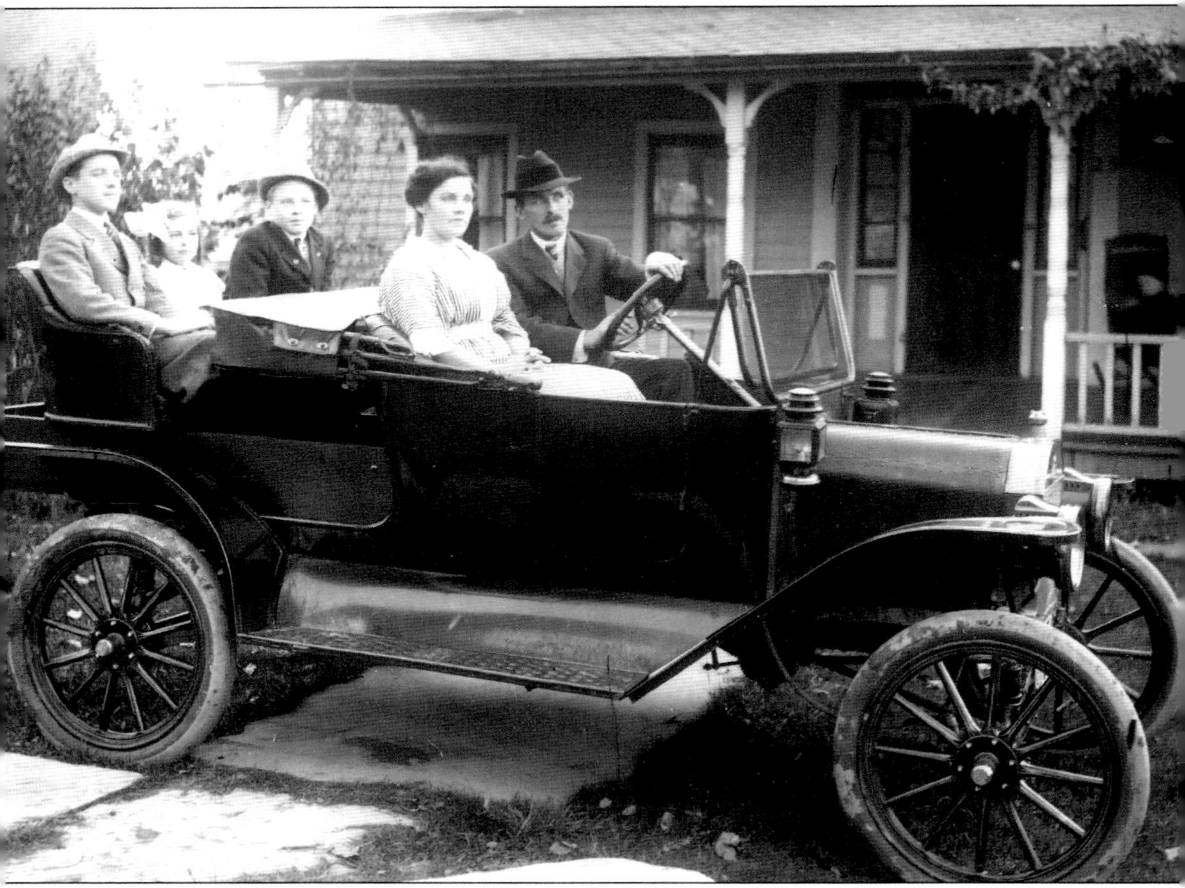

David Gilchrist and his family are enjoying an outing in their automobile. Gilchrist was a general contractor who was involved in the construction of a number of community and college buildings.

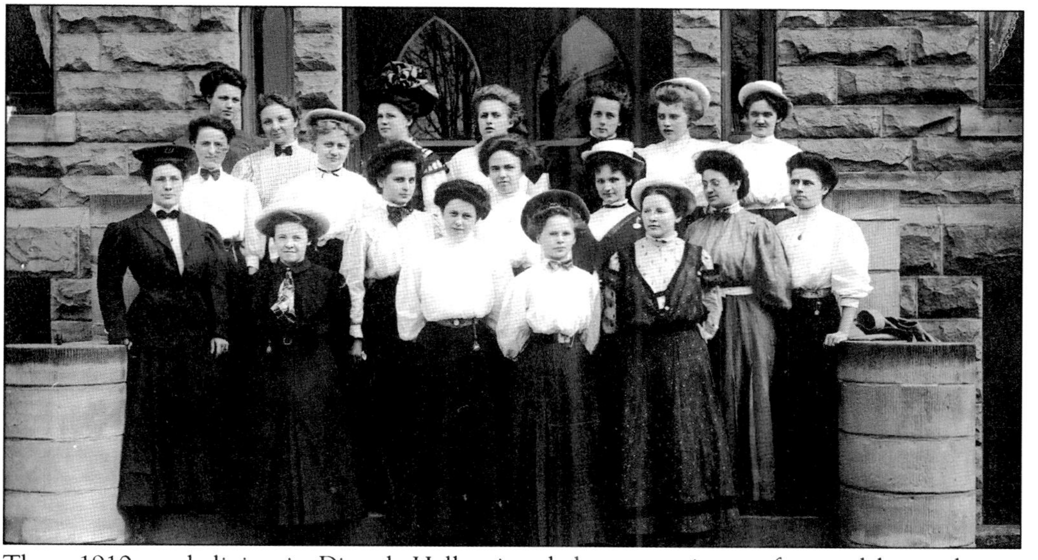

These 1910 coeds living in Dietsch Hall enjoyed the convenience of central heat, electric lights, hot water, and water closets. For this luxury, students paid $6 rent each term. Renovated in recent years, Dietsch Hall now houses the foreign language departments and the learning center. The sandstone exterior appears much the same as it did more than 100 years ago. (Courtesy of Baldwin-Wallace College.)

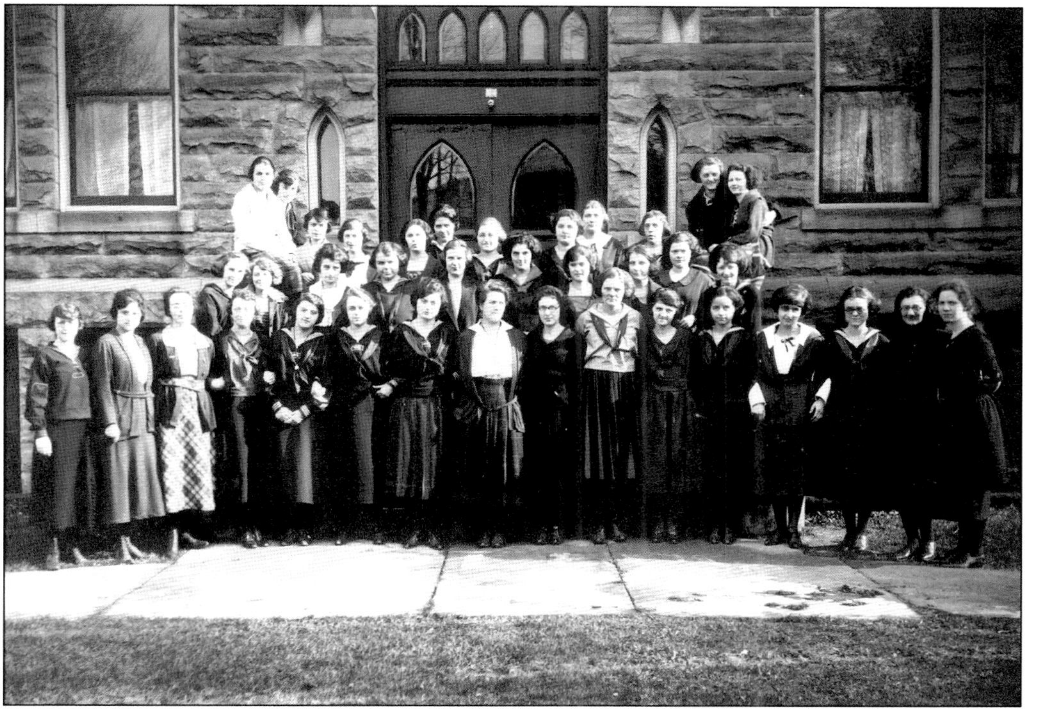

Although their attire is more relaxed than the coeds of a decade before, these 1921 B-W girls are not quite flappers. (Courtesy of Baldwin-Wallace College.)

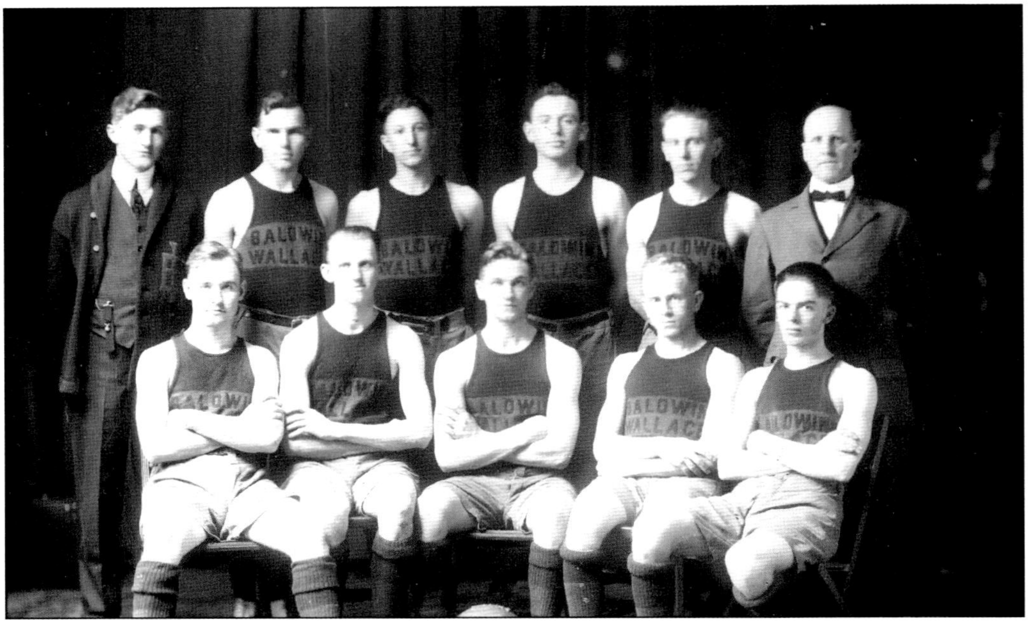

Before the two schools merged, Baldwin University and German Wallace College fielded joint athletic teams in basketball as well as football, track and field, hockey, soccer, and baseball. The 1915–1916 basketball team was one of the earliest Baldwin-Wallace College teams. From left to right are: (front row) Christ, Wessel. Captain Ansel, Herbst, and Hathaway; (back row) Gibbs, Brendt, Clancy, and Coach Wilson.

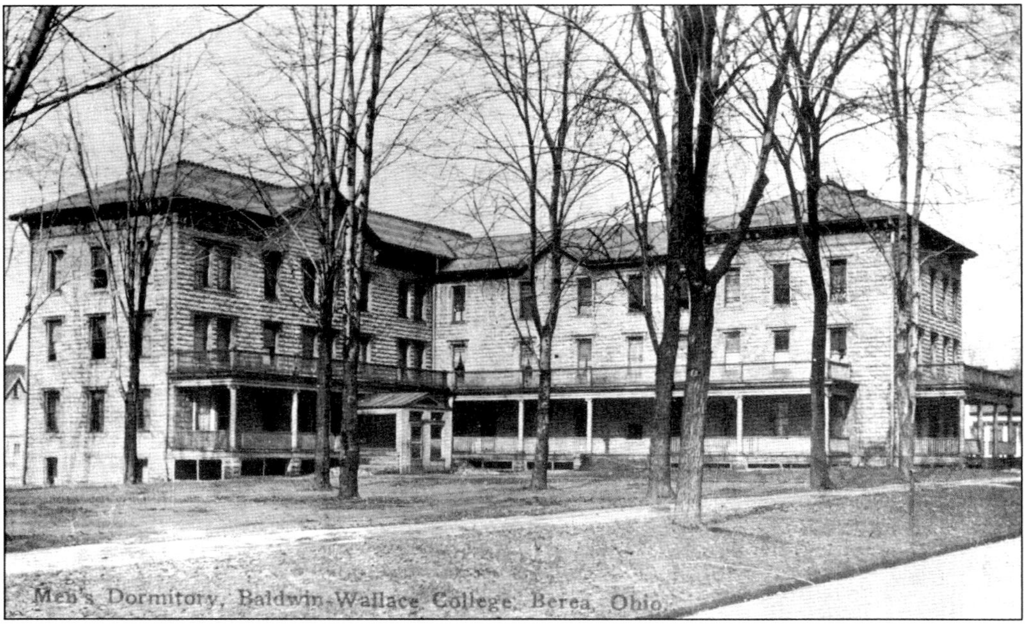

The original wing (left) of the men's dormitory at German Wallace College was built in 1851 to house orphans and the poor. The ell wing was later added, and the building was used for student housing.

Four

The German Methodist Orphan's Home

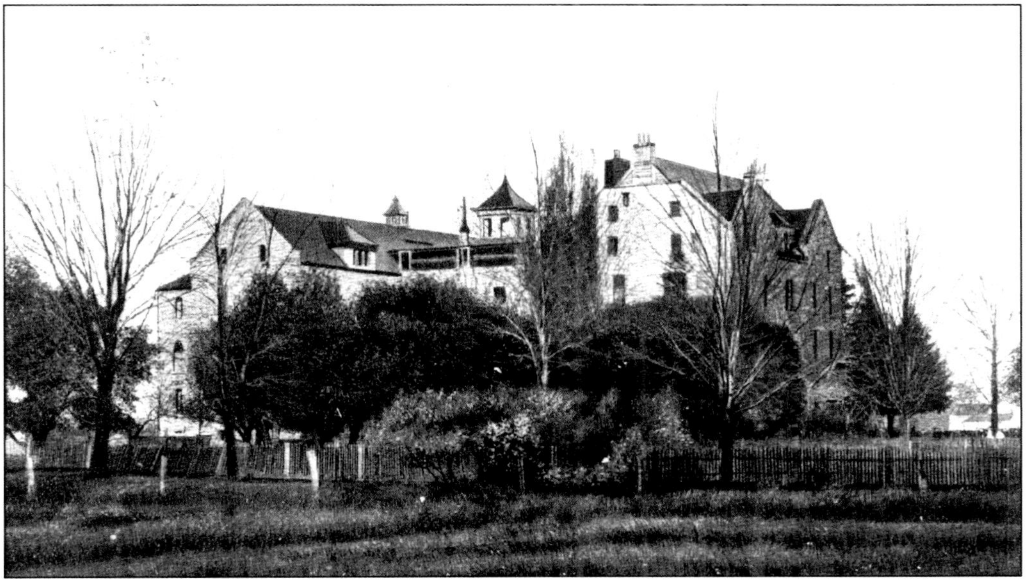

The German Methodist Orphan's Home, established by the German Methodist community in 1865, housed the poor and destitute. Many were widows and orphans of the German community whose family members had been killed in the War Between the States. Now known as the Berea Children's Home and Family Services, it offers programs to children and youth needing specialized therapeutic services.

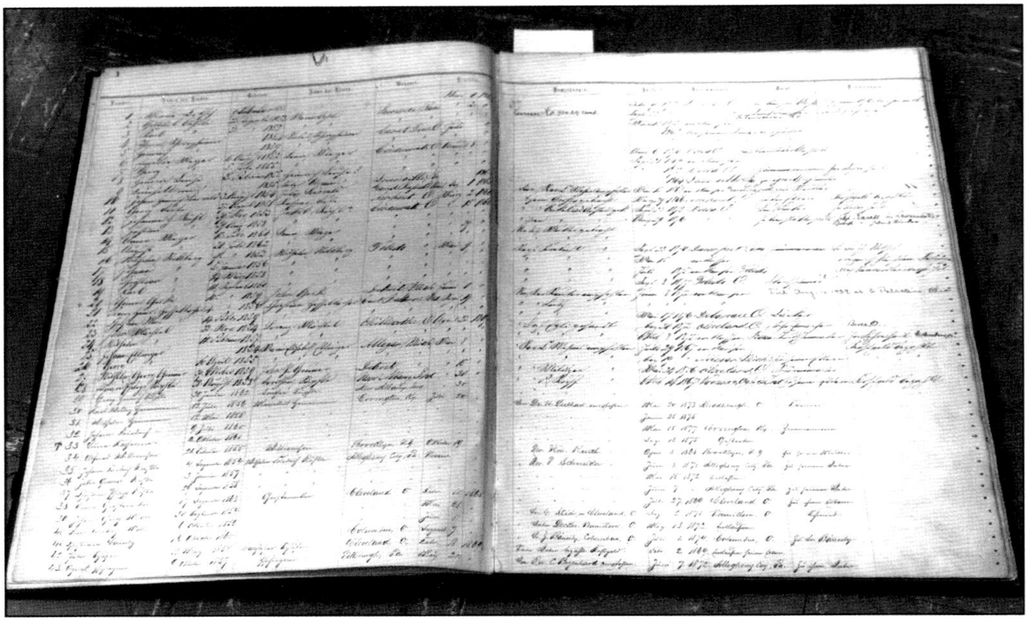

The first orphan child to be received into the home was nine-year-old Mary Bletsch in May of 1864. She remained there for 12 years. Hers is the first name in a large registration book that lists the hundreds of children who made this their home.

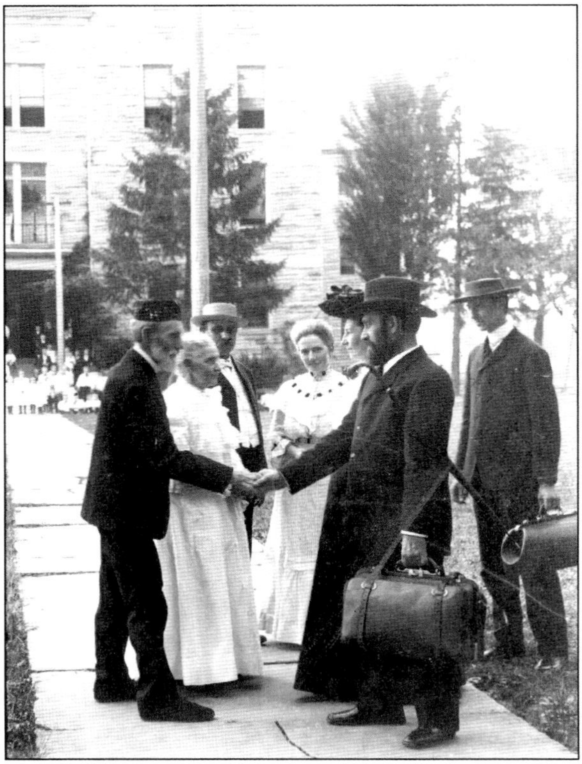

Reverend George "Pappa" Kaletsch came from southern Indiana to take over as superintendent in 1907. He and his wife remained there until 1919.

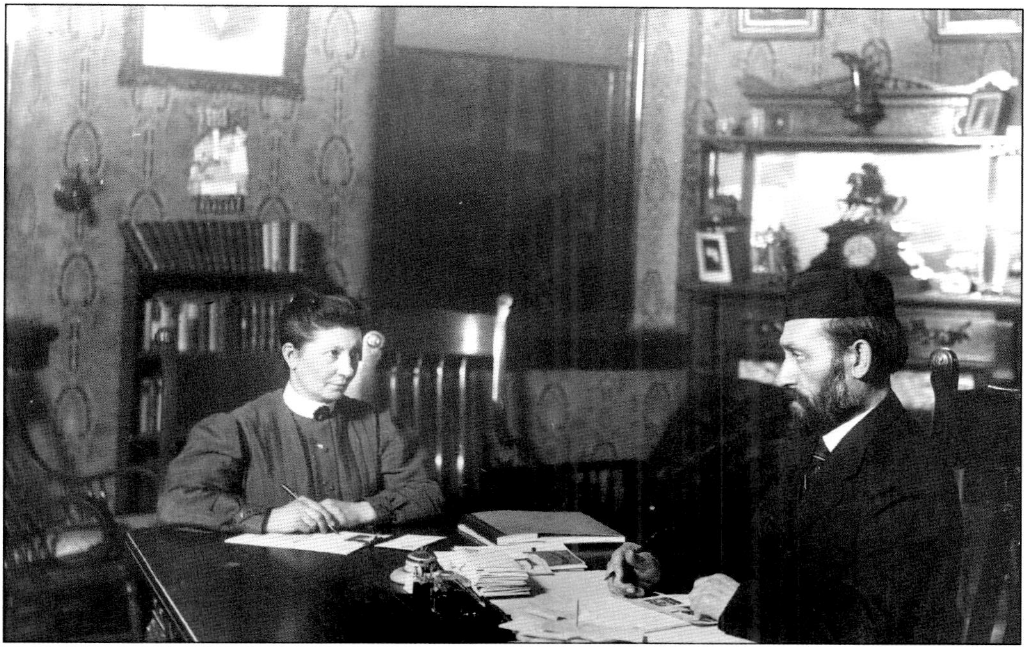

Pappa Kaletsch is shown here in his study, apparently dictating a letter to Mamma Kaletsch, who served as teacher, housemother, and secretary.

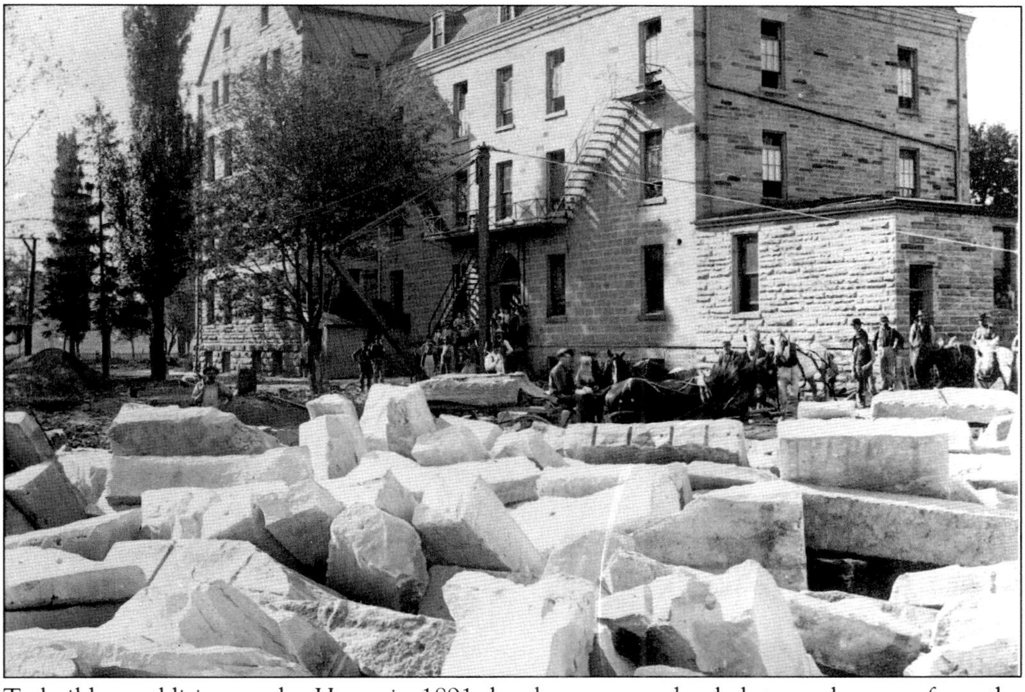

To build an addition to the Home in 1891, local quarrymen hauled stones by oxen from the nearby quarry and cut them to size on the building site and immediately laid them in position. Another wing was added in 1903.

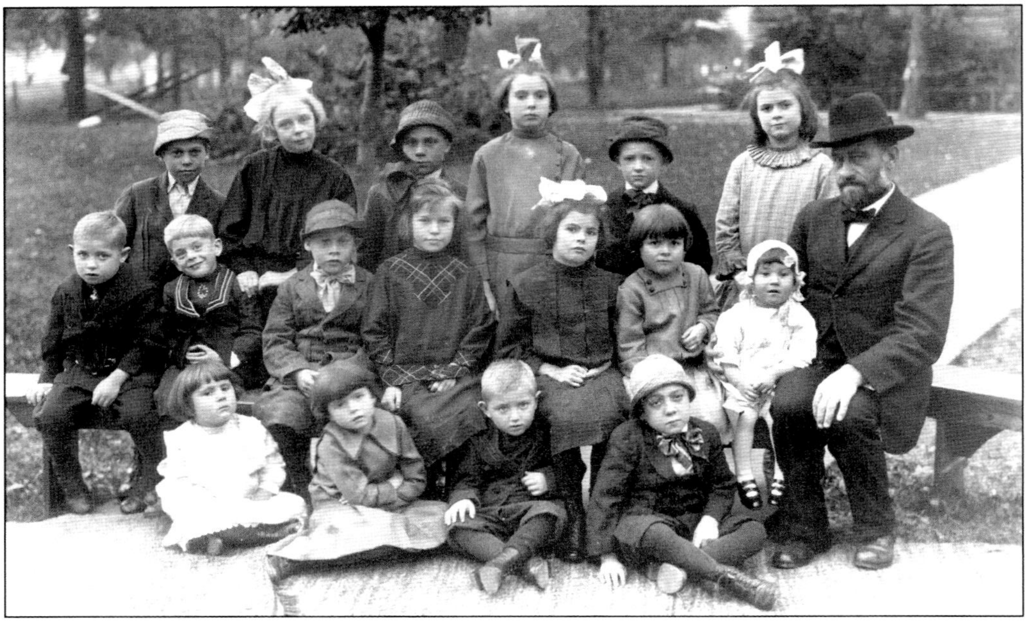

Pappa Kaletsch had a great love for children He is shown here with his adopted child on his knee. The child was left on the doorstop of the Orphanage as a foundling.

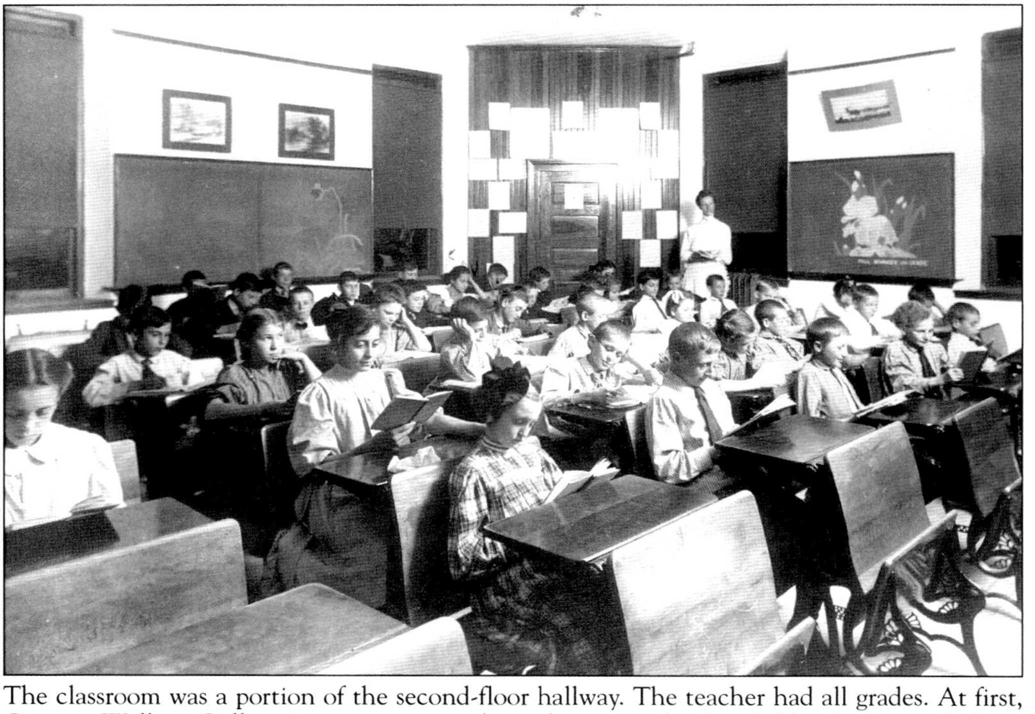

The classroom was a portion of the second-floor hallway. The teacher had all grades. At first, German Wallace College instructors or undergraduates taught the children's classes. In later years, the classes were absorbed into the Berea school district.

Mrs. Mary A. Ott of Louisville, Kentucky, gave the Ott Memorial Manual Training School in 1905, erected in honor of her husband Henry Ott and her daughter Ida.

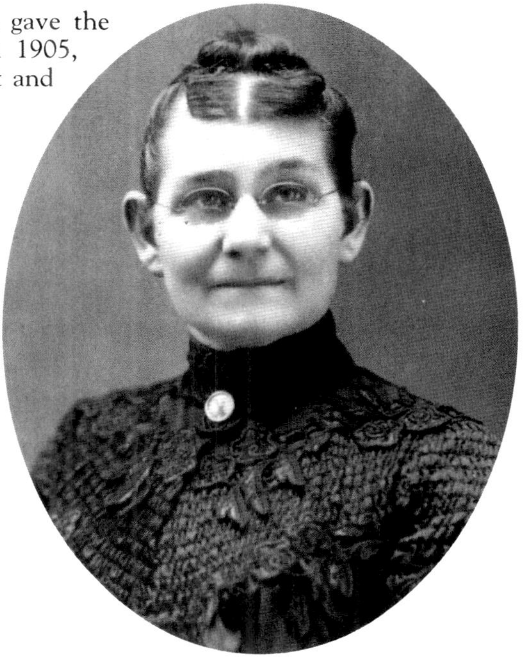

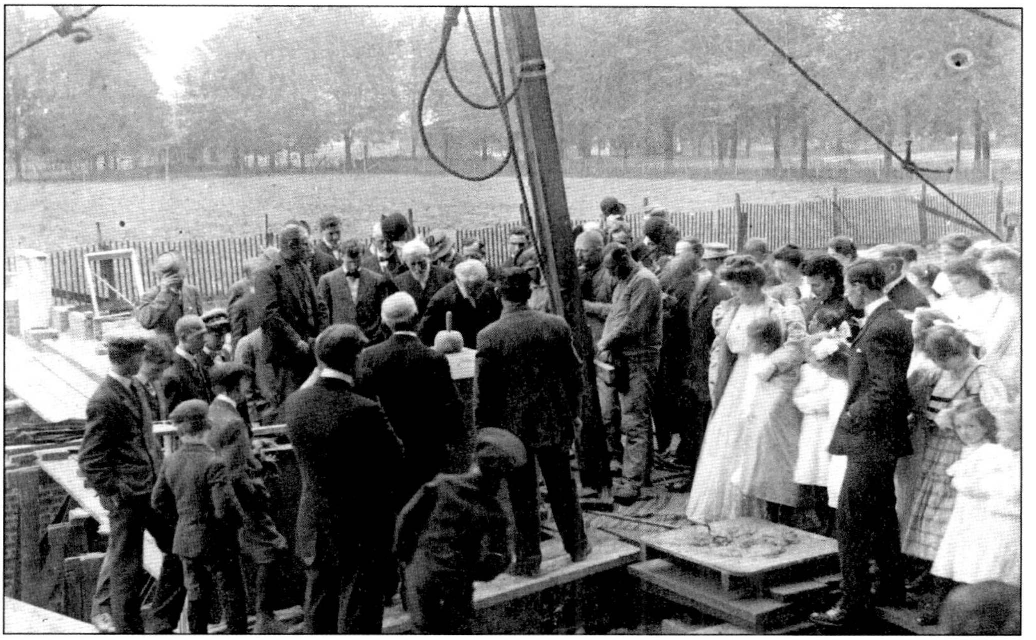

The splendidly equipped building had beautiful sandstone frescoes and the locally carved motto, "She has done what she could." Actually, this was Mrs. Ott's sentiment to commemorate Ida's many kind deeds in various ways. The dedication services were in German and English, and the orphan children presented a program.

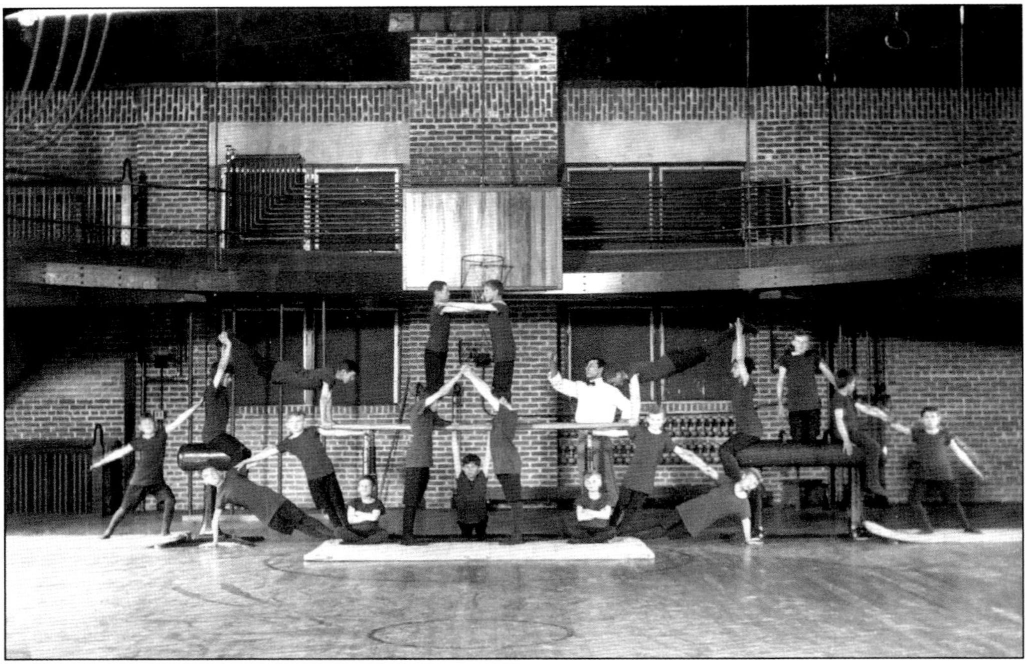

Physical training and fitness were integral parts of life at the Orphanage, at least for boys.

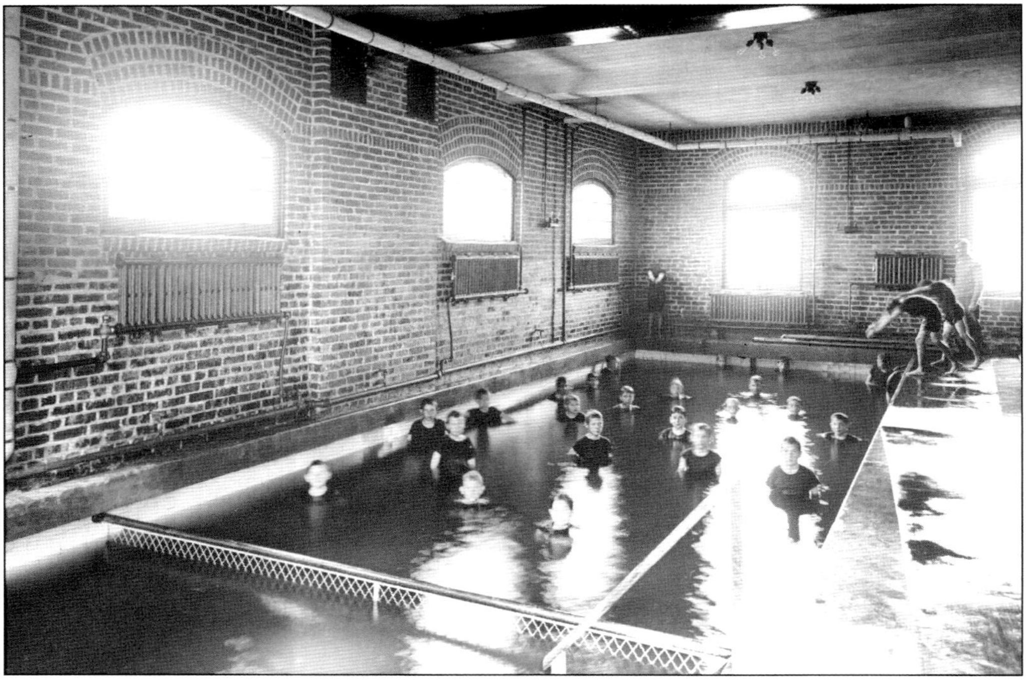

All of the children were expected to learn to swim. The heated swimming pool in the Ott Memorial Building was an amenity found in few public institutions in the early years of the 20th century; both Berea High School and Baldwin-Wallace College used it on occasion.

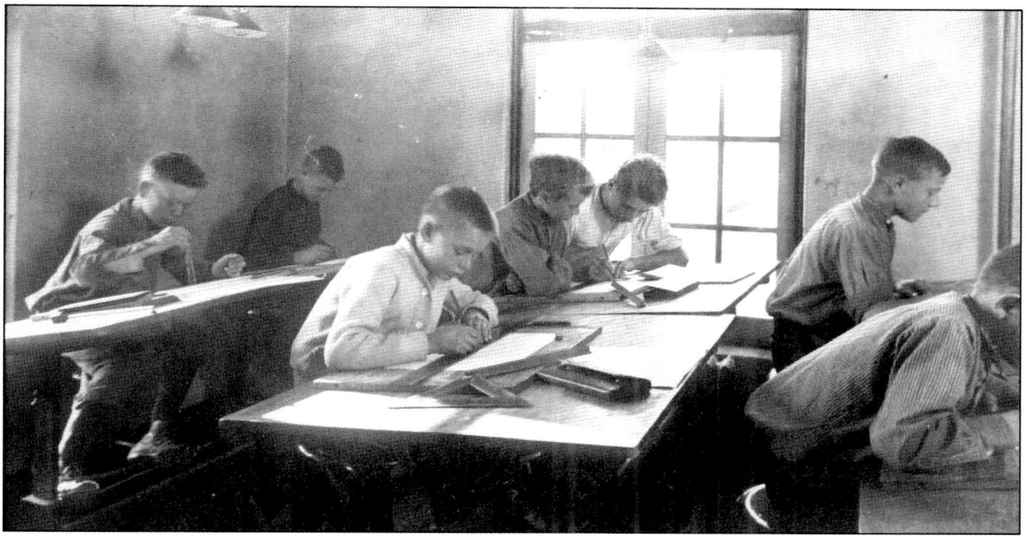

Students learned drafting on the main floor of the Ott Building. The goal of education was to provide the children with life skills to help them to become independent. From the Berea *Enterprise:* "They are taught in well-appointed schoolrooms at the home by accomplished instructors and attend the village schools of Berea. Much attention is paid to music, and those who deserve higher education are assisted at German Wallace College and Baldwin University."

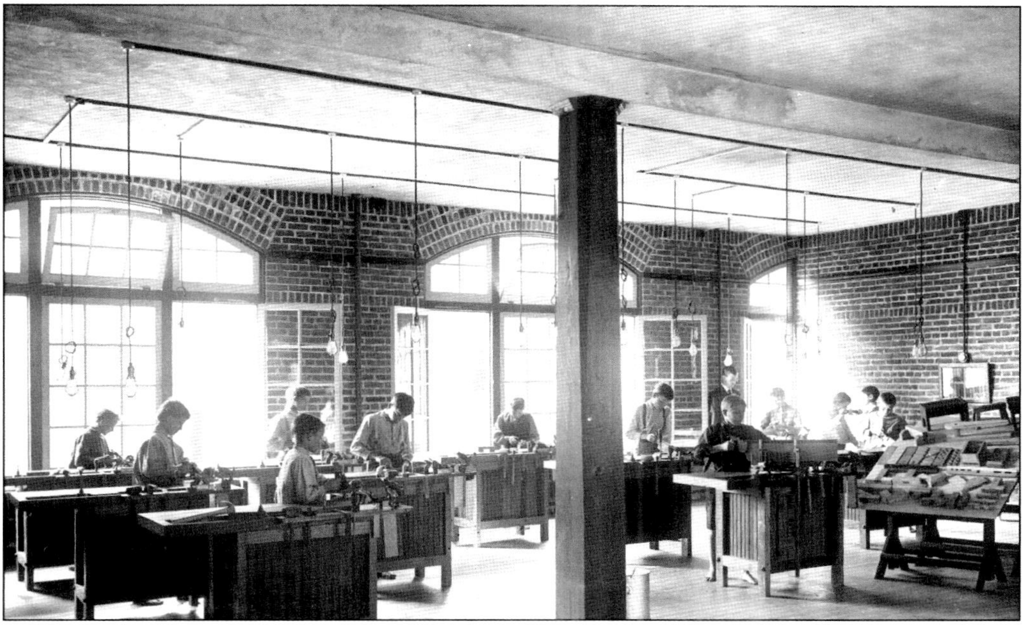

Boys learned woodworking skills as well as ironworking and horseshoeing at the Ott Memorial Manual Training School. The community respected the educational program of the Orphan's Home. From the Berea *Enterprise* on March 3, 1903: "This is a home for fatherless and motherless children of German Methodist Churches, where they are provided for until they are of age, and assisted to make the most of all that is in them."

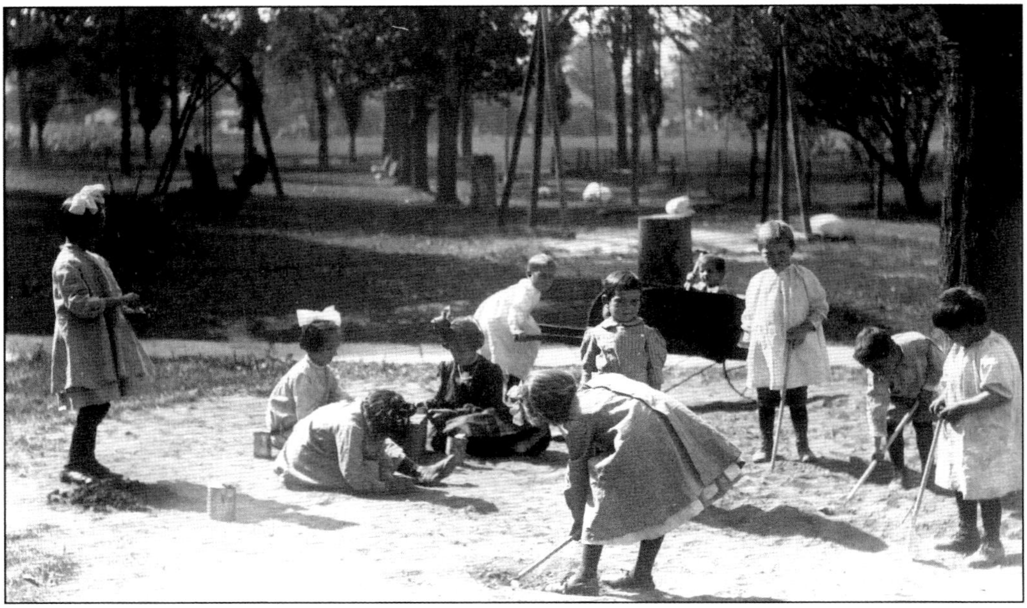

The "house kids" would gather with two wheelbarrows every evening, promptly at 5 o'clock to "pick up the yard." They circled the entire stone building, picking up all bits of debris, sticks, or stones and took them to the dump at the rear of the power house. They did this every night until the snows came.

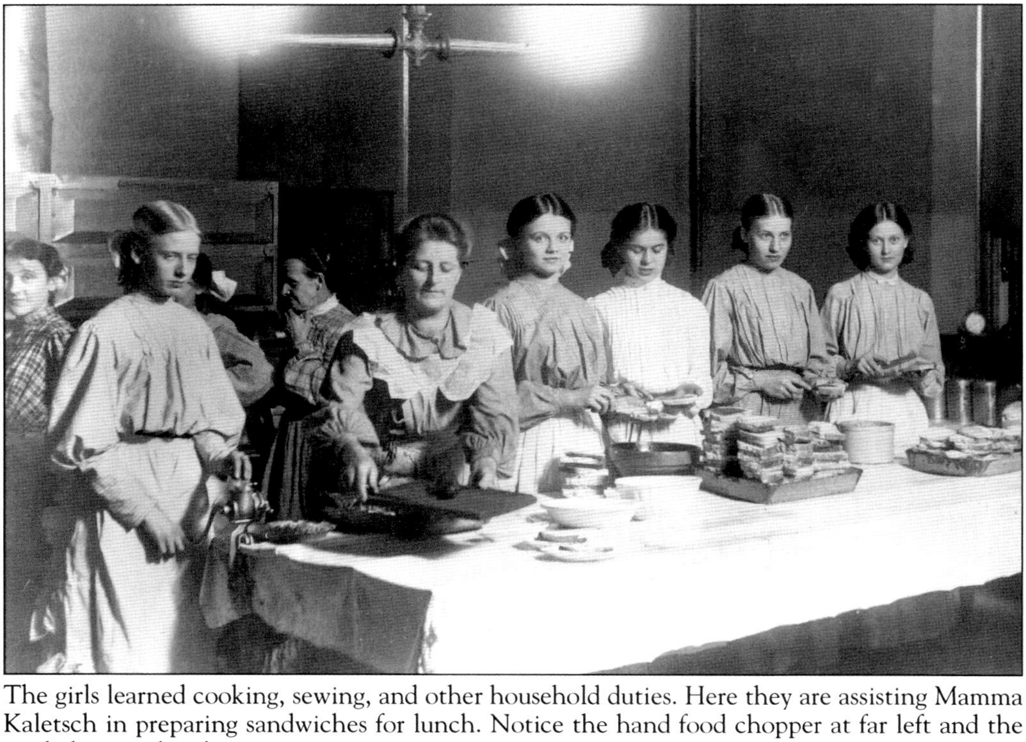

The girls learned cooking, sewing, and other household duties. Here they are assisting Mamma Kaletsch in preparing sandwiches for lunch. Notice the hand food chopper at far left and the gas lights overhead.

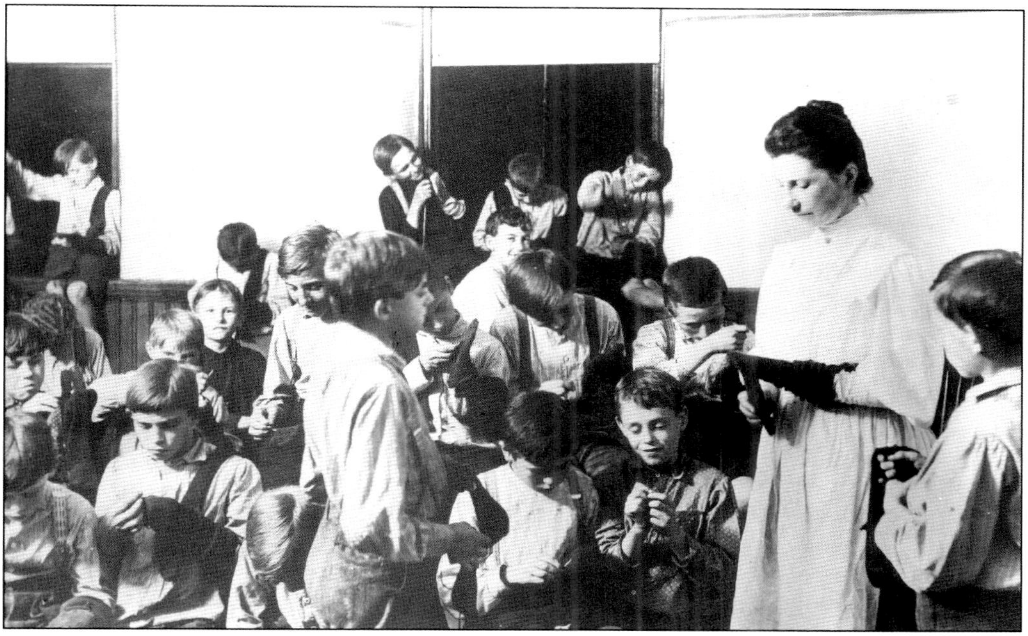

The children always called the superintendent and his wife "Pappa" and "Mamma." Here, Mamma (Selma) Kaletsch instructs the boys on the fine art of mending and darning.

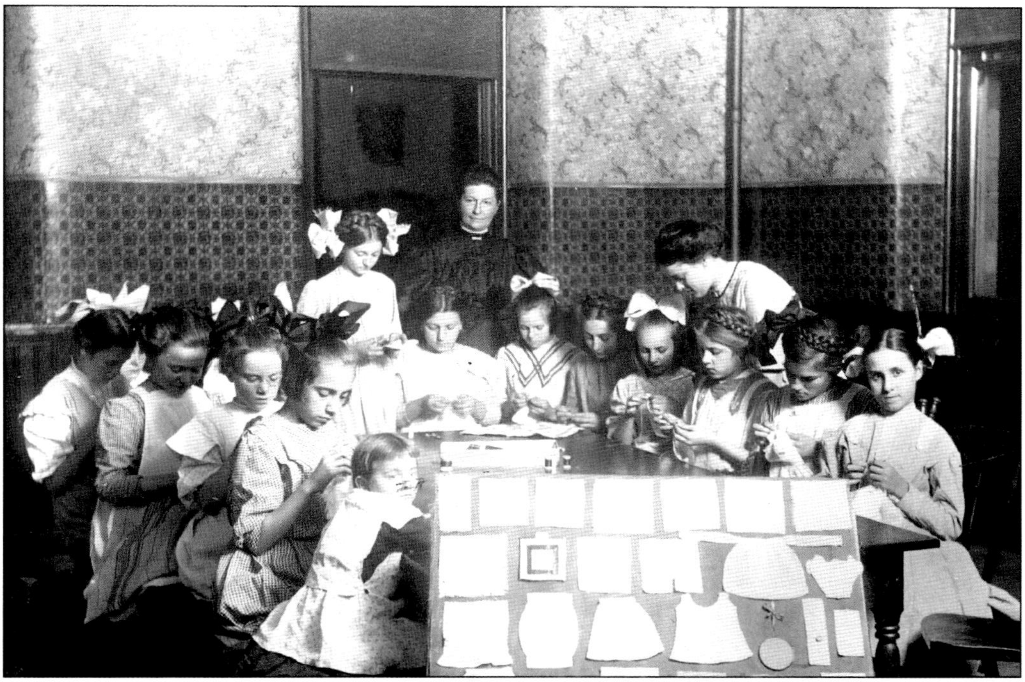

Even very young girls learned to sew and knit. From the sizes of the pattern pieces, they must have learned by making doll clothes. Notice how well groomed the girls are. Standards of personal cleanliness and neatness were very high at the Orphanage.

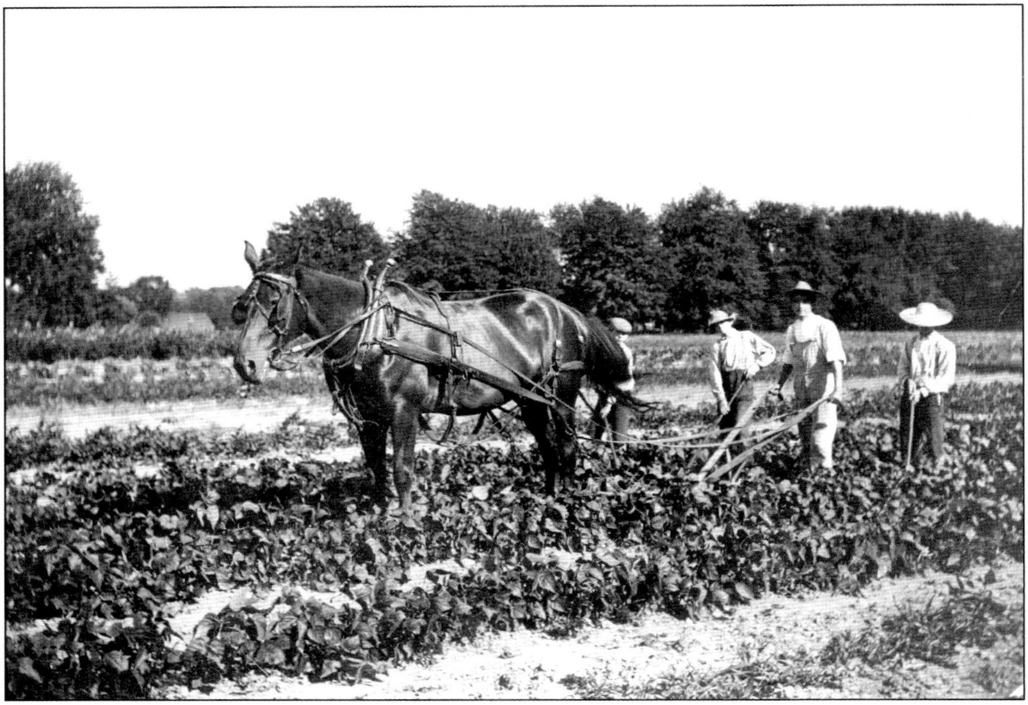

When boys reached the age of 12 through 18, they were known as "barn boys." They had farm chores beginning at 5 a.m., such as caring for horses, milking cows, planting, cultivating, and harvesting.

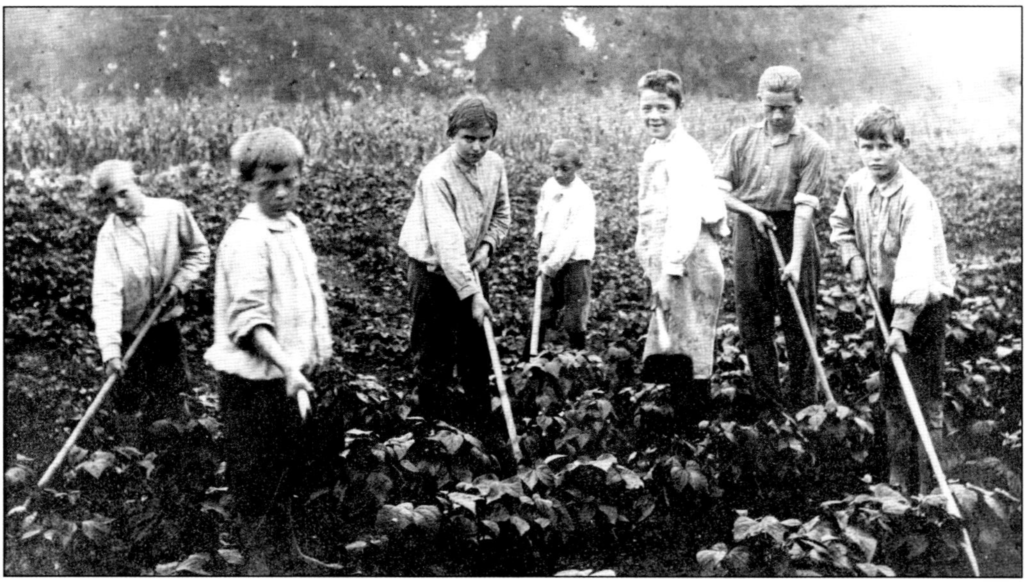

The Orphan's Home owned several nearby farms where all sorts of produce was raised, especially beans and corn and corn for silage. Even the younger boys who were "house kids" were called on to hoe the crops.

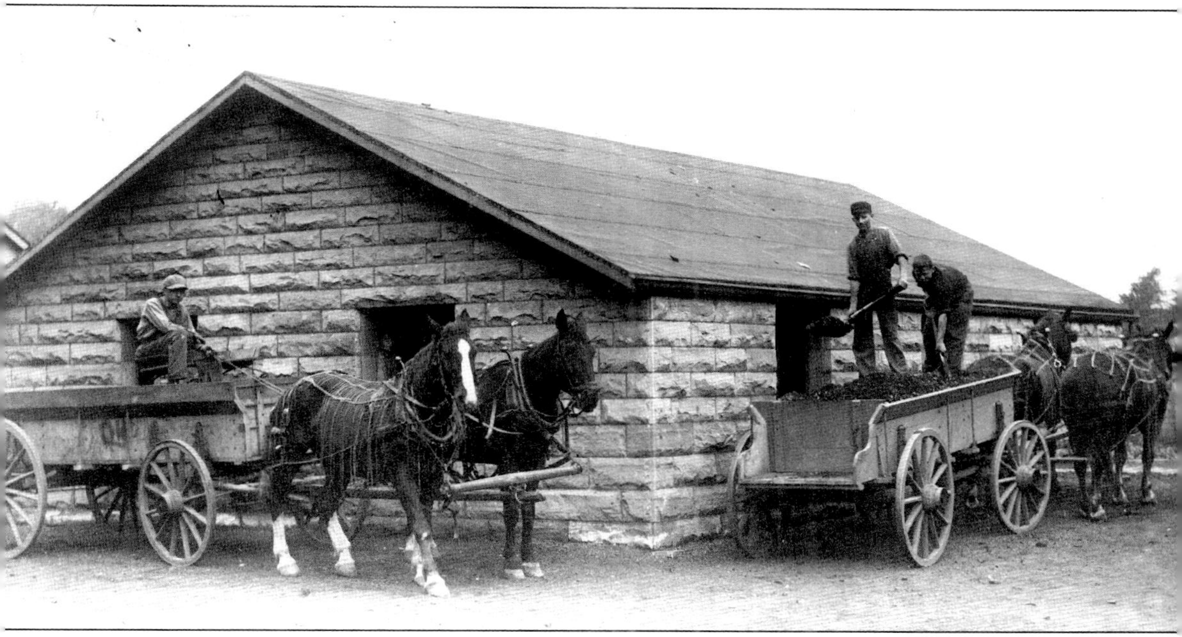

Crops and cattle furnished much of the food for the Orphanage family. In addition, the boys learned industry and responsibility from their required farm chores.

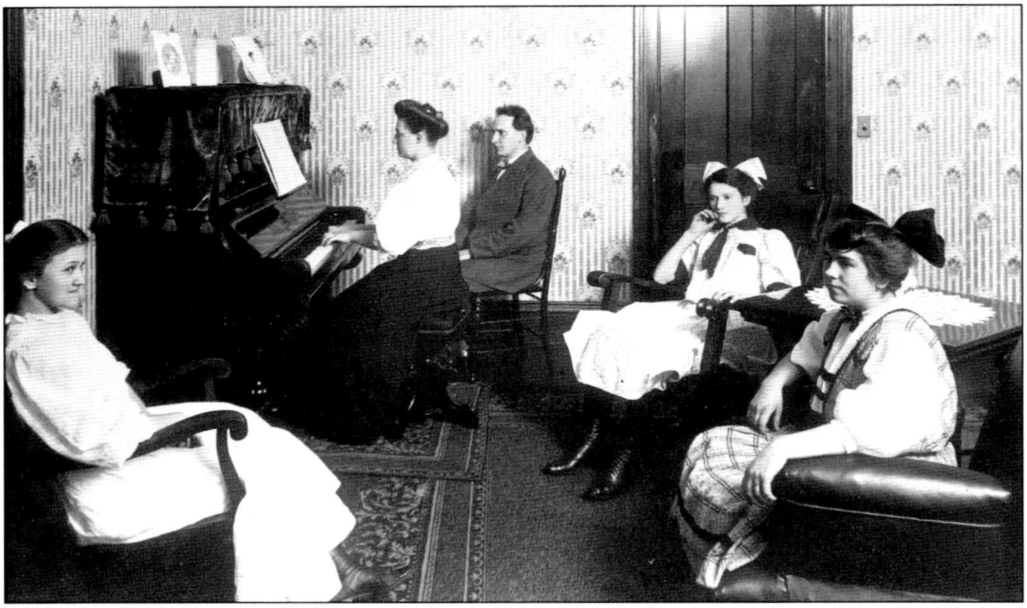

Faculty members from German Wallace College taught music to promising students at the Orphanage. Here, Professor Albert Riemenschneider listens to Mamma play while pupils wait their turn.

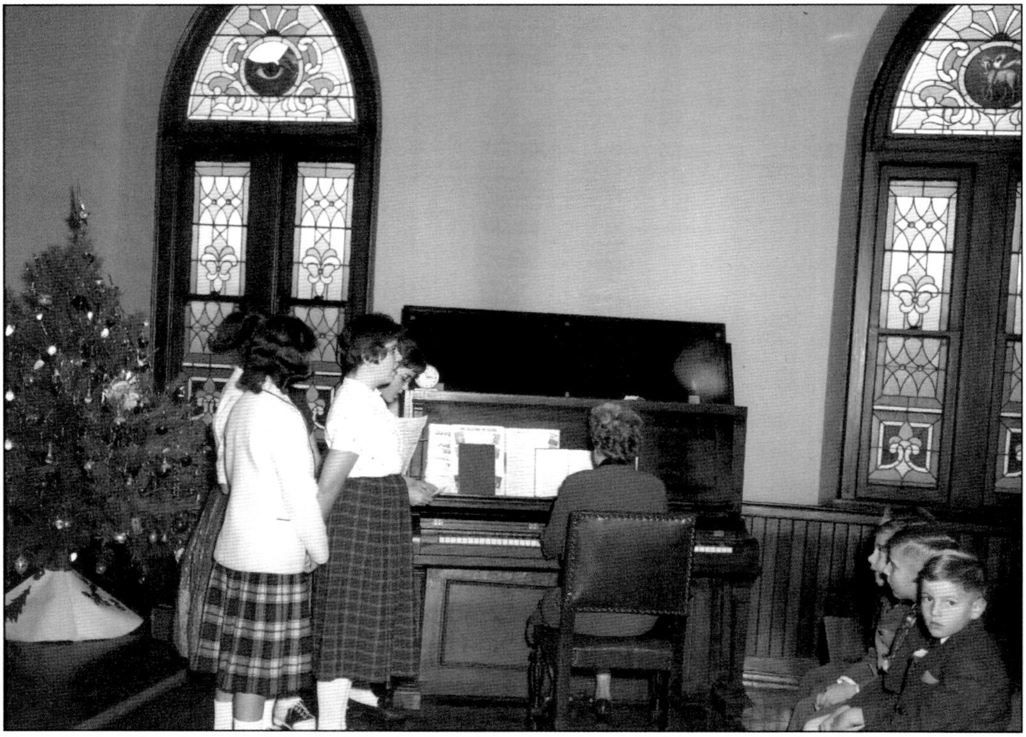

Every year, there was a Christmas party and pageant. And the 1940s, judging from the bobby socks and saddle shoes, were no exception.

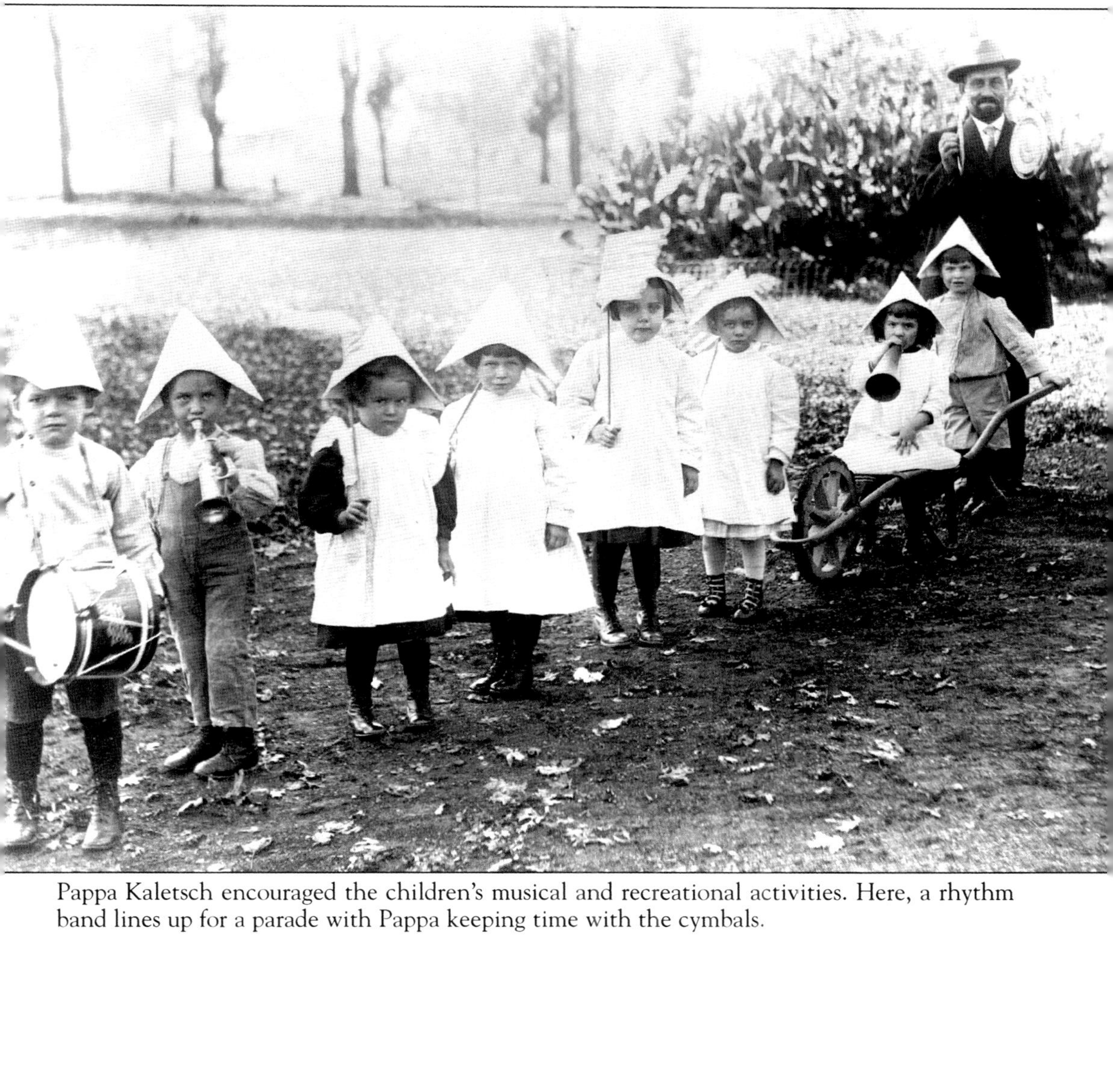

Pappa Kaletsch encouraged the children's musical and recreational activities. Here, a rhythm band lines up for a parade with Pappa keeping time with the cymbals.

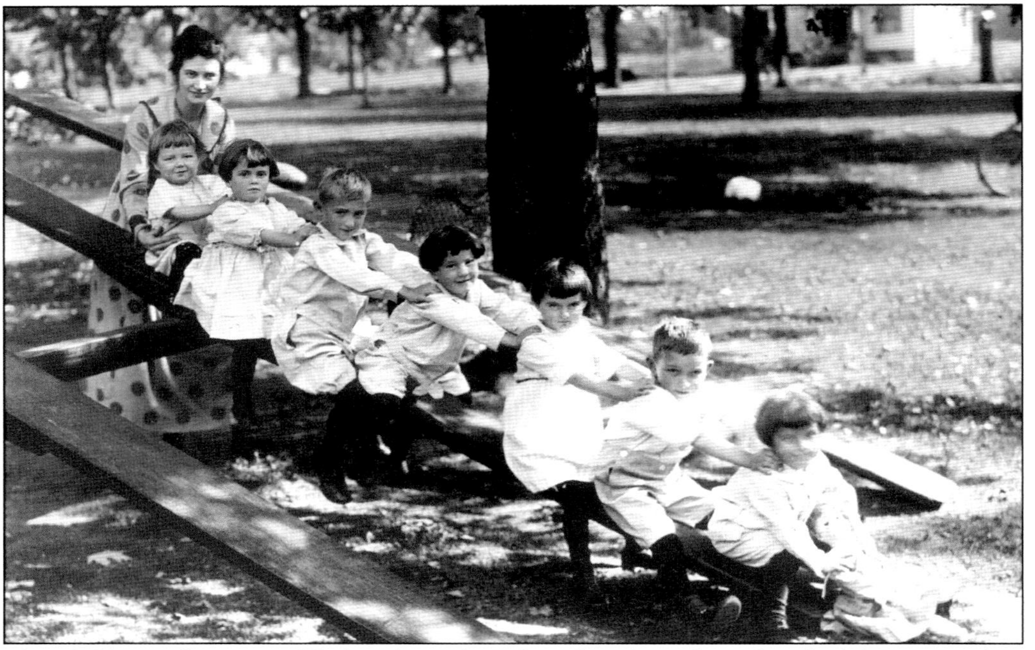

The children's days were filled with work and studies, but when they had free time, they enjoyed the spacious grounds and play areas of the Orphanage.

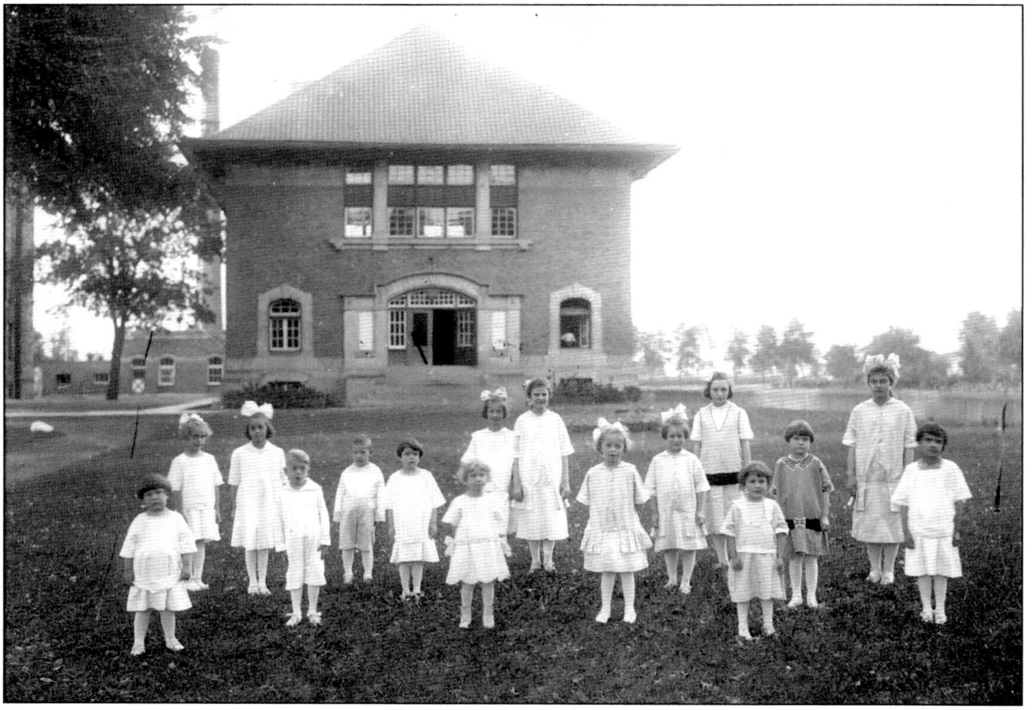

Dressed in summer whites (except the girl third from right), these youngsters pose in front of the Ott Memorial Building about 1910.

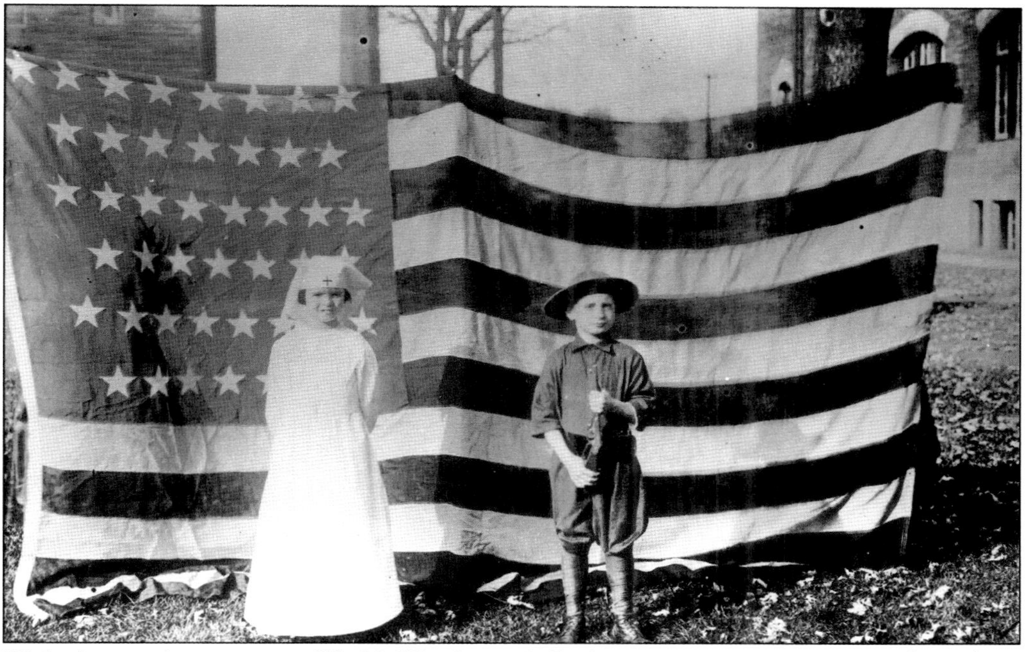

With America's entry into World War I in 1917, Americans were suspicious of anything "German." These residents of the Orphanage show their loyalty to their country.

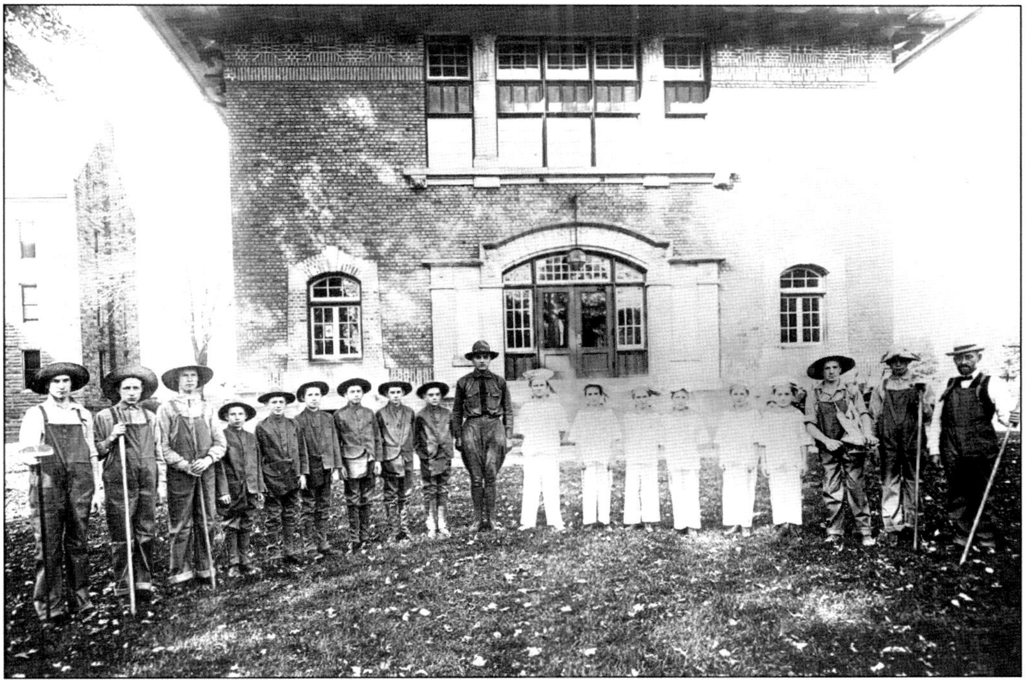

During World War I, Pappa Kaletsch (far right) organized some of the young people at the Orphanage to present a pageant depicting the importance of the farm and the military for the war effort.

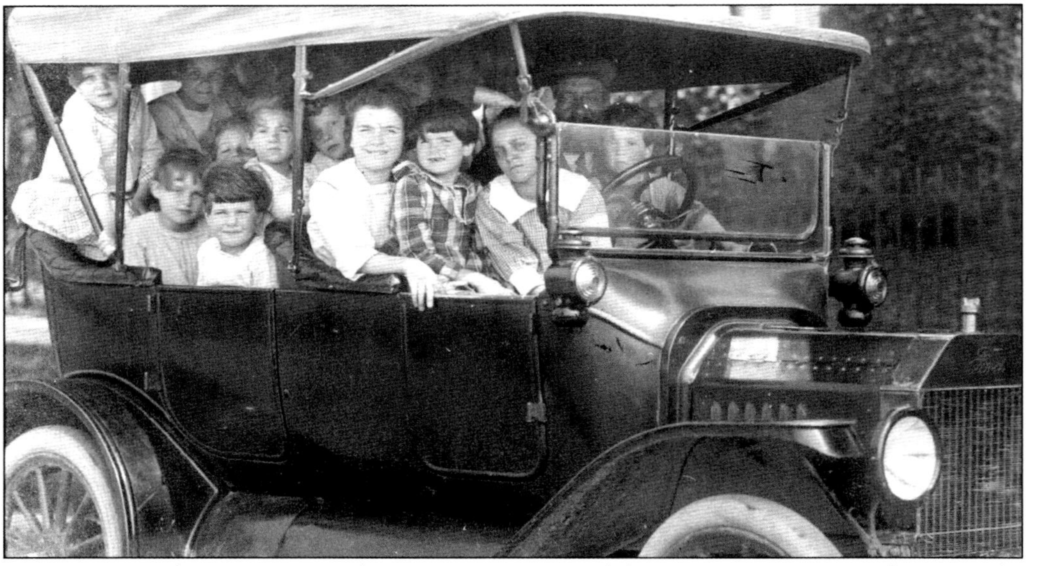

Every summer for many years, the American Automobile Association sponsored a "Day for Orphans" at Euclid Beach Park for as many as 4,000 children. Members of the club would volunteer their automobiles to take the children to the popular Cleveland amusement park. A typical carload of children is seen here, loaded and ready to move from the German Methodist Orphan's Home in Berea. "Euclid Beach was like the other side of the world to us," Henry Barr remembered. There were usually as many as 15 or 20 carloads of children from the Berea home.

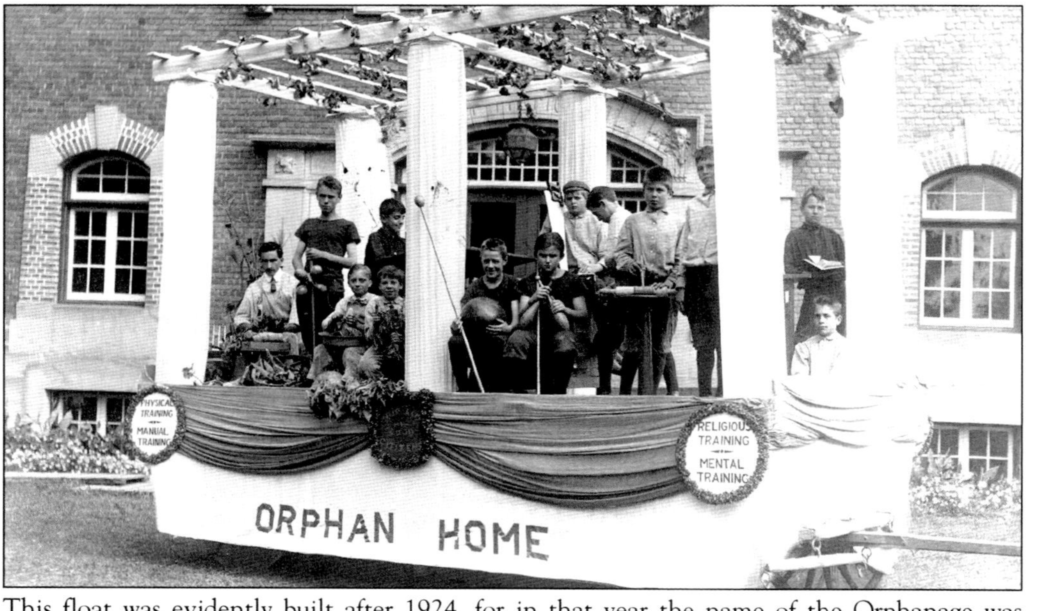

This float was evidently built after 1924, for in that year the name of the Orphanage was officially changed to the German Methodist Orphan's Home. It was becoming more of a permanent home than just a temporary refuge for children who had no parents. Apparently the goals of physical and manual training as well as religious and mental training still ranked in paramount importance.

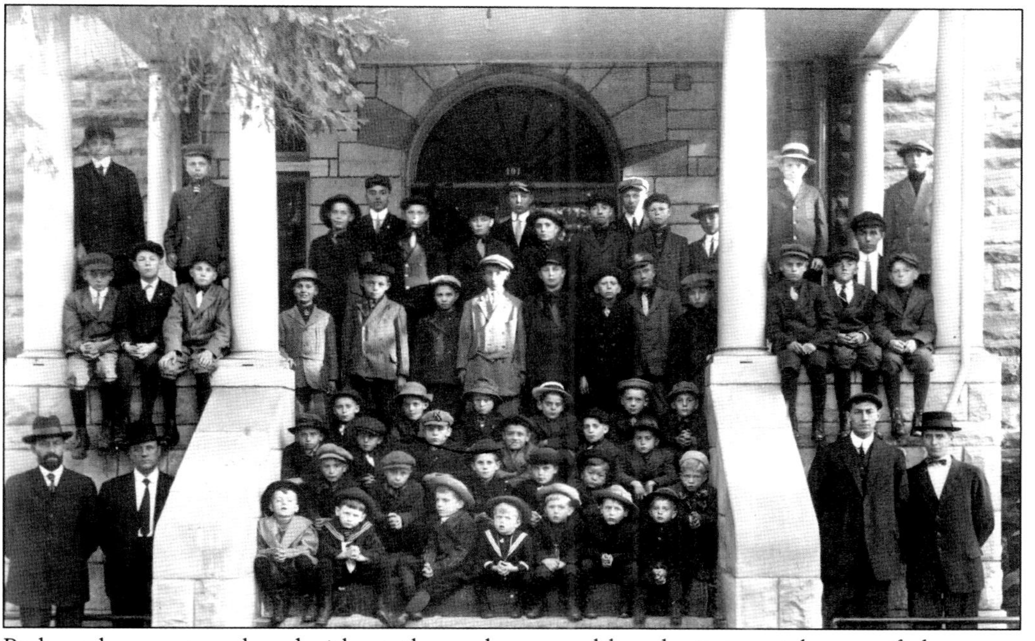

Perhaps boys outnumbered girls at the orphanage, although, it is not known if these two pictures were taken the same year. Pappa Kaletsch is at front left.

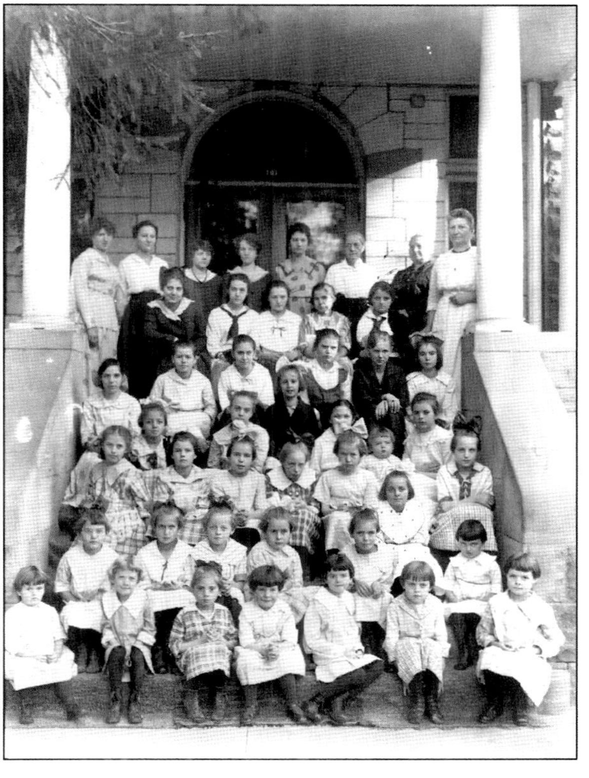

Mamma Kaletsch is at top, far right. Notice in both pictures a number of young men and women teachers or assistants. Some were college students.

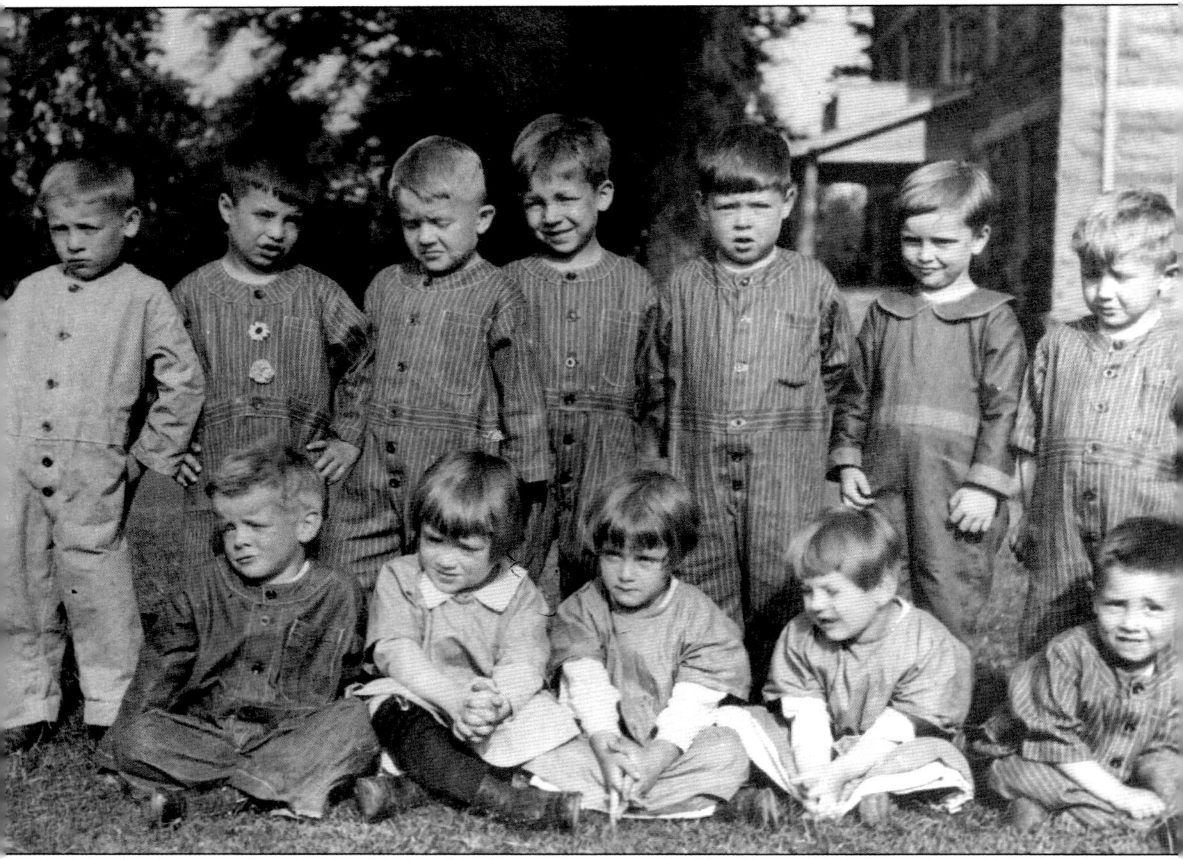

The boy in the center of the back row is Henry Barr. He came to the Orphanage in 1920 when he was five years old. His father died eight months after he was born, leaving his mother destitute with three small children. Henry lived at the Orphanage until he was 16. In his adult life, he became a well-known photographer and one of Berea's leading citizens.

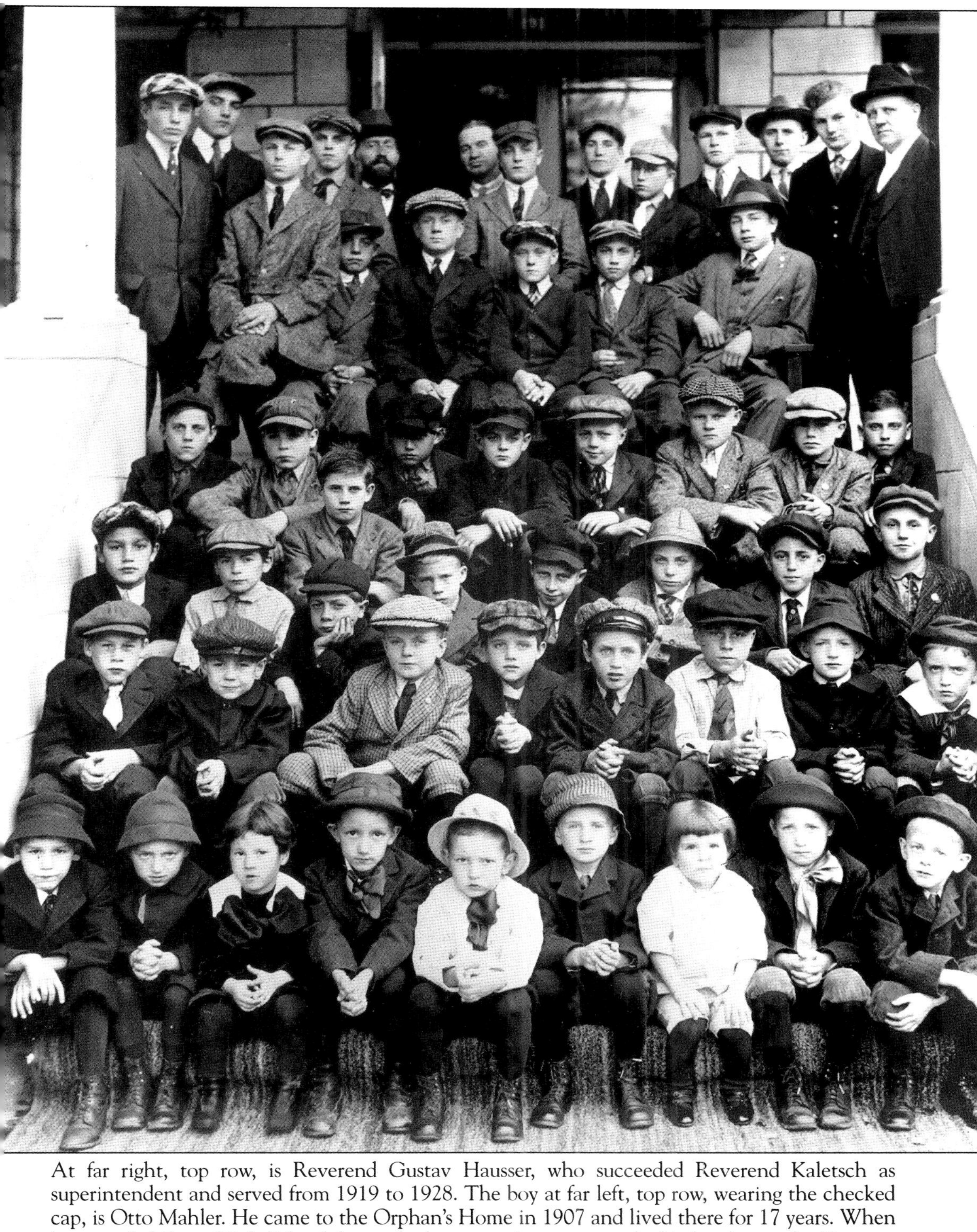

At far right, top row, is Reverend Gustav Hausser, who succeeded Reverend Kaletsch as superintendent and served from 1919 to 1928. The boy at far left, top row, wearing the checked cap, is Otto Mahler. He came to the Orphan's Home in 1907 and lived there for 17 years. When he attended Berea High School, he worked as a gym instructor and a big brother at the Home.

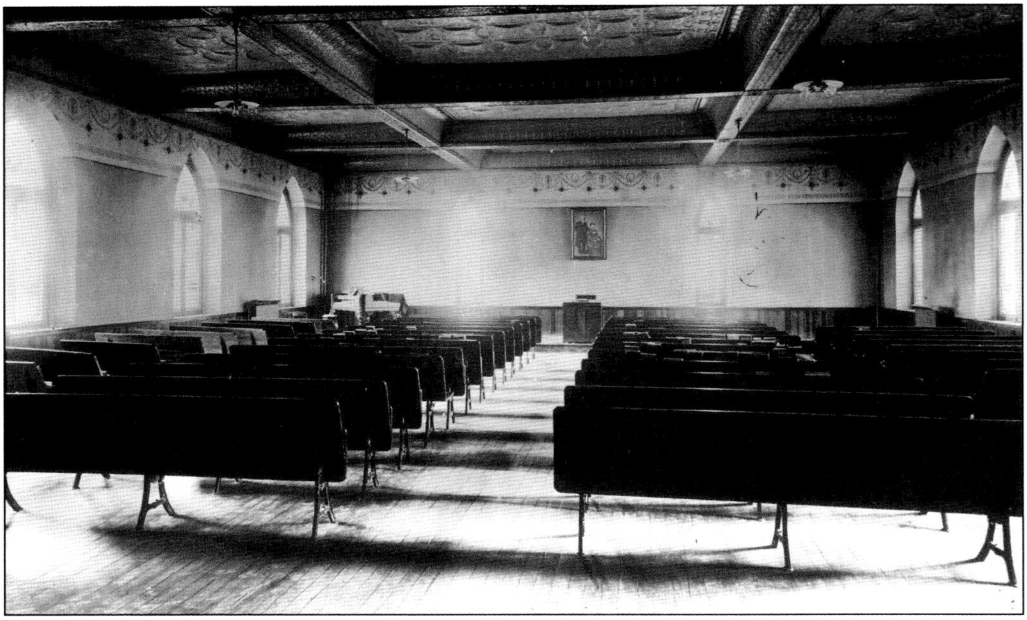

Worship services for the Orphanage family took place daily in the chapel on the second floor, centered at the rear of the main building. Note the stenciled borders, the tin ceiling, and the primitive electric light fixtures. Eight stained glass windows, 12 feet high, and five feet wide were manufactured in Germany in 1866 and were part of the original structure.

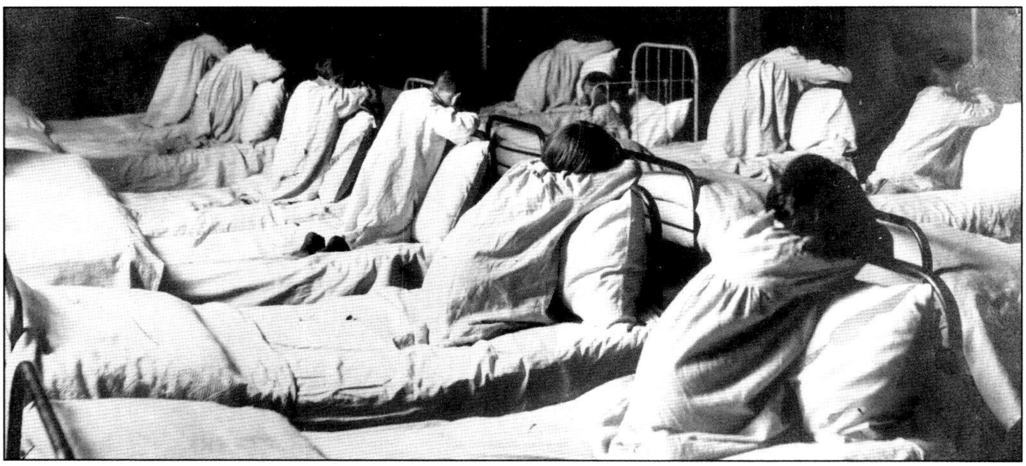

Each night the children prayed at the foot of their beds and sang this song:

Lord, a tired child am I
Soon within my bed I'll lie,
Send an angel, dear to keep
Silent watch oe'r while I sleep. Amen.

After the song, they said a prayer out loud that started like this:

Bless Pappa and Mamma and the soldiers and sailors in the heathen and foreign countries.

Five

Fires of Berea

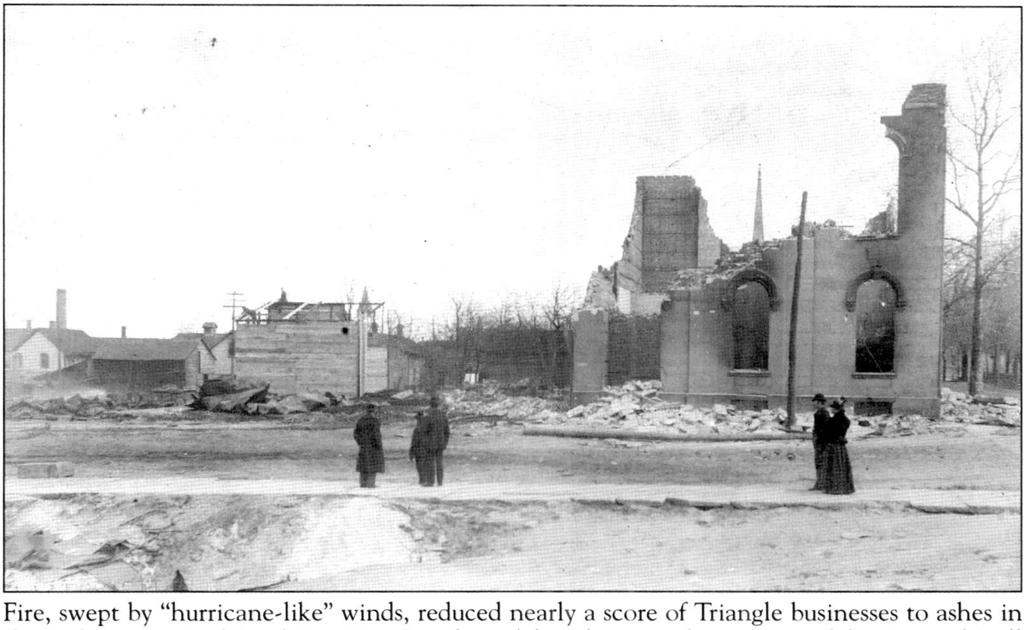

Fire, swept by "hurricane-like" winds, reduced nearly a score of Triangle businesses to ashes in the early morning of April 19, 1897. Residents (above) survey the remains of the Council Hall that had cost the village $25,000; several of the bonds were still unpaid. The fire, described by the Berea *Advertiser* as a "burning, seething mausoleum" (although there was no loss of life), started in an unoccupied tin shop supposed to be occupied by vagrants.

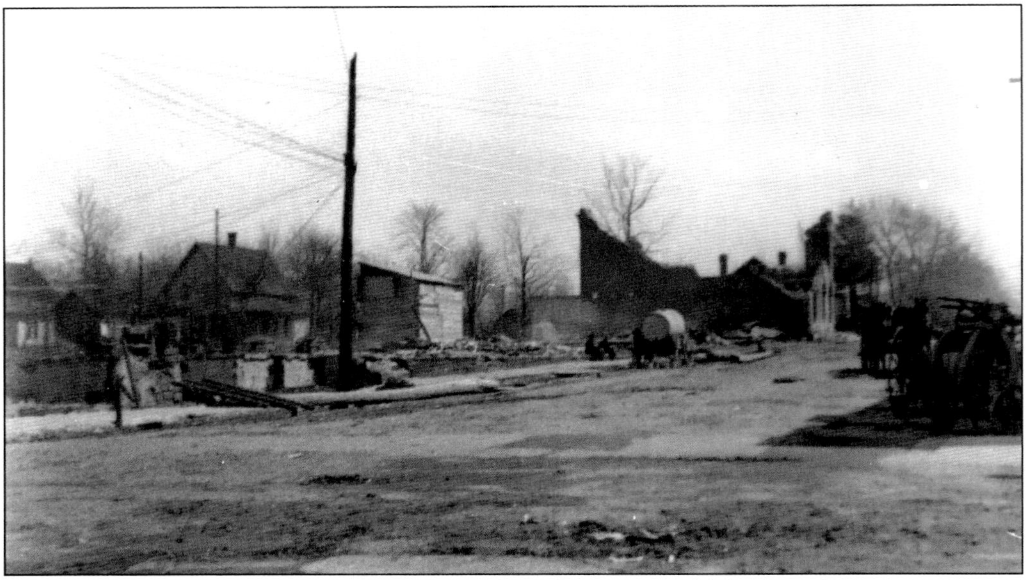

Berea's firefighting equipment, long deemed inadequate, could force only a puny spray of water from the Triangle pump. About 30 volunteers hauled water from the river in carts and in the sprinkling wagon. Following the previous summer's strike, Mayor E. Christian faced the second crisis of his tenure. He telegraphed the Cleveland Fire Department for help and led a group of volunteers into the doomed Council Hall to save records and valuable papers. (Courtesy of Jim Jaworski.)

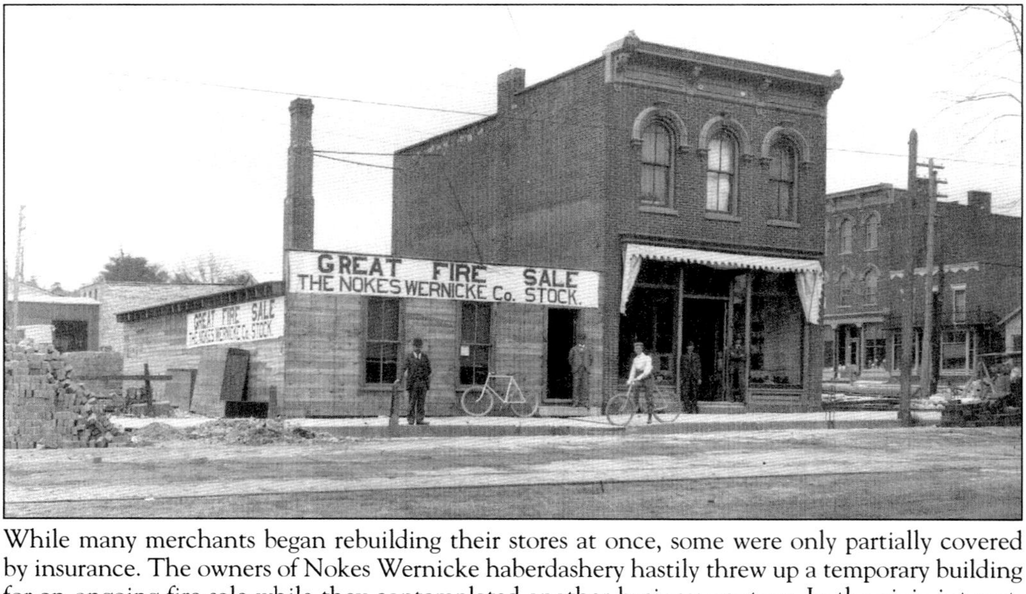

While many merchants began rebuilding their stores at once, some were only partially covered by insurance. The owners of Nokes Wernicke haberdashery hastily threw up a temporary building for an ongoing fire sale while they contemplated another business venture. In the civic interest, Mr. J.C. Nokes donated a fire whistle that was installed at the Berea Milling Company.

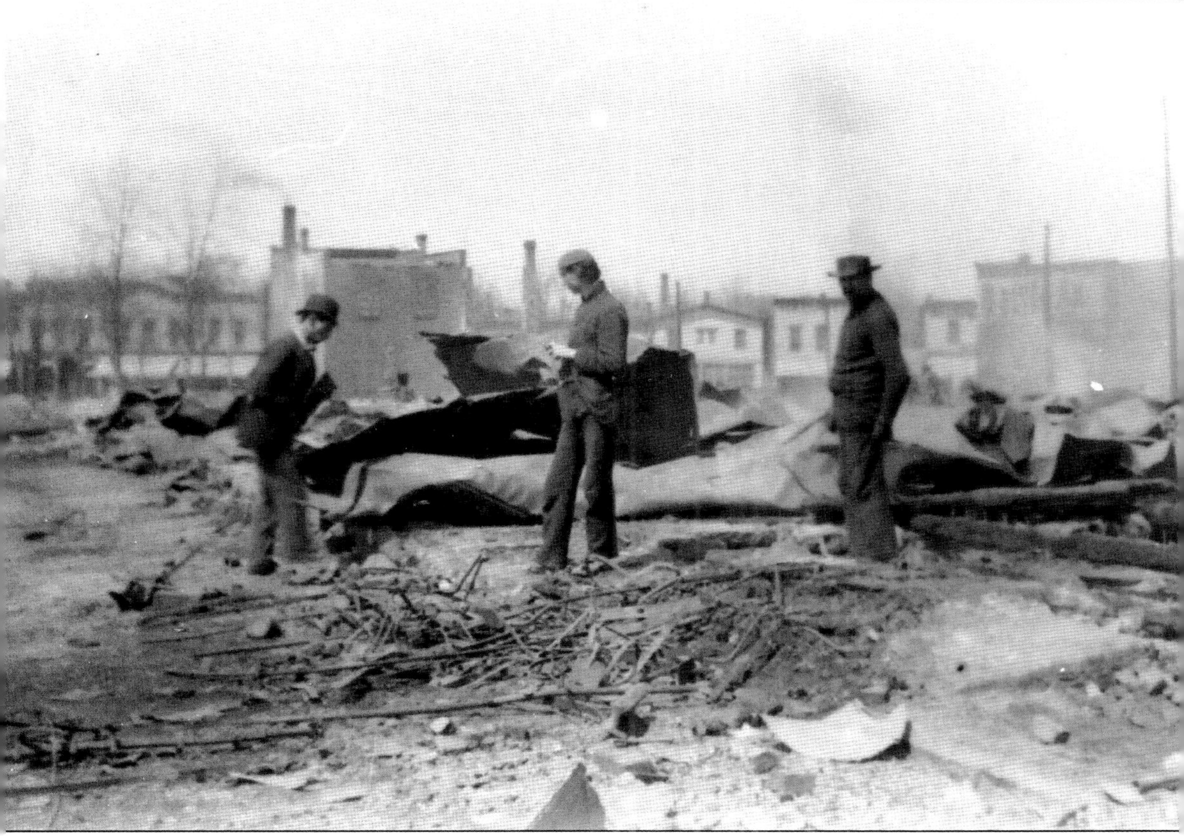

The total loss to Bereans was estimated at up to $100,000. Insurance companies refused to cover a number of buildings because of their crowded situation and Berea's poor fire protection. "Curious crowds viewed the ruins from early morning until late at night, and nearly everyone has a word of pity and sympathy for the sufferers," stated the editor of the *Advertiser*.

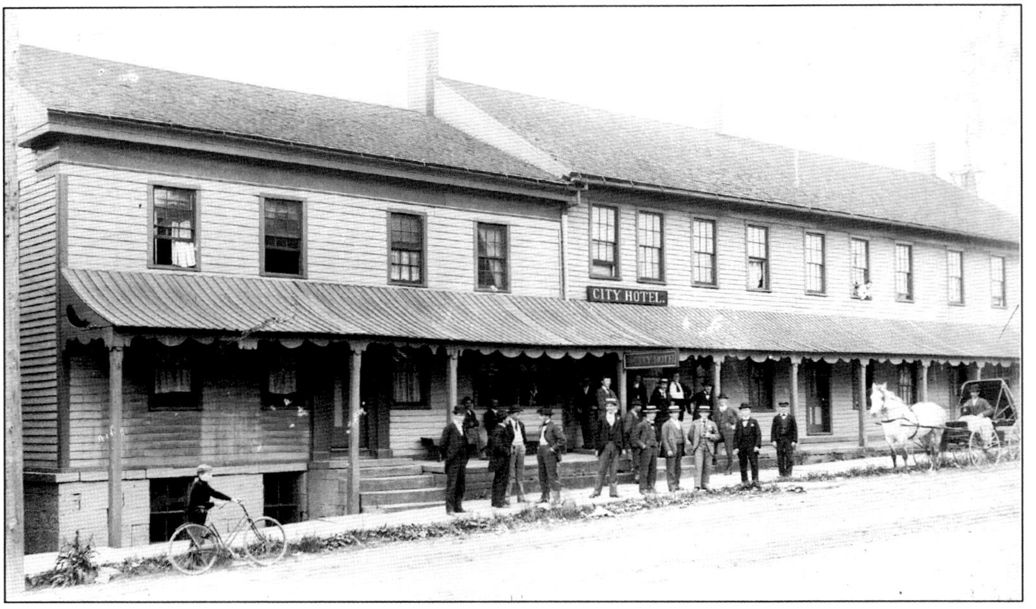

Mrs. H.N. Rockwood, owner of the City Hotel, suffered one of the heaviest losses in the 1897 fire. The frame building went up like a tinderbox. The building and its contents were valued at $3,500. Mrs. Rockwood had no insurance.

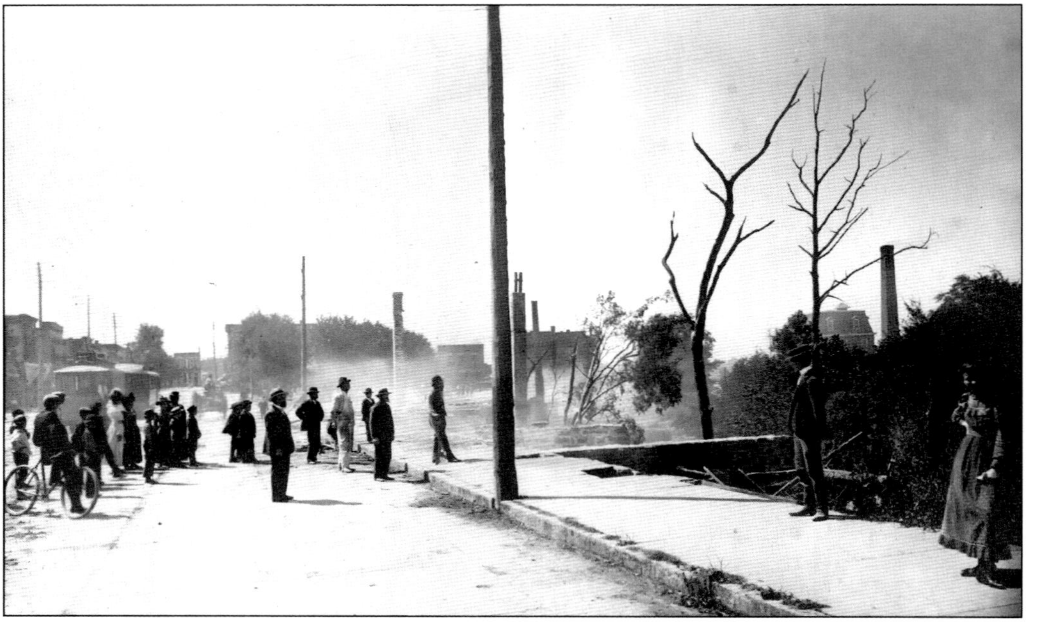

Two years later on August 14, 1899, the Triangle was again ablaze. A stiff northeast wind made businessmen know that nothing could be saved in nearly 20 blocks. The Cleveland Fire Department sent a pumper by way of the quarry railroad, but the muddy water from the Rocky River nearly ruined it. It did succeed in confining the fire to the Bullinger Block, where stone firewalls kept flames from spreading to adjacent frame stores.

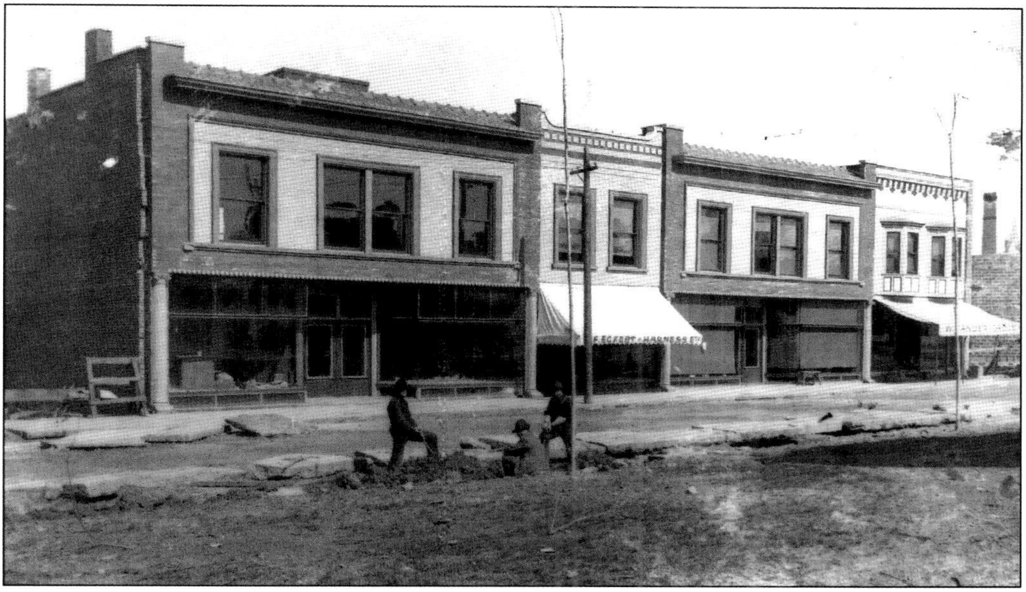

The Brown Building (left) on Factory Street was rebuilt of brick and stone after the 1899 fire. An ordinance prohibiting frame buildings had been on the books for many years, but after two disastrous fires in two years, the ruling would be more strictly enforced. (Courtesy of Jim Jaworski.)

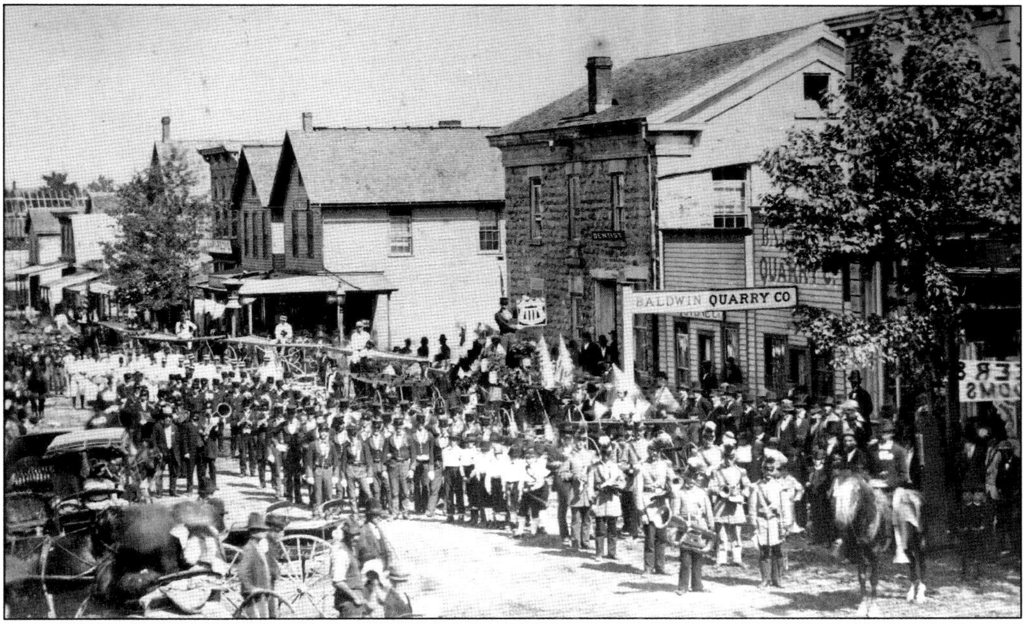

When firemen, who were all volunteers, were not fighting fires, they vied with other neighboring communities in pageantry, music, skill, and prowess. This picture shows the annual Firemen's Tournament of 1876. The picture was taken on Front Street near the Bridge Street intersection. In 1885, the Berea Fire Department was organized into three companies: True Grit Hook and Ladder Company, Cataract Engine, and the Alert Hose Company.

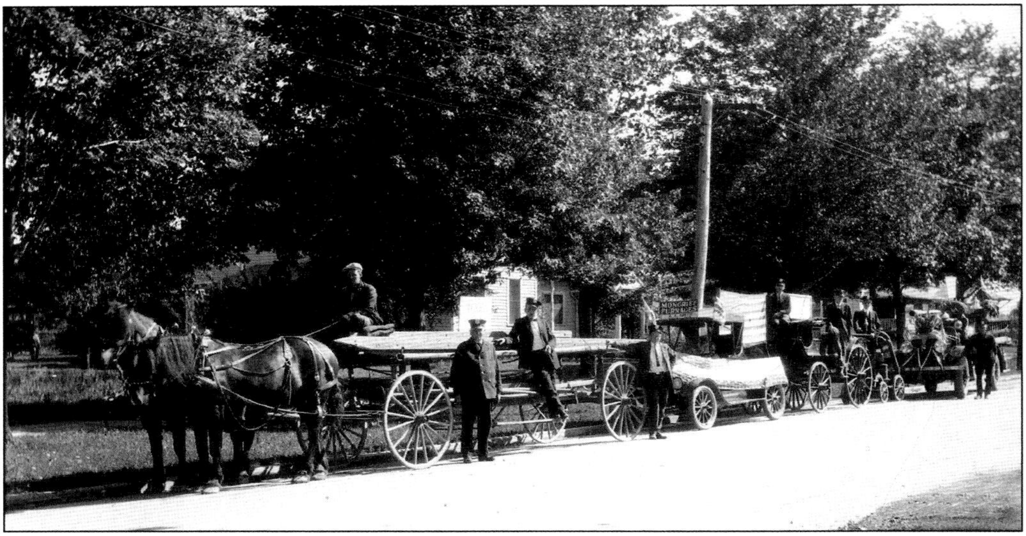

In 1936, firemen kept up the tradition by playing a key role in the Centennial Parade. Fire Chief John Nevel (standing at left), a retired Cleveland firefighter, joined the Berea force as the first full time fire chief and continued in that post until retiring in 1941 after 50 years as a firefighter.

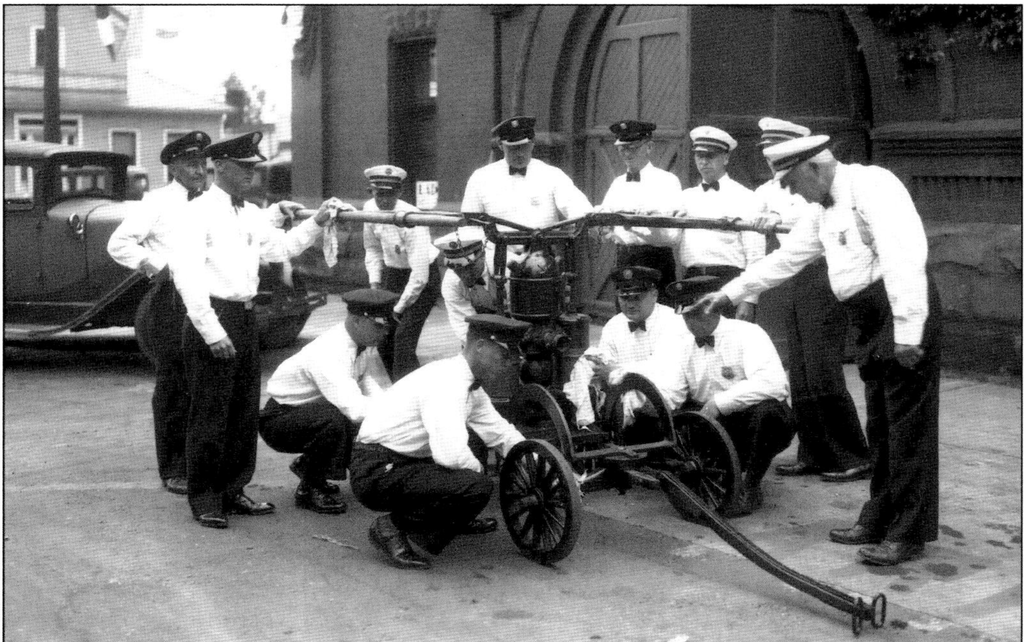

Firemen inspect the old pumper that won a trophy in the Ohio State Firemen's Association in 1947 for the oldest piece of equipment in operating condition. Purchased in 1880, it was Berea's only pumper until 1921. Berea Fire Department was organized in 1872 with 18 volunteers, ladders, a wagon, and buckets. W.L. Stearns was fire warden. Although it was in operation for many years, the old pumper often could not do the job needed during Berea's fierce fires. Water would then be hauled from the river in carts and in the sprinkling wagon.

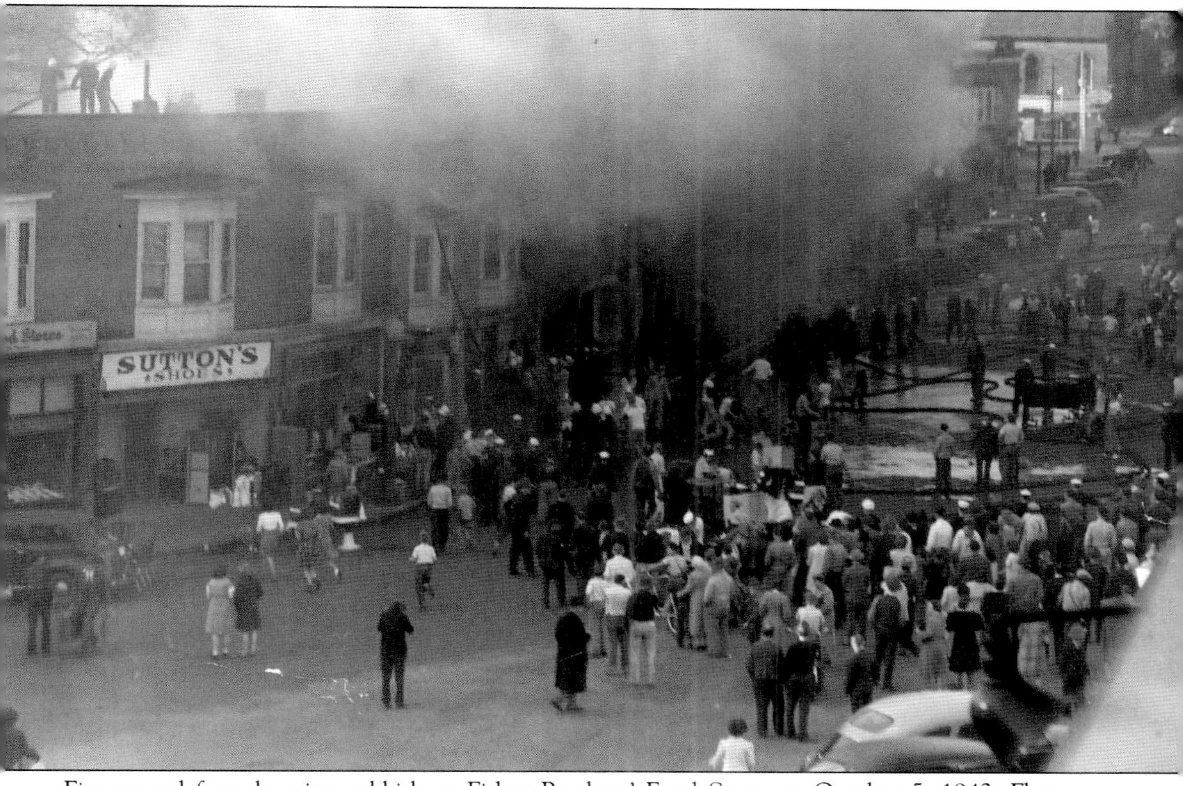

Fire started from burning rubbish at Fisher Brothers' Food Store on October 5, 1943. Flames destroyed a section of the same area along Front and Factory Streets that was devastated in the 1899 fire. Fire companies from eight neighboring towns and the Cleveland airport aided the Berea Fire Department. The only person injured was Fireman Bernard Sauerbrie, who was burned on the arm. By this time, Berea had a number of paid firemen as well as a corps of volunteers.

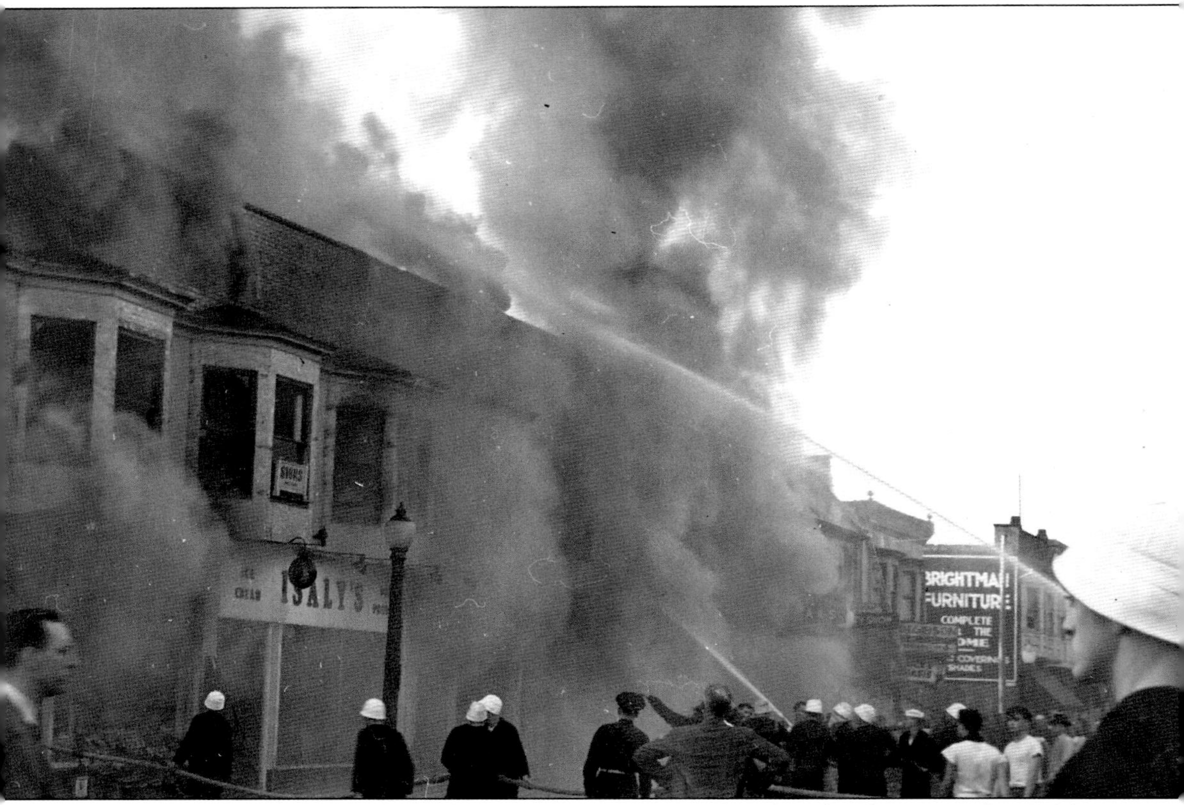

More than 50 volunteers from the Navy's V-12 program (in white hats), stationed at Baldwin-Wallace College, assisted firefighters bringing the fire of 1943 under control. Better-constructed buildings and more modern equipment aided firefighters in subduing the flames in two hours. Initial estimates of damage, however, ran as high as $200,000.

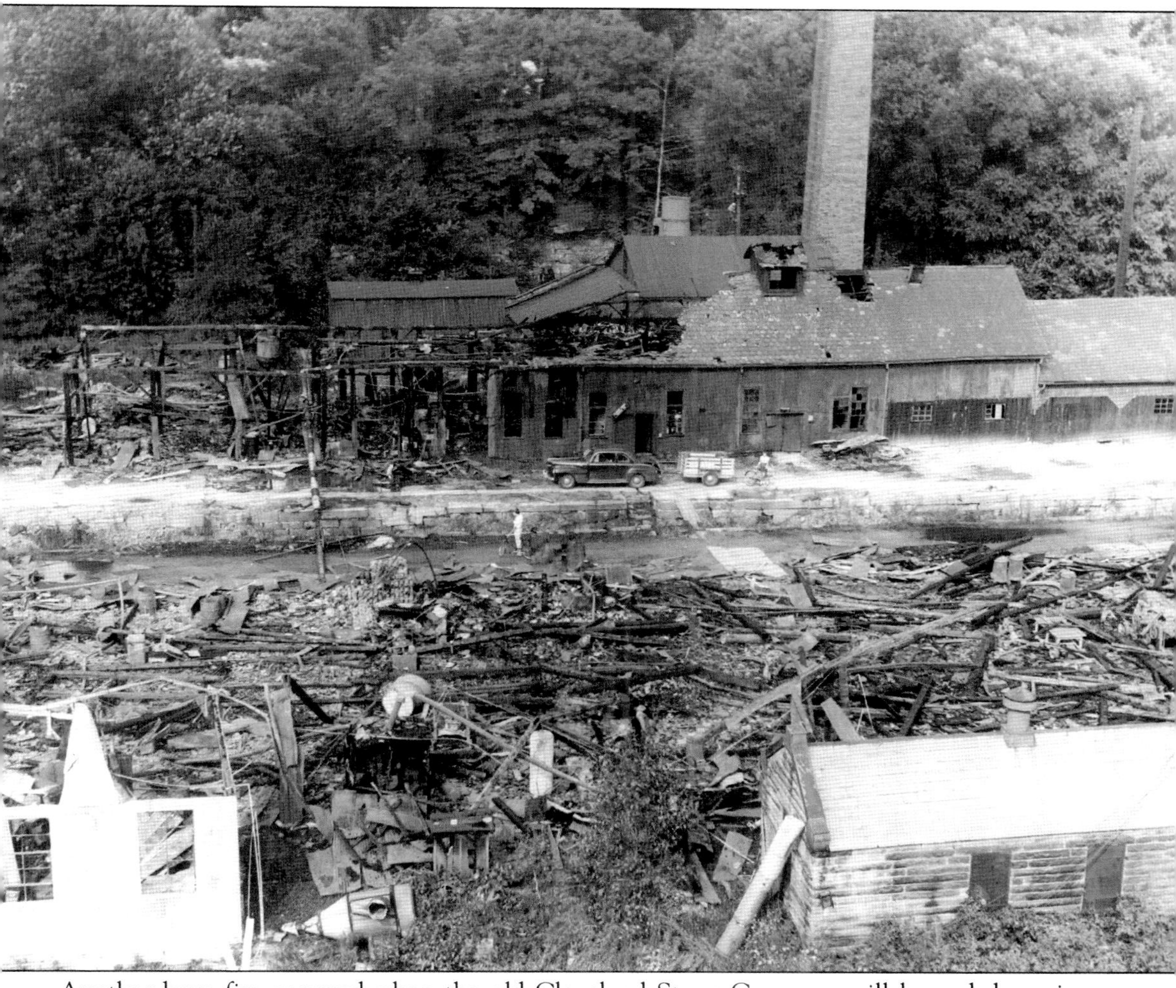

Another huge fire occurred when the old Cleveland Stone Company mill burned down in 1948. Located approximately 200 yards to the rear of what is now the Parkway Shops, the building had served as a loading area for the pony or dinky engines that carried Berea sandstone to the depot for shipment to all parts of the world.

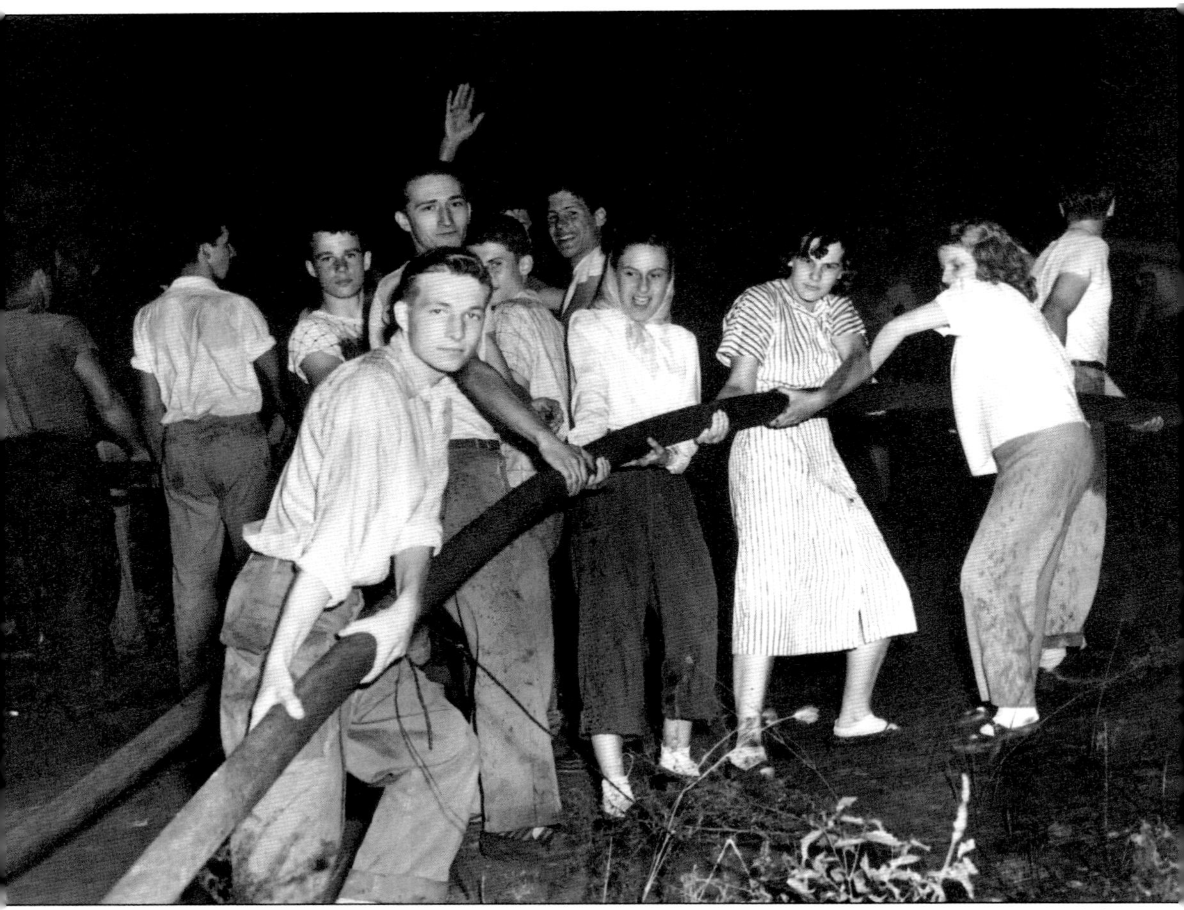

Once again, students from the college joined forces with the Berea Fire Department to fight the fire at the old mill building.

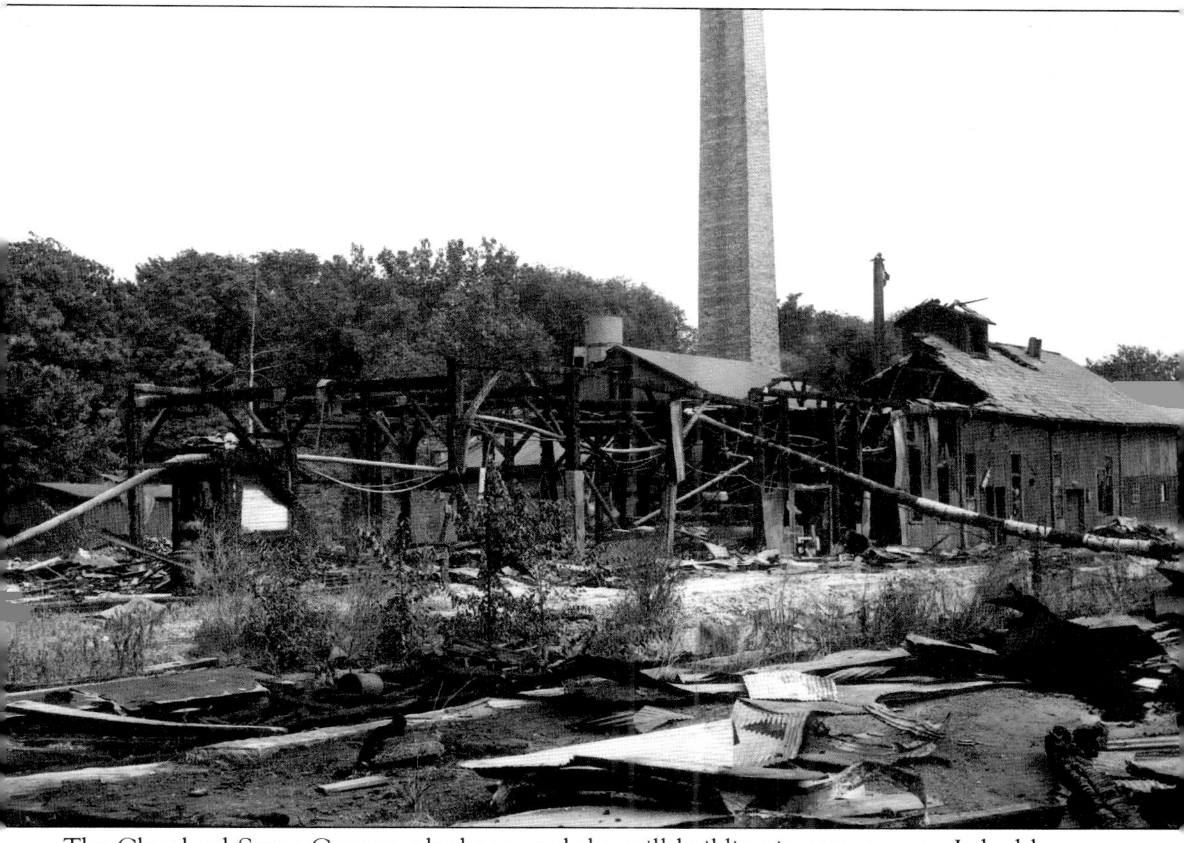

The Cleveland Stone Company had not used the mill building in recent years. It had been leased to the Dunham Company for storage.

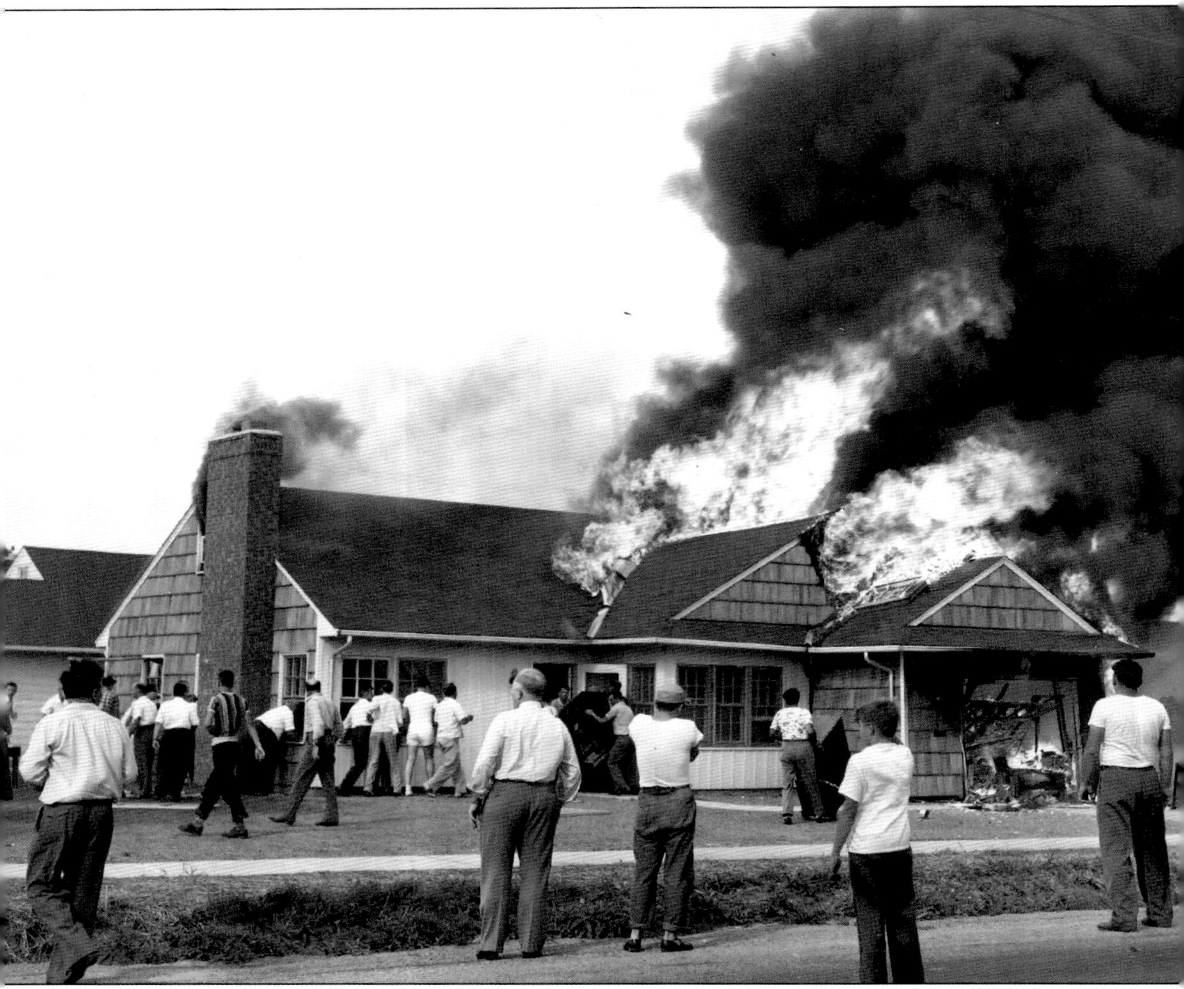

On Labor Day of 1949, round-the-world flyer Bill Odom, a participant in the Cleveland National Air Races, crashed his sleek, green P-51 Mustang into the Berea home of Bradley Laird at 36 West Street. Odom killed himself, Mrs. Jeanne Laird, 24, and the Lairds' year-old son Craig. Mrs. Laird's father, Benjamin Hoffman, was severely burned when he tried to rescue his grandson. This was the last year the races were held at Cleveland Hopkins Airport. Fifteen years later, the Cleveland Air Show was initiated at Burke Lakefront Airport and continues annually.

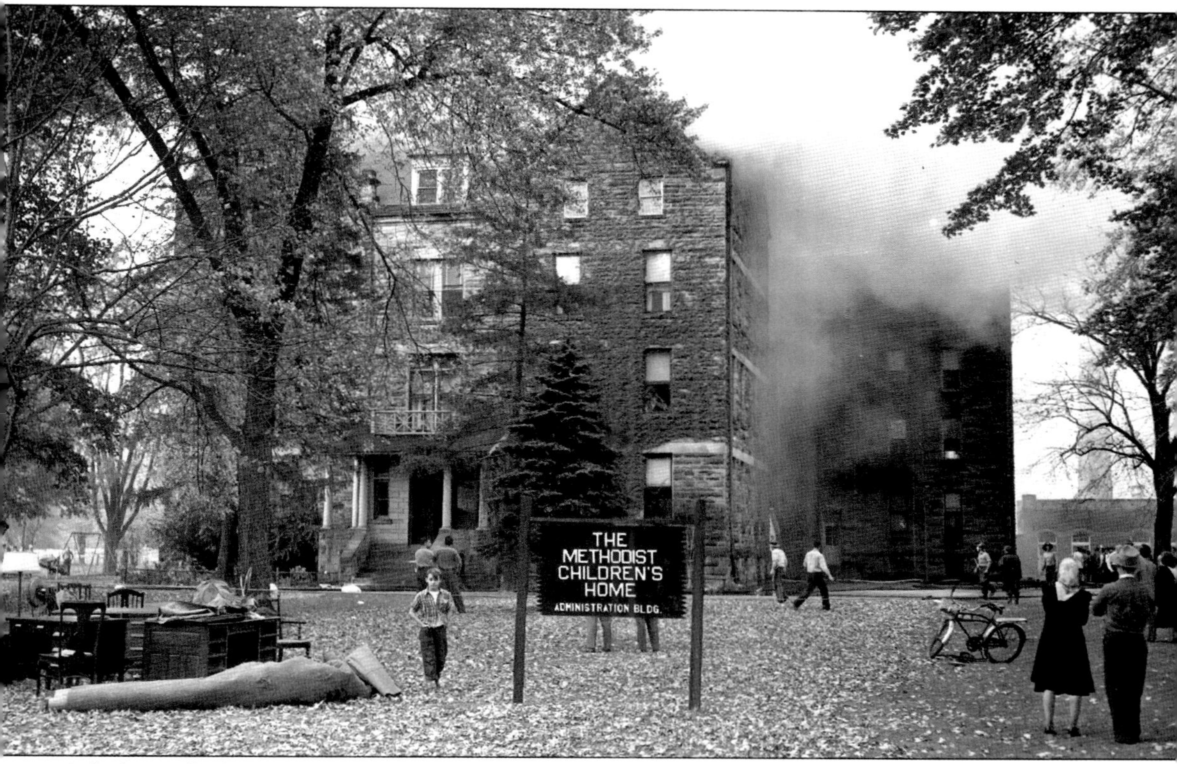

A faulty wall plug ignited a costly fire on October 30, 1950, on the fourth floor of the German Methodist Children's Home's main building. Fire swept the fourth floor and the roof and then traveled down the elevator shaft to the basement. Damage to the structure was estimated at about $110,000 but was adequately covered by insurance.

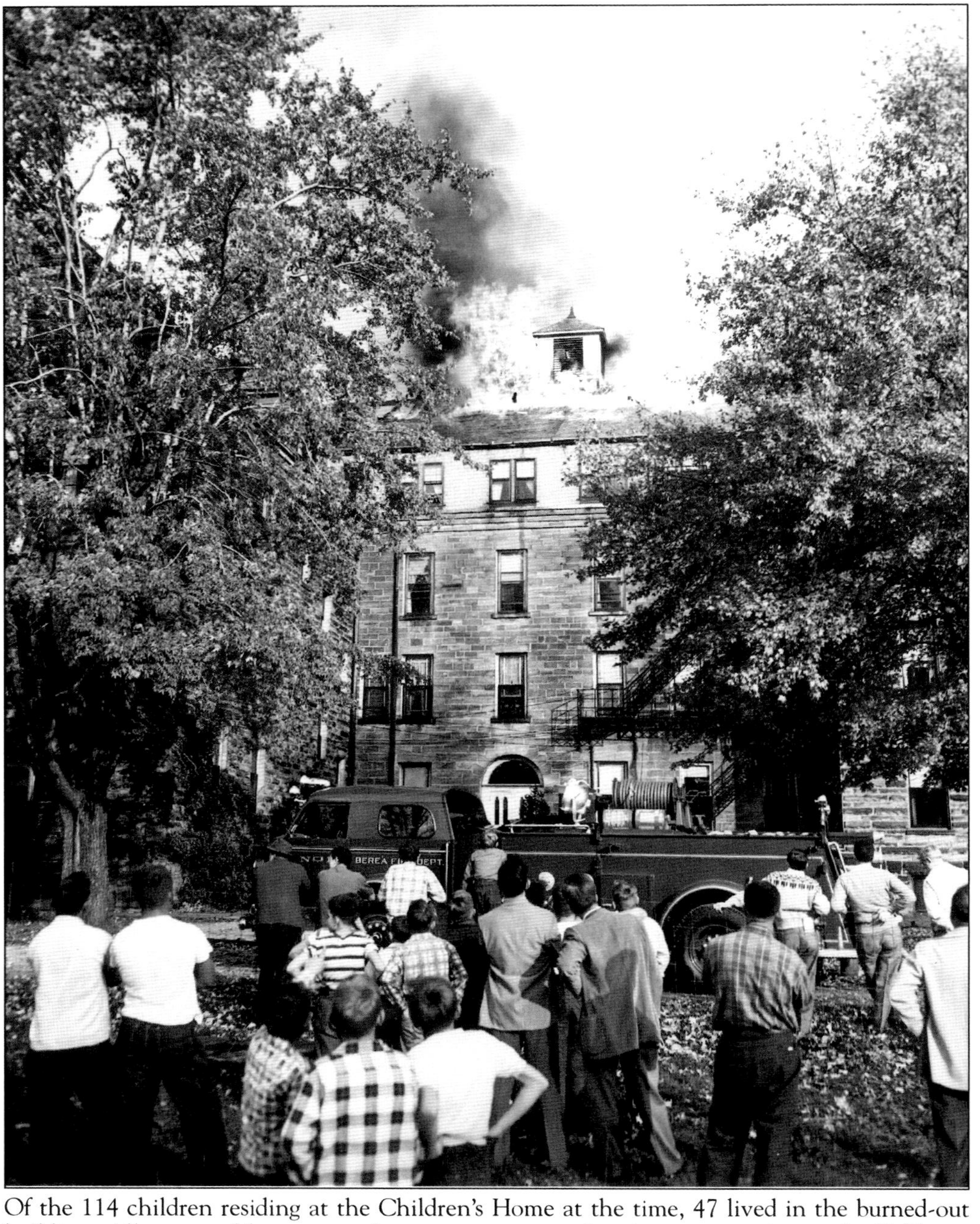

Of the 114 children residing at the Children's Home at the time, 47 lived in the burned-out building. All were safely evacuated to an emergency dormitory set up in nearby Baldwin-Wallace field house. The Red Cross supplied cots, bedding, pajamas, towels, and soap. The Children's Home revised its policy of housing children on upper floors of the buildings.

Six

More than a Suburb

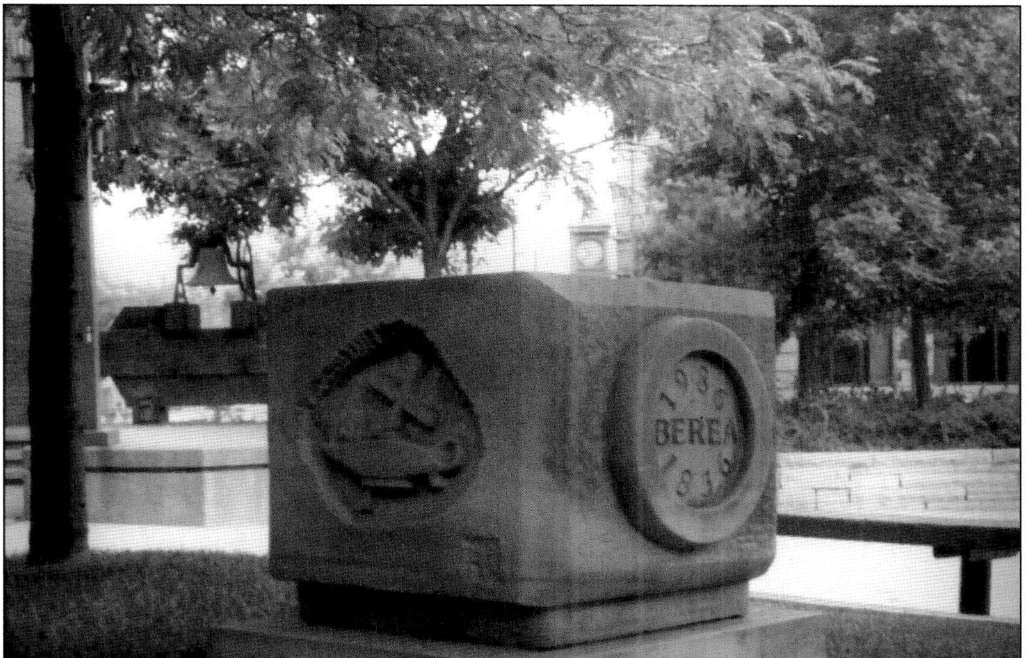

Berea artist Thomas Harmon designed and sculpted this memorial as a gift to his community and its citizens to commemorate Berea's sesquicentennial in 1986. The sculpture of Berea sandstone bears the lamp of learning on which is superimposed the cross, symbolizing Christian education; on the opposite side is a grindstone. These are the two foundations of Berea's heritage.

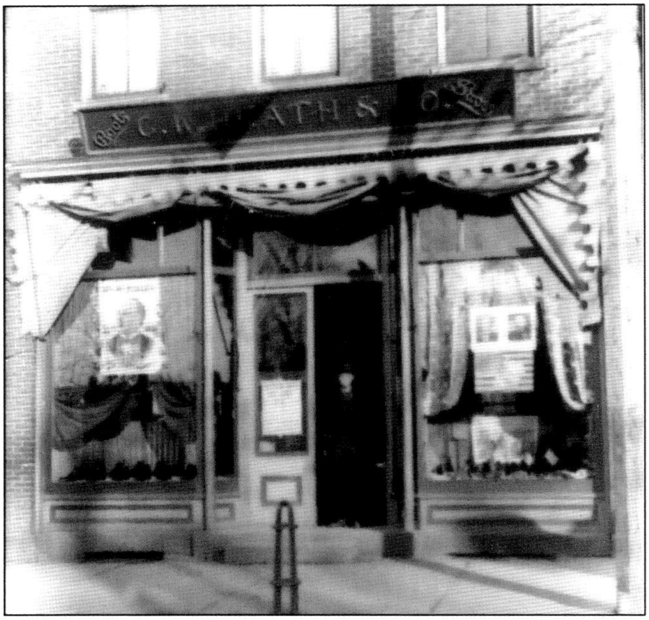

C.W. Heath's Shoe Store displays its colors for an 1896 rally for Republican presidential candidate and Ohio native son William McKinley. Berea, a GOP stronghold, turned out 5,000 strong for the rally. According to the *Advertiser*, businessmen, professionals, professors, and a good number of farmers, even former Democrats, were united on McKinley and sound money, as opposed to the Free Silver policies of his opponent, William Jennings Bryan.

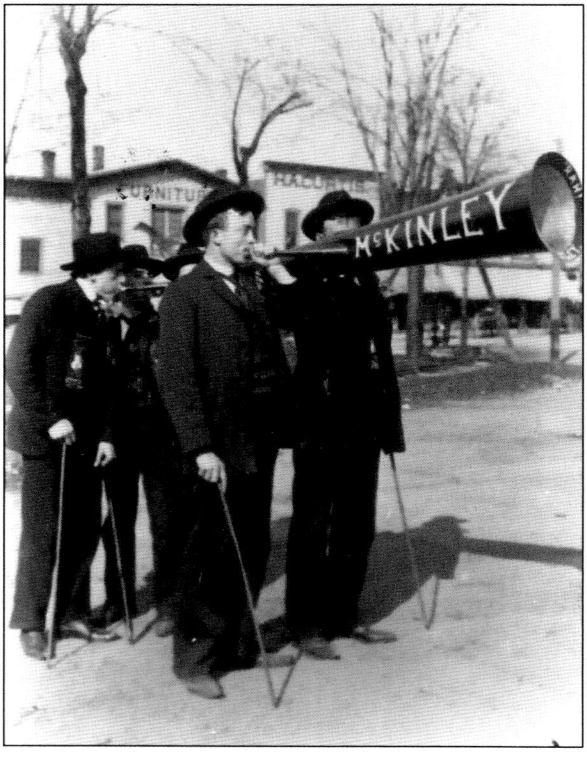

Young and old favored McKinley. A few weeks before the election, 400 Bereans, including nearly 100 cheering students from Baldwin University and German Wallace College, boarded the McKinley excursion train at Berea's Union Depot and headed to Canton for one of McKinley's famous "front porch" campaign visits. Although McKinley rarely left his frail wife, Ida, he ran one of the first heavily financed propaganda campaigns, largely through the support of Cleveland industrialist, Marcus Hanna.

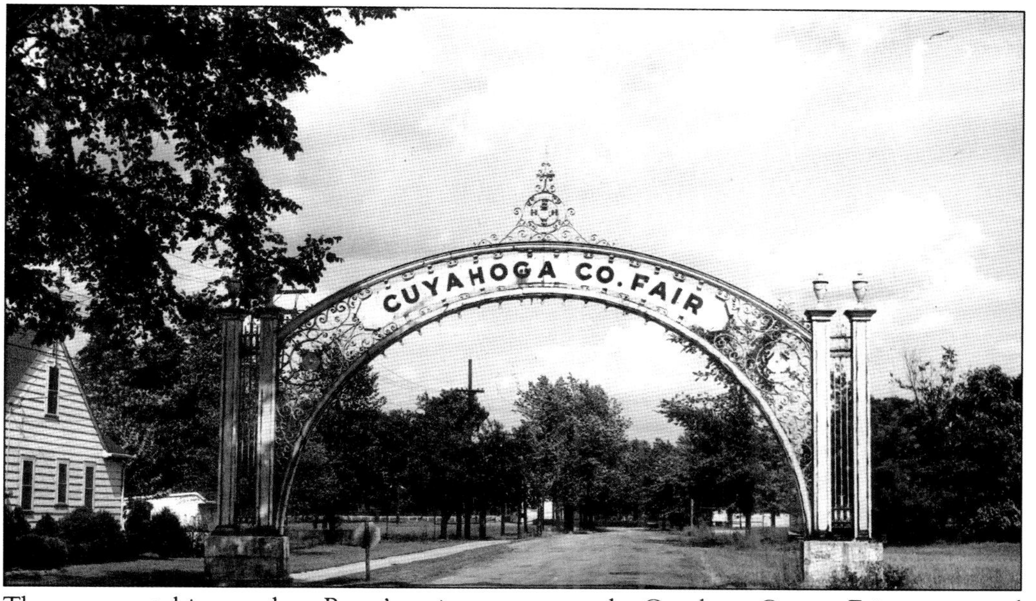

The ornamental iron arch at Berea's main entrance to the Cuyahoga County Fair was erected by Fred J. Hartman whose low bid was $2,390. Originally, there had been another county fairgrounds in Chagrin Falls because of the size of the county. By 1914, the county commissioners decided to abandon the Chagrin Falls site, which was a great advantage to Berea. That year, all of the buildings were lighted, and a new dance hall opened.

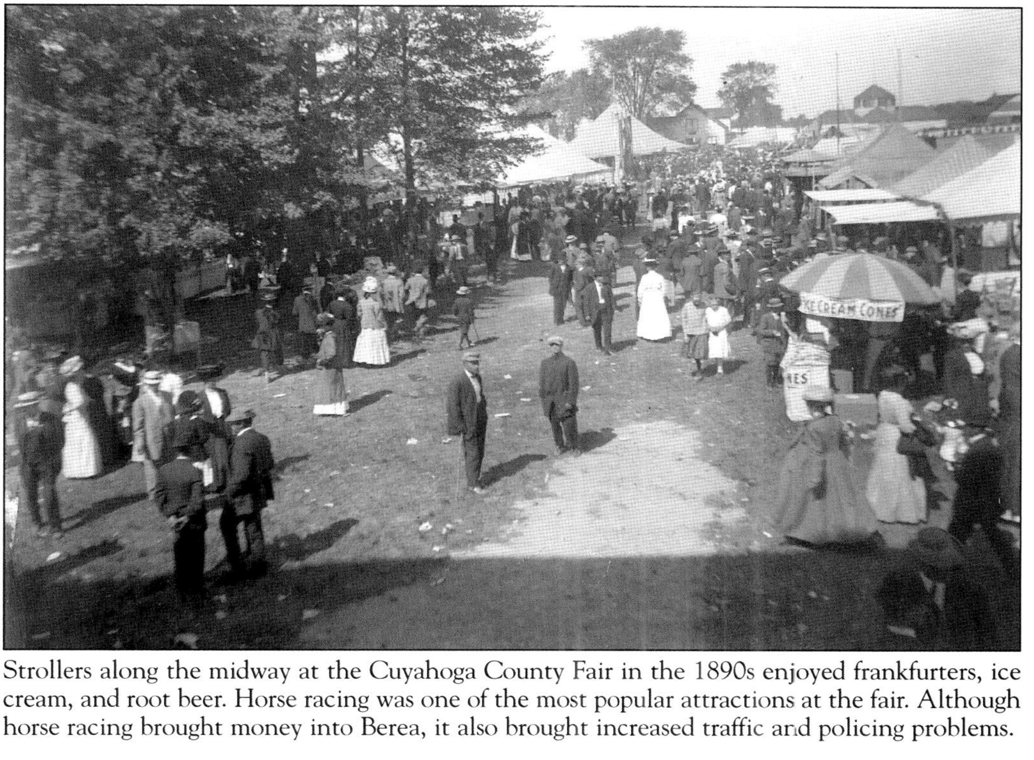

Strollers along the midway at the Cuyahoga County Fair in the 1890s enjoyed frankfurters, ice cream, and root beer. Horse racing was one of the most popular attractions at the fair. Although horse racing brought money into Berea, it also brought increased traffic and policing problems.

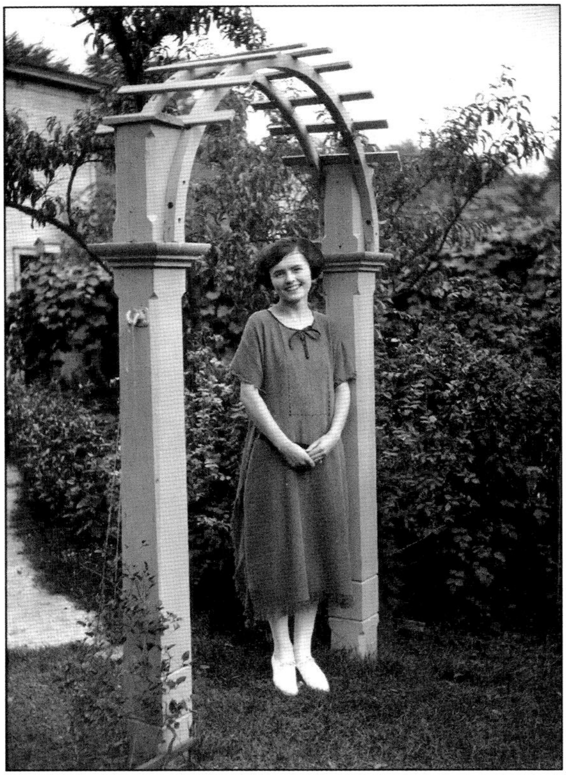

A young Dorothy Marks is standing in her back yard at 108 Seminary Street in 1924. Without the efforts and generosity of Berea native Dorothy Marks McKelvey, this book could never have been written. Educated at Baldwin-Wallace College, she became the college historian in 1950, a post she held until her death in 1985. In her will, she left a treasury of Berea lore to the Berea Historical Society.

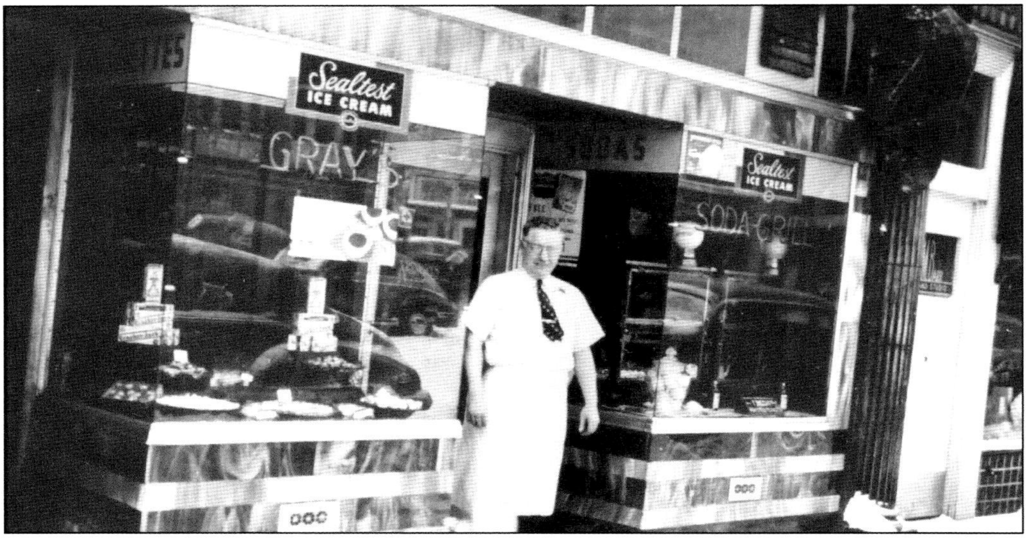

Otto Mahler stands in the doorway of Gray's Candy Kitchen. He worked at Gray's when he was in high school, and after graduating from Baldwin-Wallace College, he bought the popular confectionery from Mr. and Mrs. George Gray. In 1967, he received the first Grindstone Award, now given annually by the Berea Chamber of Commerce to an outstanding citizen. Otto spent 17 years of his life in the German Methodist Orphan's Home and served as a trustee in his later years.

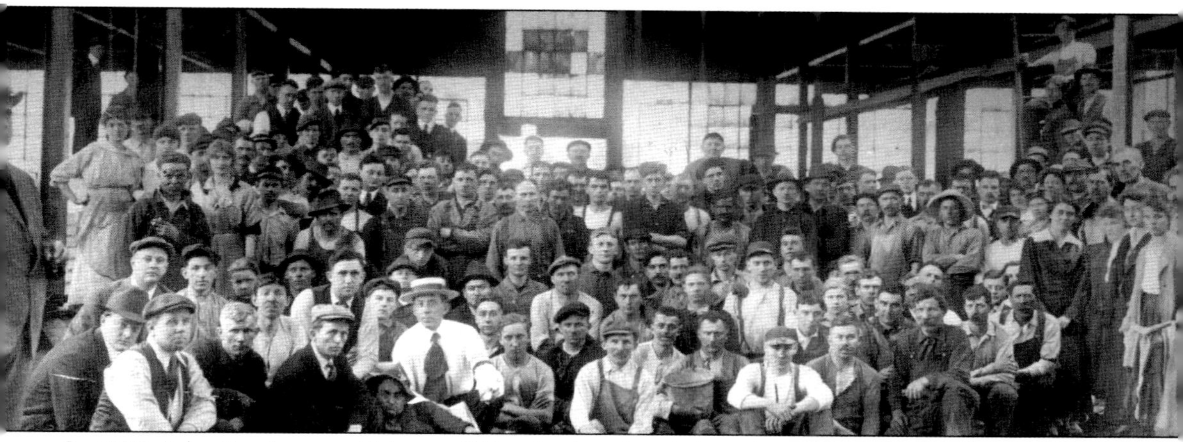

In 1899, John Dunham and his son, Wiley J., abandoned their foundry at Hinckley in Medina County and moved to Berea to an abandoned mill along the river. They made steel land rollers and harrows and weeders. In 1916, the Dunham Company began making castings for auto and tractor manufacturers. Eventually, Dunham's employed 350 people and shipped carloads of products throughout the Midwest agricultural belt.

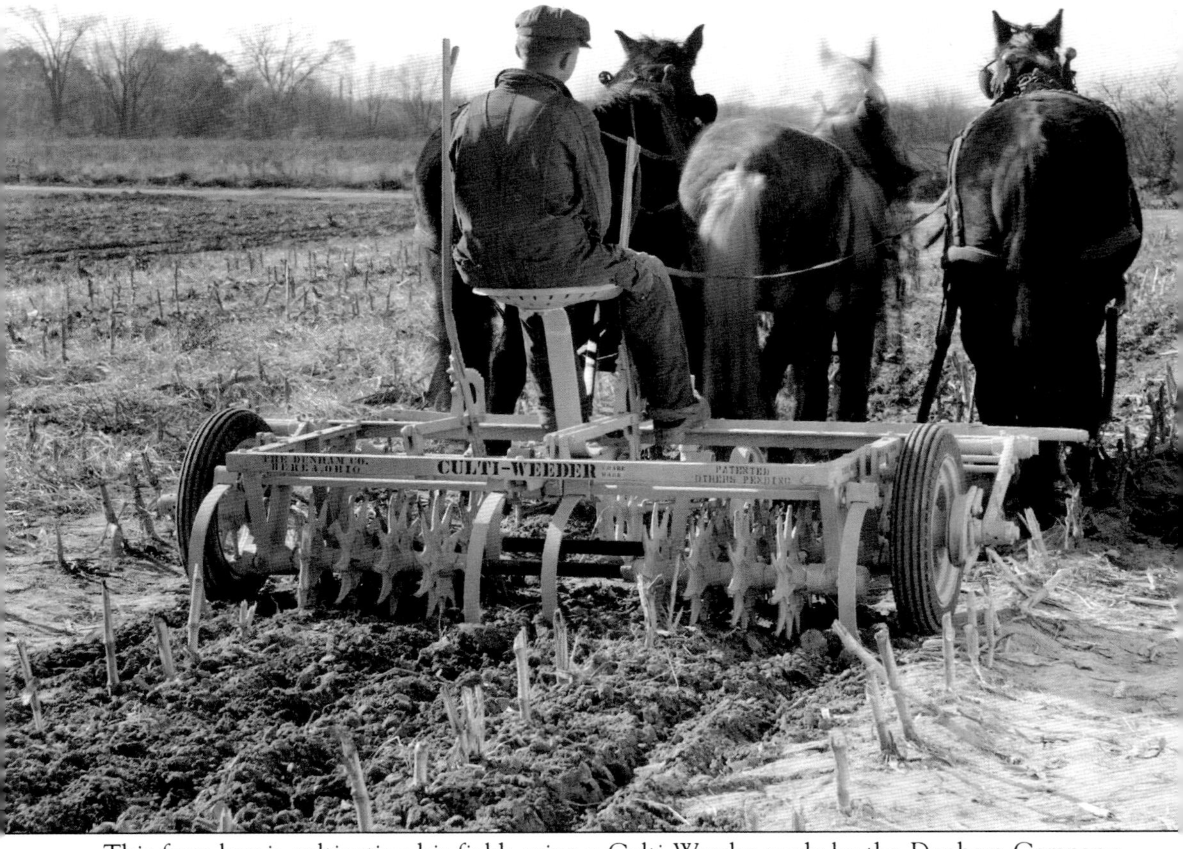

This farm boy is cultivating his fields using a Culti-Weeder made by the Dunham Company. The Dunham Company patented a number of agricultural tools that were shipped throughout the Midwest agricultural belt bearing the name of Berea. In 1914, Dunham's patented the Culti-Packer to replace the steel land rollers. It became their main agricultural product.

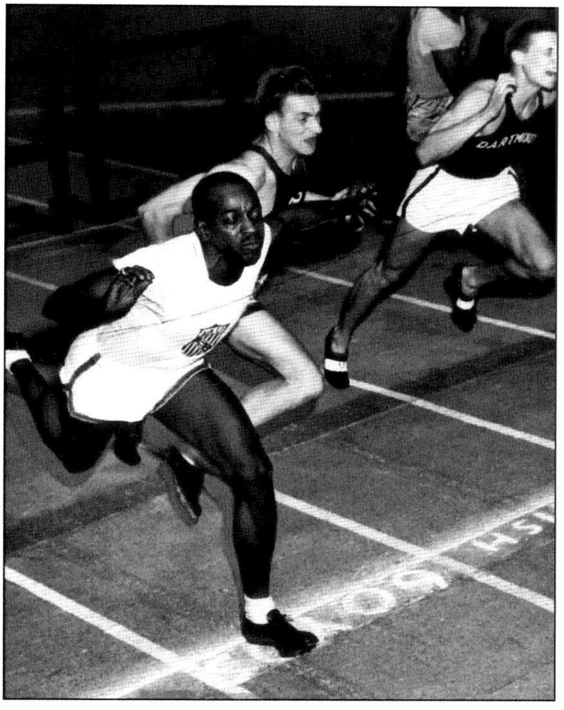

Harrison Dillard, Cleveland native and Baldwin-Wallace College graduate, won the AAU national indoor 60-yard hurdles seven years in a row. Since he was eight years old, Harrison Dillard had been running makeshift hurdles made out of junked auto seats in Cleveland alleys. At a state high school track meet at Ohio State, visiting alumnus and Olympic medalist Jesse Owens noticed Harrison's tattered shoes and gave the boy a pair of his own. They wore the same size—eight and a half.

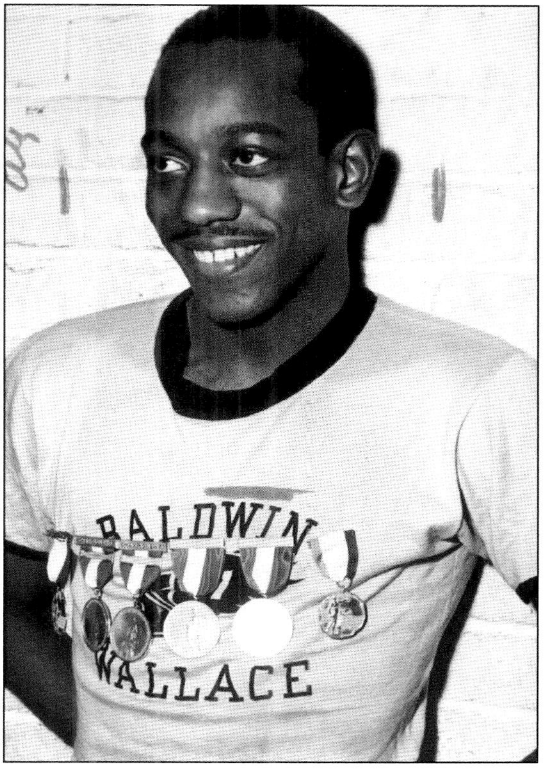

Harrison Dillard had a jersey filled with medals before he went to London to the 1948 Olympics. There, he tied the world record for the 100-meter hurdles and was part of the winning 4 x 100 relay team. In 1952, at the Helsinki Olympics, he won the 110-meter hurdles and again was part of the winning relay team. He was named the nation's outstanding amateur athlete in 1953.

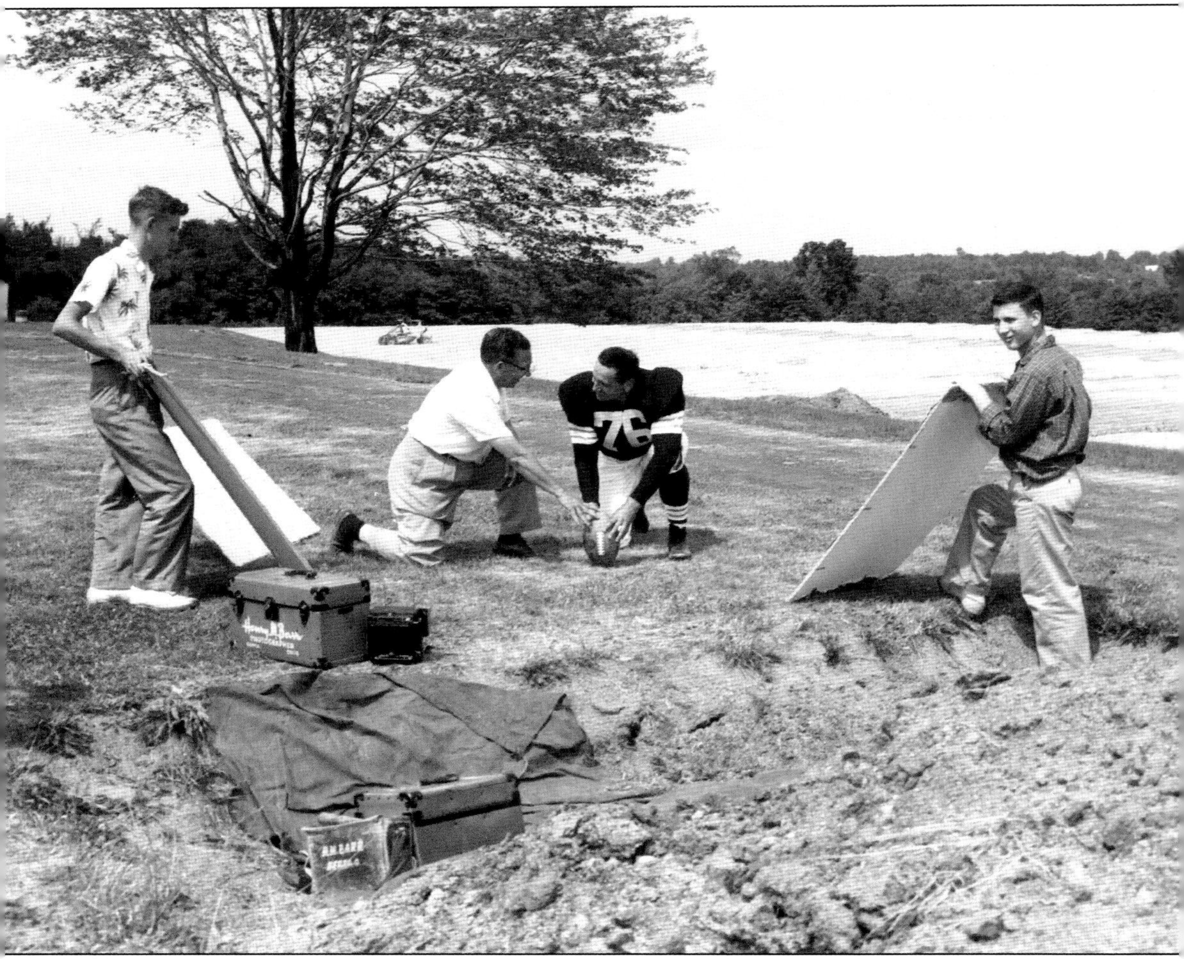

Berea photographer Henry Barr is showing All-American Cleveland Brown Lou "the Toe" Groza how to position a football—for the best photographic advantage. Henry Barr spent his youth at the German Methodist Orphan's Home in Berea and later worked for fellow "home mate" Otto Mahler at Gray's Candy Kitchen. After serving in the U.S. Signal Corps in World War II as a photographer, he established a photography business in Berea. Henry Barr became a civic leader, serving on both the City Council and the Berea School Board. He never forgot his early years at the Orphan's Home, and he was a trustee there for many years.

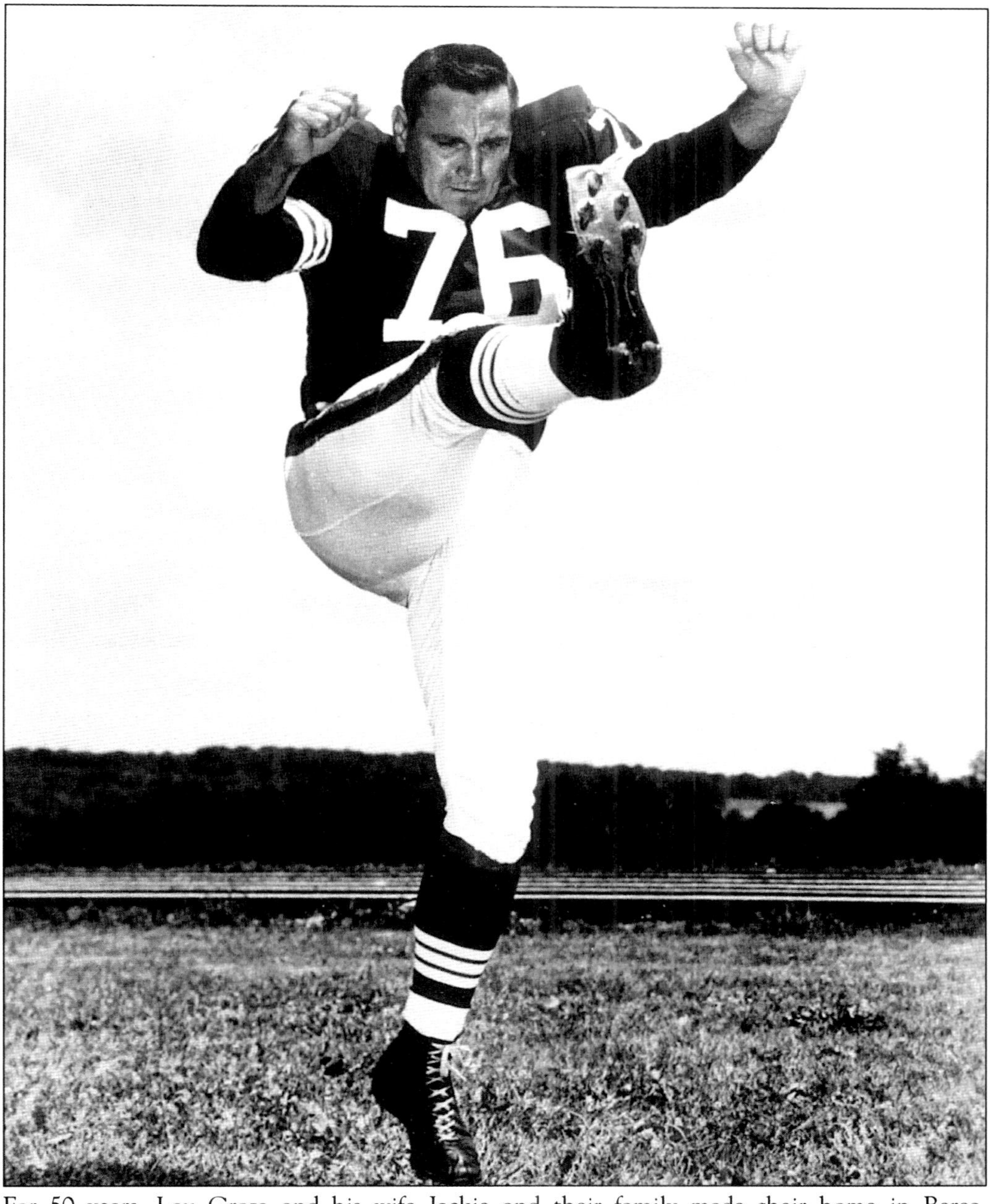

For 50 years, Lou Groza and his wife Jackie and their family made their home in Berea, headquarters for the Cleveland Browns. For 21 seasons, Lou Groza wore number 76 as the Browns' place kicker. He was named to the NFL Hall of Fame in 1974. Lou Groza brought credit to his community as a humble, sincere man, a good neighbor, who championed many civic causes and chaired many charity events. In 1990, the community presented Lou with its Grindstone Award and named him Berea's Outstanding Citizen. In 1999, the Browns' headquarters was assigned the new address of 76 Lou Groza Boulevard. Lou died on November 29, 2000.

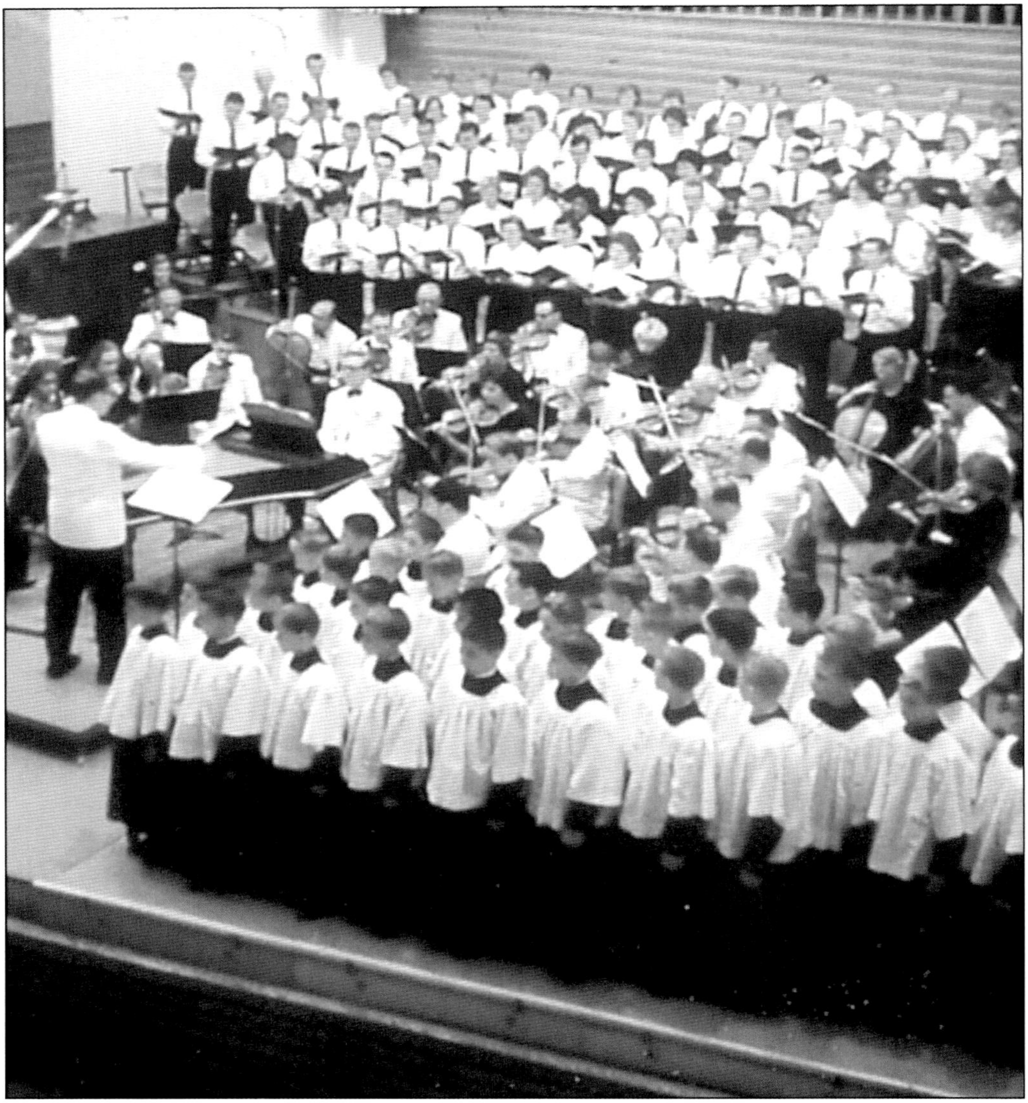

Thousands of classical music lovers throng to Berea in May of each year for the Bach Festival, held annually since 1933. Professor Albert Riemenschneider and his wife Selma organized this oldest collegiate Bach Festival in the United States. Internationally known artists participate. The Riemenschneider Bach Institute at Baldwin-Wallace College, the research arm for the festival, is a world renowned Bach center. It is the guardian of priceless Bach-related manuscripts and first editions, and it publishes the *Bach Journal* twice yearly, featuring articles by international Bach scholars. It is sent to subscribers in approximately 30 countries.

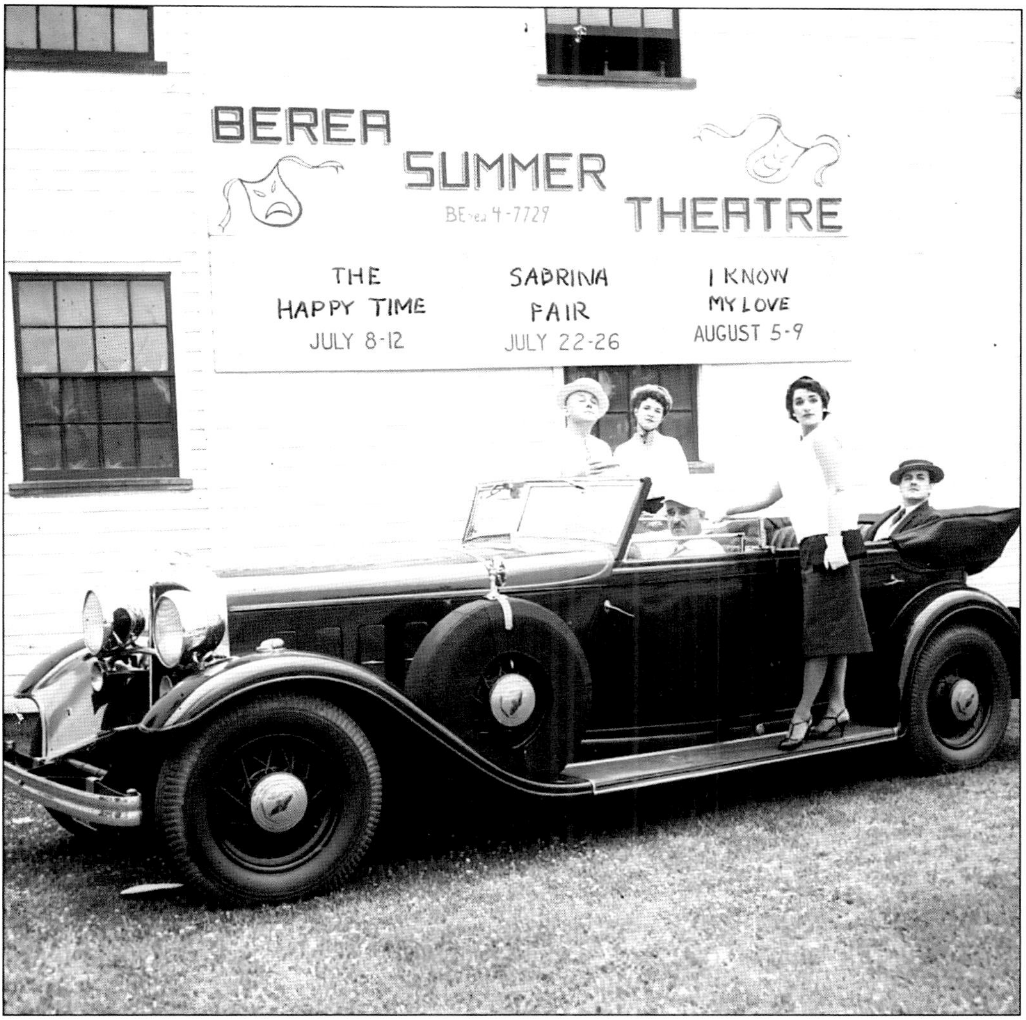

The Berea Summer Theatre celebrated the opening of its second season in 1958 with Samuel Taylor's *The Happy Time*. The cast advertised the play by driving through Berea streets in one of Howard Wyles' vintage automobiles. Howard is at the wheel, Karen Wyles is on the running board, and John Krich is in the rear seat. The others are unknown. The Berea Summer Theatre met first in the old recreation hall and in 1972 moved to the Baldwin-Wallace College Art and Drama Center. Berea Summer Theater operated until 2002, drawing patrons from many surrounding communities.

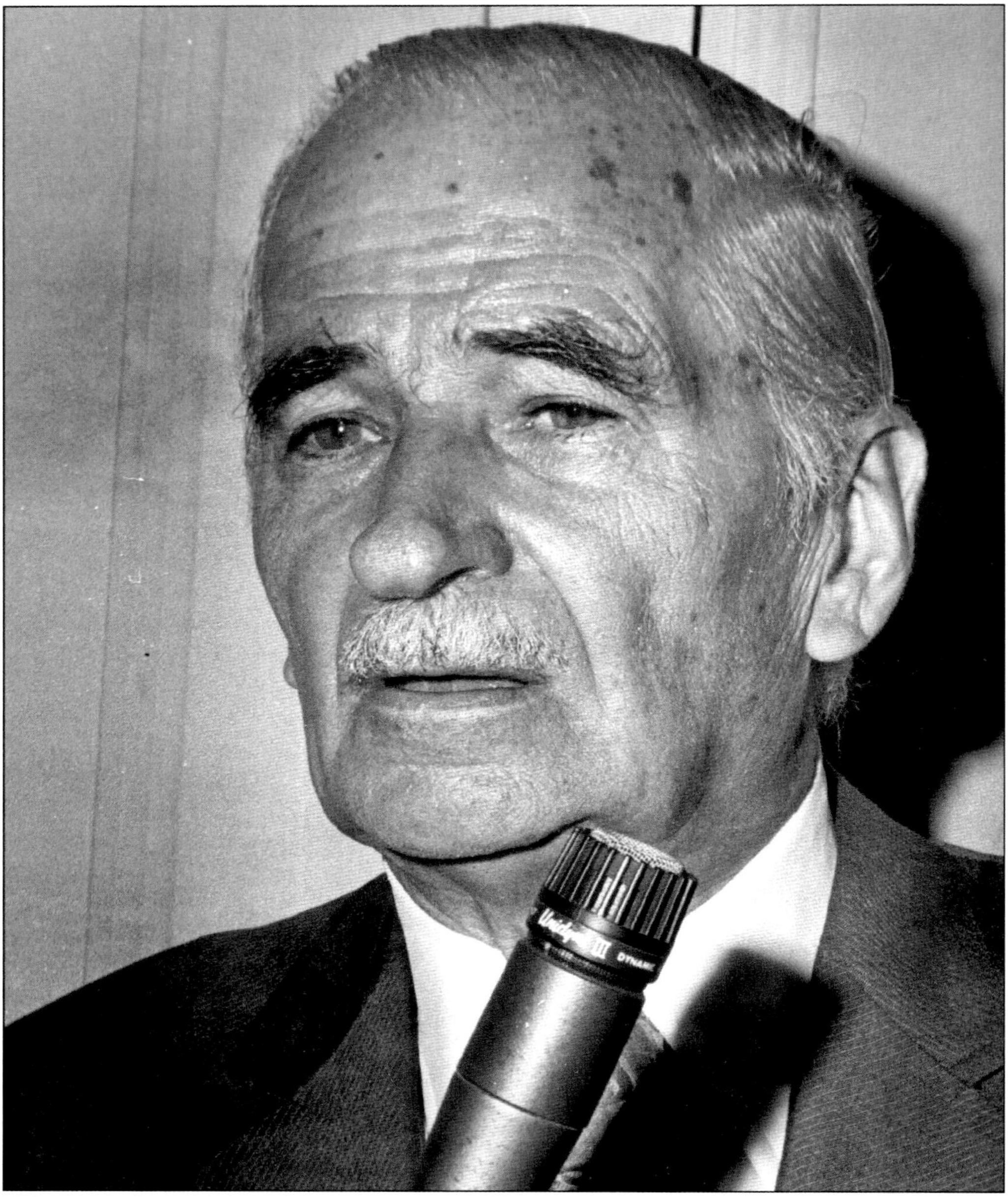

Pulitzer Prize winning cartoonist Edward D. Kuekes, whose family moved to Berea from Pittsburgh when he was 12, went to work as an editorial artist for the Cleveland *Plain Dealer* in 1922 after working there three months for free. In that same year, he married Clara Gray in Berea. They had two sons, Edward and George. By 1939, Kuekes had accumulated numerous credits and awards for his work, and editor Paul Bellamy named him chief editorial cartoonist for the *Plain Dealer*, replacing the late James (Hal) Donahey. Medals and certificates of awards for his editorial cartoons include 10 Freedom Foundation awards, the Sigma Delta Chi Distinguished Service Award, and recognition by the National Conference of Christians and Jews. His collections of cartoons are housed at Syracuse University and at the Ohio State University School of Journalism. In 1987, he died of a heart ailment at age 85. He is buried in Berea.

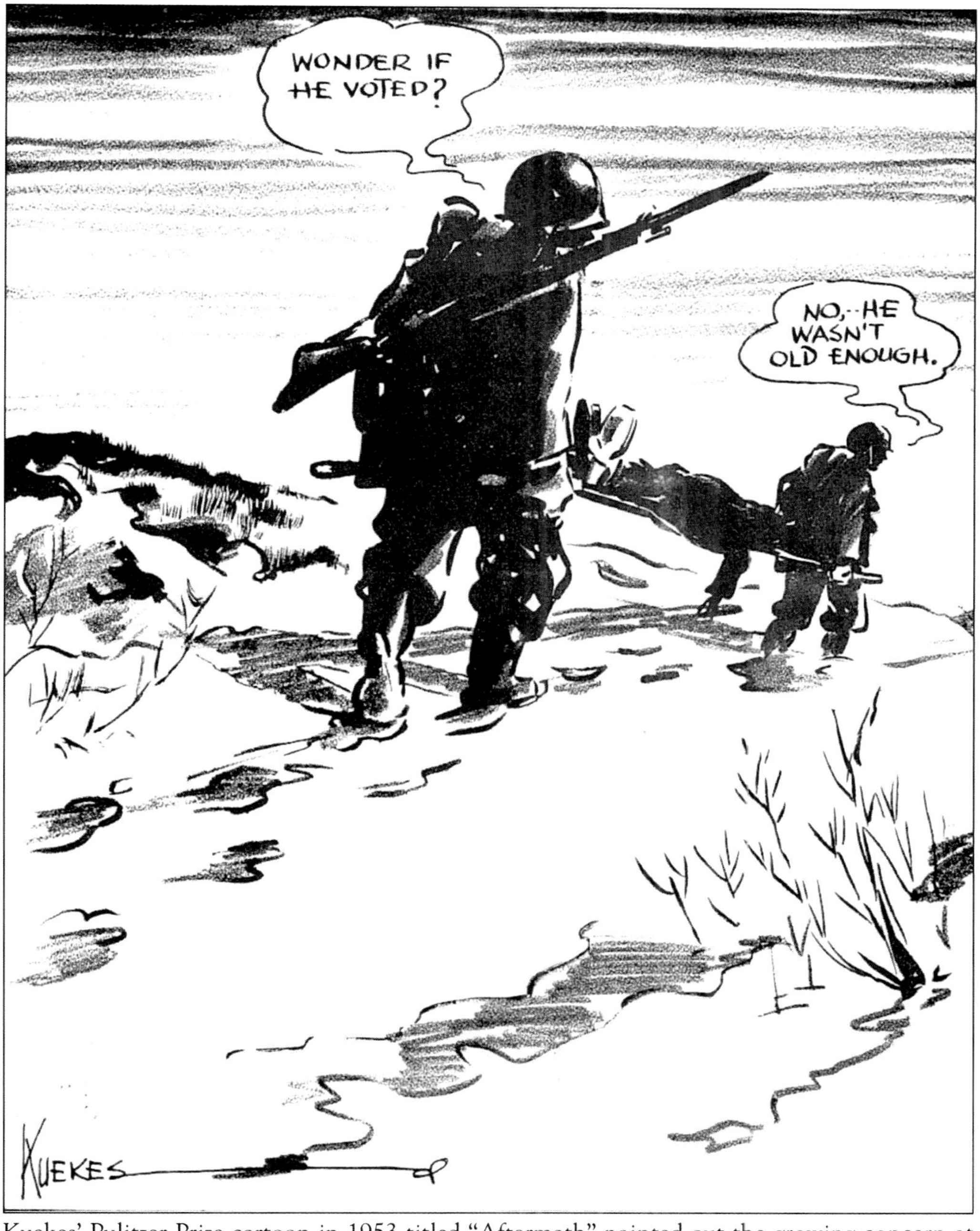

Kuekes' Pulitzer Prize cartoon in 1953 titled "Aftermath" pointed out the growing concern at the time of the Korean armistice that 18-year olds who were drafted into the military were not eligible to vote until they were 21. Kuekes' trademark was his spare, dramatic renderings that immediately drove home a single visual point.

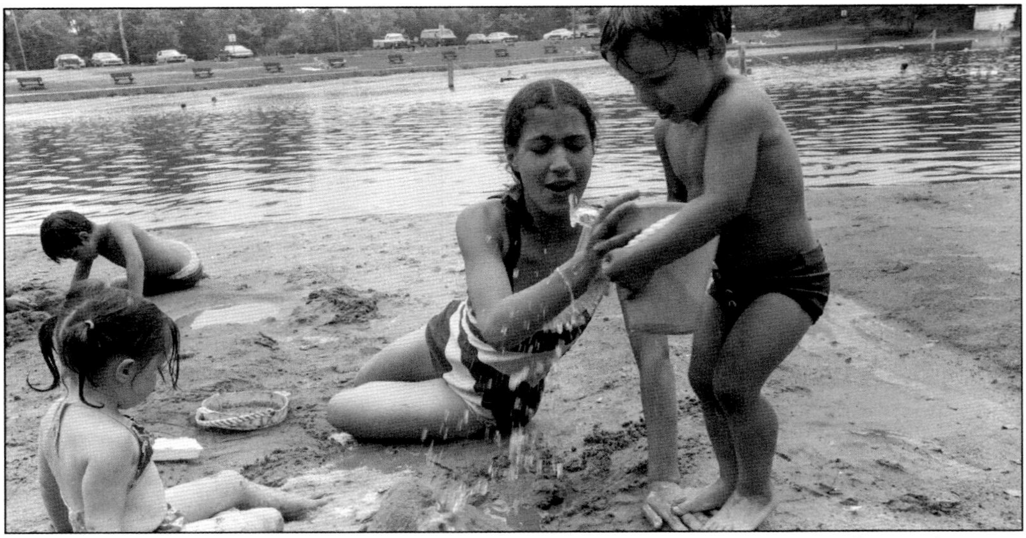

Rose Rodriguez entertains three-year olds Beth Regan and David Palmer at Wallace Lake, once the center of a bruising, backbreaking industry, the sandstone quarries. In 1931, the quarry owners donated a 54-acre tract of waste quarry land to the City of Berea. In turn, the city donated it to the Cleveland Metropolitan Park Board. After many years of negotiations for more acreage and efforts of 2,000 workers from the WPA (Work Projects Administration), and $2.5 million, the park opened in 1941.

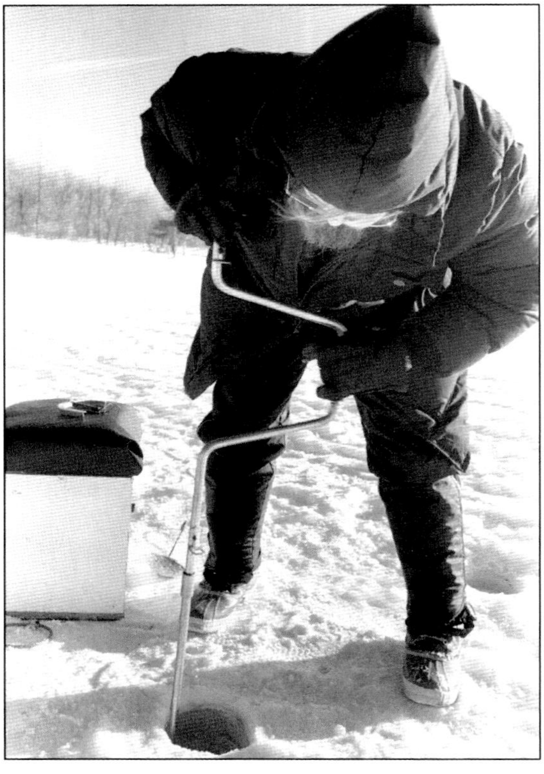

Coe Lake, formerly Big Quarry, now offers Bereans recreational activity all year long. On a February day, Ralph Pitts (top) bores a new hole in the ice for his line.

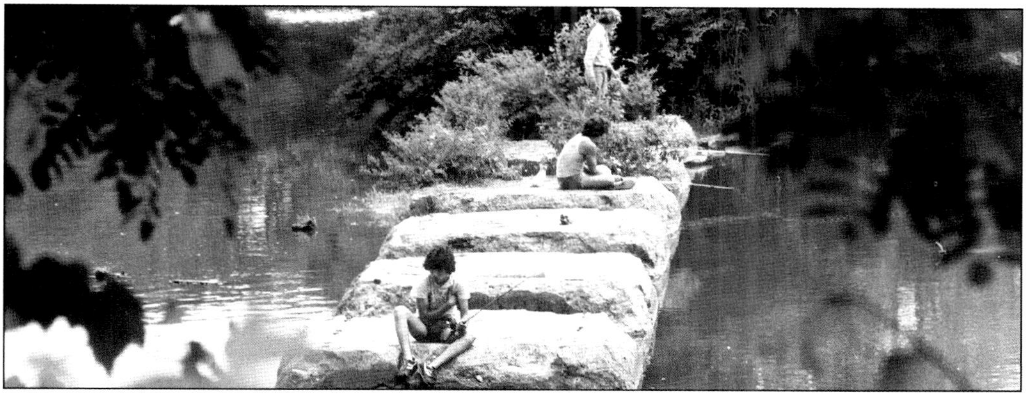

These boys are angling from the crankshaft pedestal supports for sidewalk polishing beds.

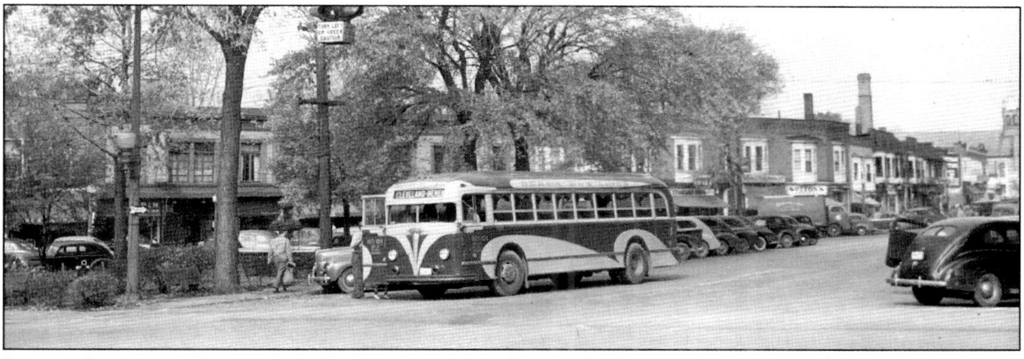

Just as they started an interurban train service by using their own vision and enterprise, Berea business leaders developed an interurban bus system that became a model in the area. This sparked competition between the buses and interurban trains and kept fares reasonable. The Berea Bus Company was a family operated business. H.W. Wilchek was secretary and general manager; his brother Frank and nephew R.L. Weber were the operating personnel, garage men, and business managers.

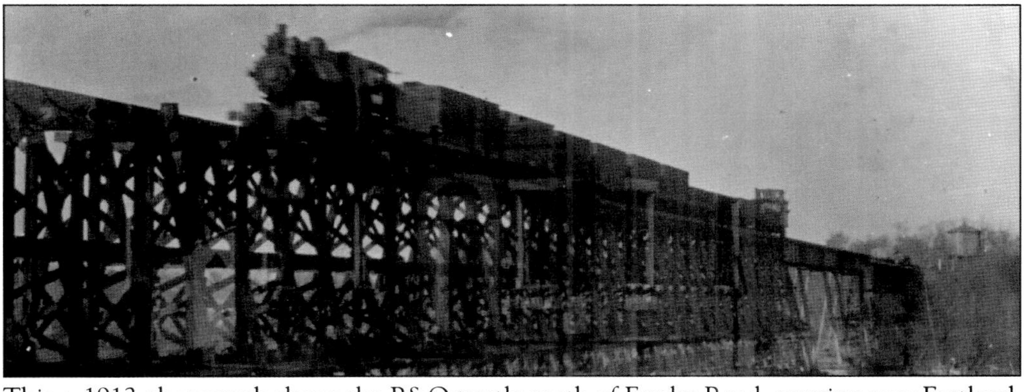

This *c.* 1912 photograph shows the B&O trestle south of Fowles Road, crossing over Eastland. It is now earth-filled from Eastland into Strongsville.

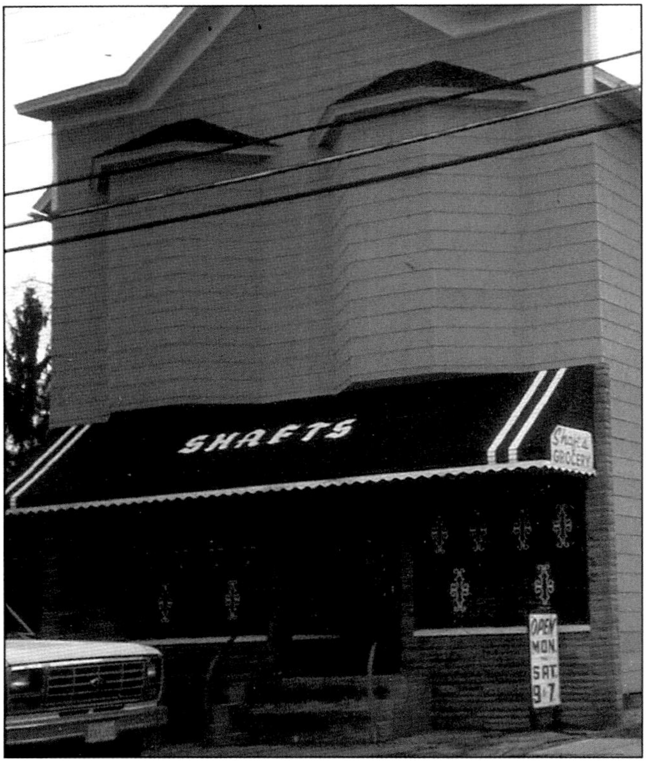

A true mom and pop store and still thriving, Shaft's Grocery was started in 1901 by Joseph and Mary Yanke Shaft and has operated continually on Fowles Road. Joseph was a quarryman, and Mary ran the store. Even today, "People come here where they are treated like neighbors and friends," said Loretta Juergens, granddaughter of Joseph and Mary. Unlike the town's two supermarkets, Shaft's never opened on Sunday, and it closes at 7 o'clock every evening.

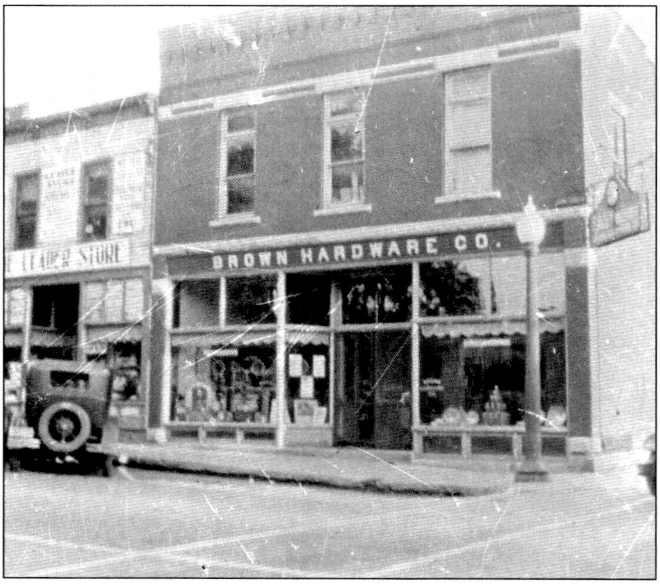

Brown Hardware was and is still a Berea institution, offering personal attention and service as well as support to community enterprises. Originally founded in 1873 and located near the Triangle, it was displaced by an urban renewal project in the 1970s. Though now situated on the edge of town, customers can still buy nails by the handful, get a screen door repaired, or find out the name of a competent plumber.

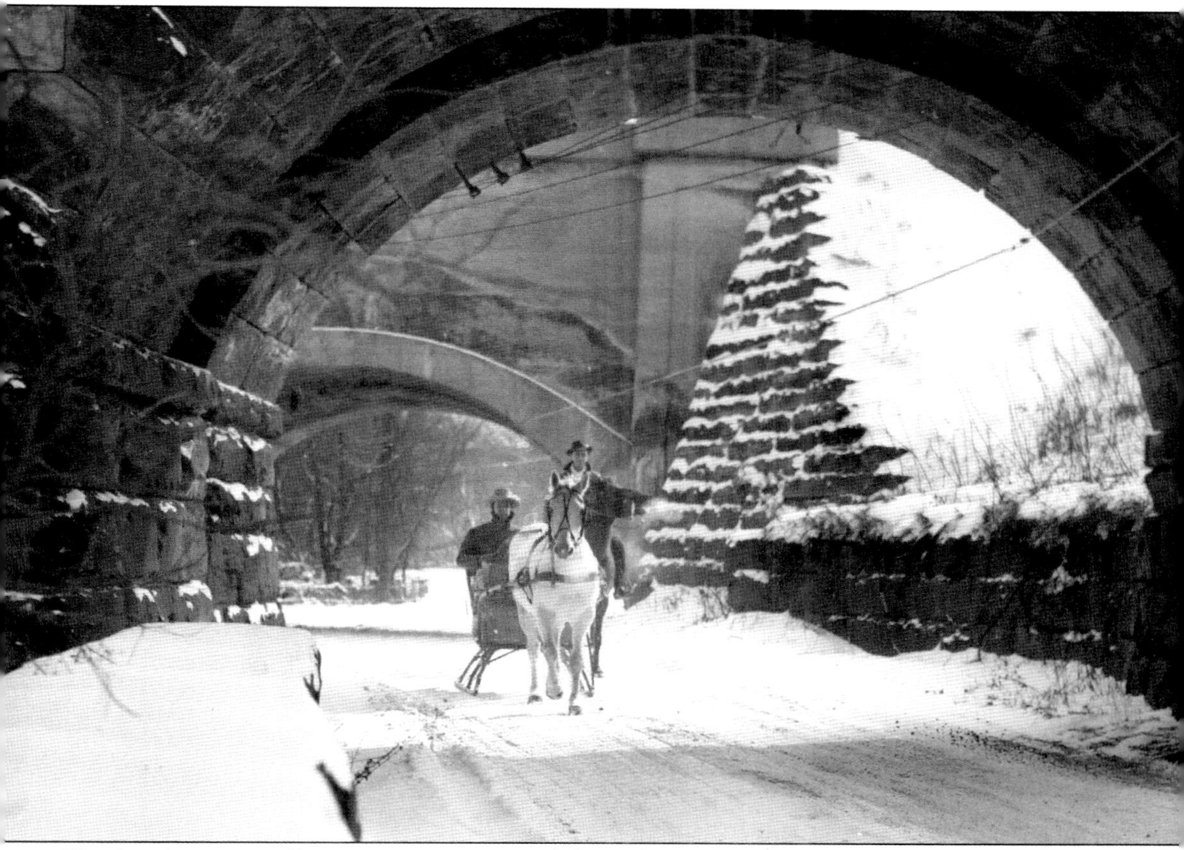

Sleigh rides were still common in 1948, and the railroad bridges at The Rocks have always been a photographer's favorite setting. This stretch of Barrett Road was once considered "out in the country."

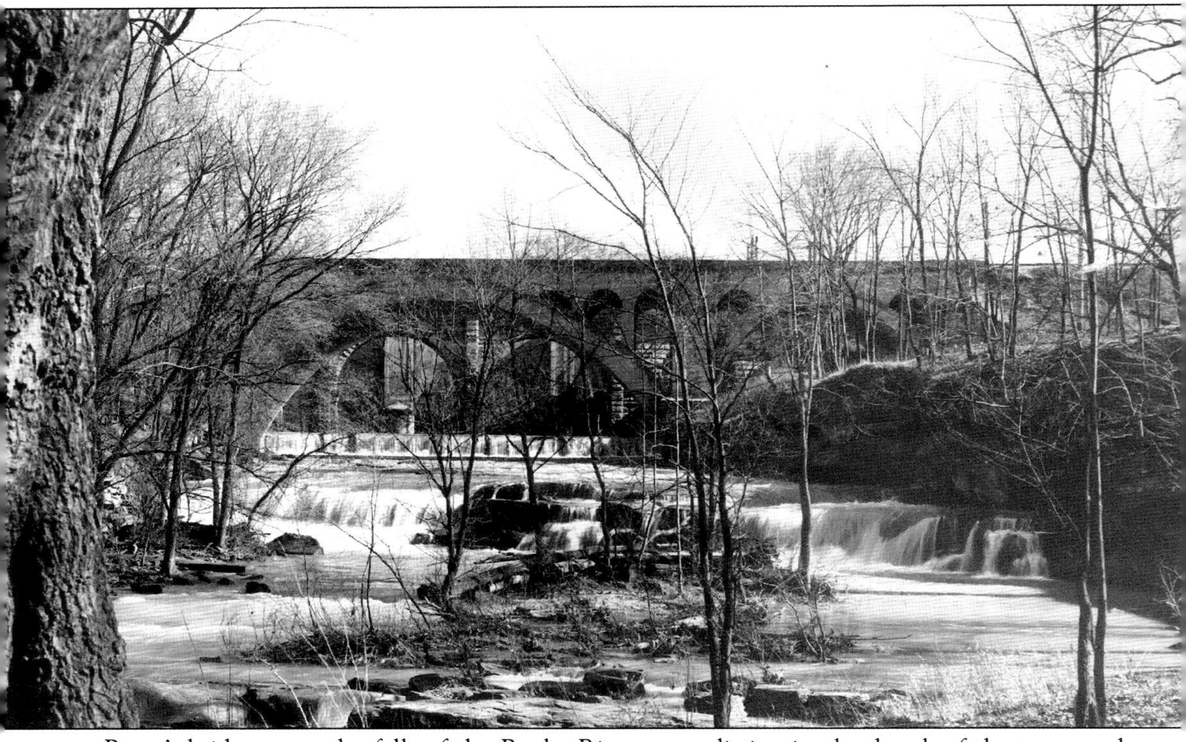

Berea's bridges over the falls of the Rocky River are a distinctive landmark of the town and emphasize the town's history and its uniqueness.